FIFTH EDITION

"THEY SAY / I SAY"

The Moves That Matter in Academic Writing

GERALD GRAFF

CATHY BIRKENSTEIN

both of the University of Illinois at Chicago

CAT Custom Edition
UC San Diego

This volume has been customized by the school for which it was published, to give you the best educational value. Chapters and pages may have been altered, added, deleted, or rearranged. Pagination and chapter numbers may be non-sequential. This volume is meant solely for use at this school.

NORTON
CUSTOM

W · W · NORTON & COMPANY

NEW YORK | LONDON

W. W. Norton & Company has been independent since its founding in 1923, when William Warder Norton and Mary D. Herter Norton first published lectures delivered at the People's Institute, the adult education division of New York City's Cooper Union. The firm soon expanded its program beyond the Institute, publishing books by celebrated academics from America and abroad. By midcentury, the two major pillars of Norton's publishing program—trade books and college texts—were firmly established. In the 1950s, the Norton family transferred control of the company to its employees, and today—with a staff of five hundred and hundreds of trade, college, and professional titles published each year—W. W. Norton & Company stands as the largest and oldest publishing house owned wholly by its employees.

Printed in the United States of America

Includes material from the following:

They Say / I Say, Fifth Edition (Gerald Graff and Cathy Birkenstein)
Copyright © 2021, 2018, 2017, 2014, 2010, 2009, 2006 by W. W. Norton & Company, Inc.
The Norton Field Guide to Writing, Fifth Edition (Richard Bullock and Maureen Daly Goggin)
Copyright © 2019, 2016, 2013, 2010, 2009, 2007, 2006 by W. W. Norton & Company, Inc.

Director of custom strategy: Susan Brennan
Associate director: Katie Hannah
Managing editor, College: Marian Johnson
Associate editor: Alexandra Gakos
Assistant editor: Samantha Knoerzer
Editorial assistant: Alana Pérez
Production supervisor: Lindsay Fischer
Production assistant: Caroline Hewitt
Design director: Rubina Yeh
Custom cover designer: Michael Wood
Text permissions managers: Megan Schindel and Bethany Salminen
Photo permissions managers: Stacey Stambaugh and Mike Cullen

978-0-393-87960-5

W. W. Norton & Company, Inc., 500 Fifth Avenue, New York, NY 10110
wwnorton.com

W. W. Norton & Company Ltd., 15 Carlisle Street, London W1D 3BS

INTRODUCTION

Welcome to Sixth College and the Culture, Art, and Technology program!

The Culture, Art, and Technology Program at Sixth College offers students exciting and varied scholarly opportunities centered on exploring and interrogating the intersection of culture, art, and technology. From the origins of civilization to the history of Hollywood and the future of the environment, students in CAT engage with big questions about where we've come from, who we are, and where we are going. Driving CAT are questions about how technology, art, and culture shape, determine, and interrogate the lives we lead, our ideas of self and community.

Each quarter we offer a selection of interdisciplinary writing courses, which take a variety of approaches to thinking about the intersection of culture, art, and technology. CAT 1, CAT 2, and CAT 3 are Sixth College's core sequence and these classes foreground critical reading, argumentative writing, research, and collaboration. CAT 2 and 3, offered in the Winter and Spring respectively, are six-unit writing-intensive courses that fulfill the UC-wide writing requirements. Our upper-division CAT 125 course invites students to think about public rhetoric, practical communication, and writing after college.

This textbook is meant to serve as your guide to writing during the core sequence and more broadly in college, no matter what course you are taking. In the CAT core sequence, you will learn to ask questions, write ethical and compelling arguments, and do creative and collaborative research. While the topics hopefully pique your interest, the skills that we are teaching—with this textbook as a base—are meant to help you succeed in your other college courses, be it writing a lab report, crafting a grant proposal, drafting an email to a professor, or collaborating on the next big idea.

The later chapters on cover letters and résumés are there to provide you a resource for CAT 125, as you begin to think of writing and communication after college. In CAT 125, we ask you to think about writing practically and for public audiences: how do you present your expertise and experience to potential employers? Graduate schools? And future colleagues?

In CAT we aim to teach you to think critically and creatively across media while also preparing you for success in college and the world beyond. As a living-learning community, we believe that students' engagement must extend beyond the classroom, and we hope to foster a community that helps students engage the world around them ethically, critically, and compassionately.

CONTENTS

CONTENTS

PART 3. TYING IT ALL TOGETHER

PART 4. IN SPECIFIC ACADEMIC CONTEXTS

PART 5. PROCESSES

PART 6. DOING RESEARCH

PART 7. GENRES

PART 8. MEDIA/DESIGN

CONTENTS

For
Aaron David

PREFACE
TO THE FIFTH EDITION

SINCE IT WAS FIRST PUBLISHED over a decade ago, this book has been dedicated to the idea that our own views are most thoughtfully formed in conversation with the views of others, including views that differ from our own. When students work with one of this book's templates like "They say that _______, and I concede _______. But _______," they see their beliefs from another side and, in our view, are therefore able to produce more compelling arguments.

As the twenty-first century unfolds, however, the increasingly polarized state of our society is making it harder to listen to those who see things differently than we do. With the recent outbreak of the coronavirus pandemic, for instance, those for and against the seemingly simple act of wearing a protective face mask have come to occupy two noncommunicating universes. The wider such divisions become, the harder it is to find anyone who is willing to seriously consider viewpoints that oppose their own. Too often we either avoid difficult discussions altogether, or we talk only with like-minded people, who often reinforce our preexisting assumptions and insulate us from serious challenge.

In this fifth edition of our book, therefore, we continue to emphasize the importance of getting outside our isolated silos and listening to others, even when—especially when—we may not like what we hear.

WHAT'S NEW IN THIS EDITION

"What I Really Want to Say Is . . .": Revising Substantially. This new chapter takes on one of the more formidable challenges faced by college students: how to move beyond superficial revision and improve a composition in a genuinely substantial way. It presents revision not as a matter of simply correcting spelling or moving a sentence or two but as a process students can use to discover what it is they really want to say. More specifically, the chapter encourages students to reread their writing with an eye to whether, for instance, they have accurately represented their sources, inadvertently contradicted themselves or lost their train of thought, or included "uh-oh" moments, as we refer to them, that are out of step with their larger intentions and aims.

New Exercises. Each main chapter (Chapters 1–13) now includes three exercises, which give students an opportunity to apply the chapter's advice. Instructors can either use theseexercises for in-class work or assign them as homework. Many exercises include a short passage for reading and writing practice and also prompt students to join conversations on **theysayiblog.com**.

WHAT'S ONLINE

"They Say / I Say" comes with more online options than ever—all of which are available separately for a low cost. Visit **digital.wwnorton.com/theysay5** for access, or contact your Norton representative for more information or help with any of the resources that follow.

Ebooks provide an enhanced reading experience. Convenient and affordable, the Norton ebooks can be used on any device and let students highlight ideas, bookmark passages, take notes, and even listen to the text.

Online tutorials give students hands-on practice using the rhetorical moves that this book emphasizes. Each tutorial helps students analyze an essay with an eye to these "moves that matter" and then use the book's templates to craft a response.

InQuizitive for Writers delivers adaptive, game-like exercises to help students practice editing and working with sources, including fact-checking. InQuizitive for Writers includes *The Little Seagull Handbook*, so students get two books for the price of one.

Instructor's Guide includes expanded in-class activities, sample syllabi, summaries of each chapter and reading, and a chapter on using the online resources, including the tutorials and the book's blog.

"They Say / I Blog" provides current readings that use the rhetorical moves covered in the book, along with questions that prompt students to join conversations online. Updated twice a month by Laura J. Panning Davies of SUNY Cortland, the blog provides a rich archive of additional readings on important issues. Check it out at **theysayiblog.com**.

Resources for your learning management system (LMS) provide high-quality Norton content for your online, hybrid, or in-person course. Customizable resources include assignable writing prompts from **theysayiblog.com**, quizzes on editing and documentation, style guides, student essays, and more.

Even as we have updated *"They Say / I Say"* and added more online components, our basic goals remain unchanged: to help students master the all-too-rare skill of engaging closely with others, particularly those who challenge what we say. Our additions, that is, are meant to reinforce our long-standing goal of demystifying academic discourse by identifying its key moves in forms that students can put into practice. Given the deeply divided society we live in, this practice of engaging in dialogue and entertaining counterarguments seems more urgent than ever.

PREFACE

Demystifying Academic Conversation

EXPERIENCED WRITING INSTRUCTORS have long recognized that writing well means entering into conversation with others. Academic writing in particular calls on writers not simply to express their own ideas but to do so as a response to what others have said. The first-year writing program at our own university, according to its mission statement, asks "students to participate in ongoing conversations about vitally important academic and public issues." A similar statement by another program holds that "intellectual writing is almost always composed in response to others' texts." These statements echo the ideas of rhetorical theorists like Kenneth Burke, Mikhail Bakhtin, and Wayne Booth as well as recent composition scholars like David Bartholomae, John Bean, Patricia Bizzell, Irene Clark, Greg Colomb, Lisa Ede, Peter Elbow, Joseph Harris, Andrea Lunsford, Elaine Maimon, Gary Olson, Mike Rose, John Swales and Christine Feak, Tilly Warnock, and others who argue that writing well means engaging the voices of others and letting them in turn engage us.

Yet despite this growing consensus that writing is a social, conversational act, helping student writers actually participate in these conversations remains a formidable challenge. This book aims to meet that challenge. Its goal is to demystify academic writing by isolating its basic moves, explaining them clearly, and representing them in the form of templates.

In this way, we hope to help students become active participants in the important conversations of the academic world and the wider public sphere.

HIGHLIGHTS

- *Shows that writing well means entering a conversation*, summarizing others ("they say") to set up one's own argument ("I say")
- *Demystifies academic writing*, showing students "the moves that matter" in language they can readily apply
- *Provides user-friendly templates* to help writers make those moves in their own writing
- *Shows that reading is a way of entering a conversation*—not just of passively absorbing information but of understanding and actively entering dialogues and debates

HOW THIS BOOK CAME TO BE

The original idea for this book grew out of our shared interest in democratizing academic culture. First, it grew out of arguments that Gerald Graff has been making throughout his career that schools and colleges need to invite students into the conversations and debates that surround them. More specifically, it is a practical, hands-on companion to his book *Clueless in Academe: How Schooling Obscures the Life of the Mind*, in which he looks at academic conversations from the perspective of those who find them mysterious and proposes ways in which such mystification can be overcome. Second, this book grew out of writing templates that Cathy Birkenstein developed in the 1990s for use in writing and literature courses she was teaching. Many students, she found, could readily grasp what it meant to support a thesis with evidence, to entertain a counterargument, to identify a textual contradiction, and ultimately to summarize and respond to challenging arguments, but they often had trouble putting these concepts into practice in their own writing. When Cathy sketched out templates on the board, however, giving her students some of the language and patterns that these sophisticated moves require, their writing—and even their quality of thought—significantly improved.

This book began, then, when we put our ideas together and realized that these templates might have the potential to open up and clarify academic conversation. We proceeded from the premise that all writers rely on certain stock formulas that they themselves didn't invent—and that many of these formulas are so commonly used that they can be represented in model templates that students can use to structure and even generate what they want to say.

As we developed a working draft of this book, we began using it in first-year writing courses that we teach at UIC. In classroom exercises and writing assignments, we found that students who otherwise struggled to organize their thoughts, or even to think of something to say, did much better when we provided them with templates like the following:

- ▸ In discussions of __________, a controversial issue is whether __________. While some argue that __________, others contend that __________.
- ▸ This is not to say that __________.

One virtue of such templates, we found, is that they focus writers' attention not just on what is being said but also on the *forms* that structure what is being said. In other words, they make students more conscious of the rhetorical patterns that are key to academic success but often pass under the classroom radar.

THE CENTRALITY OF "THEY SAY / I SAY"

The central rhetorical move that we focus on in this book is the "they say / I say" template that gives our book its title. In our view, this template represents the deep, underlying structure, the internal DNA as it were, of all effective argument. Effective persuasive writers do more than make well-supported claims ("I say"); they also map those claims relative to the claims of others ("they say").

Here, for example, the "they say / I say" pattern structures a passage from an essay by the media and technology critic Steven Johnson:

> For decades, we've worked under the assumption that mass culture follows a path declining steadily toward lowest-common-denominator standards, presumably because the "masses" want dumb, simple pleasures and big media companies try to give the masses what they want. But . . . the exact opposite is happening: the culture is getting more cognitively demanding, not less.
>
> Steven Johnson, "Watching TV Makes You Smarter"

In generating his own argument from something "they say," Johnson suggests *why* he needs to say what he is saying: to correct a popular misconception.

Even when writers do not explicitly identify the views they are responding to, as Johnson does, an implicit "they say" can often be discerned, as in the following passage by Zora Neale Hurston:

> I remember the day I became colored.
>
> Zora Neale Hurston, "How It Feels to Be Colored Me"

In order to grasp Hurston's point here, we need to be able to reconstruct the implicit view she is responding to and questioning: that racial identity is an innate quality we are simply born with. On the contrary, Hurston suggests, our race is imposed on us by society—something we "become" by virtue of how we are treated.

As these examples suggest, the "they say / I say" model can improve not just student writing but student reading comprehension as well. Since reading and writing are deeply reciprocal activities, students who learn to make the rhetorical moves represented by the templates in this book figure to become more adept at identifying these same moves in the texts they read. And if we are right that effective arguments are always in dialogue with other arguments, then it follows that in order to understand the types of challenging texts assigned in college, students need to identify the views to which those texts are responding.

Working with the "they say / I say" model can also help with invention, finding something to say. In our experience, students best discover what they want to say not by thinking about a subject in an isolation booth but by reading texts, listening closely to what other writers say, and looking for an opening through which they can enter the conversation. In other words, listening closely to others and summarizing what they have to say can help writers generate their own ideas.

THE USEFULNESS OF TEMPLATES

Our templates also have a generative quality, prompting students to make moves in their writing that they might not otherwise make or even know they should make. The templates in this book can be particularly helpful for students who are unsure about what to say or who have trouble finding enough to say, often because they consider their own beliefs so self-evident that they need not be argued for. Students like this are often helped, we've found, when we give them a simple template like the following one for entertaining a counterargument (or planting a naysayer, as we call it in Chapter 6):

- **Of course some might object that __________. Although I concede that __________, I still maintain that __________.**

What this particular template helps students do is make the seemingly counterintuitive move of questioning their own beliefs, of looking at them from the perspective of those who disagree. In so doing, templates can bring out aspects of students' thoughts that, as they themselves sometimes remark, they didn't even realize were there.

Other templates in this book help students make a host of sophisticated moves that they might not otherwise make: summarizing what someone else says, framing a quotation in one's own words, indicating the view that the writer is responding to, marking the shift from a source's view to the writer's own view, offering evidence for that view, entertaining and answering counterarguments, and explaining what is at stake in the first place. In showing students how to make such moves, templates do more than organize students' ideas; they help bring those ideas into existence.

PREFACE

"OK—BUT TEMPLATES?"

We are aware, of course, that some instructors may have reservations about templates. Some, for instance, may object that such formulaic devices represent a return to prescriptive forms of instruction that encourage passive learning or lead students to put their writing on automatic pilot.

This is an understandable reaction, we think, to kinds of rote instruction that have indeed encouraged passivity and drained writing of its creativity and dynamic relation to the social world. The trouble is that many students will never learn on their own to make the key intellectual moves that our templates represent. While seasoned writers pick up these moves unconsciously through their reading, many students do not. Consequently, we believe, students need to see these moves represented in the explicit ways that the templates provide.

The aim of the templates, then, is not to stifle critical thinking but to be direct with students about the key rhetorical moves that it comprises. Since we encourage students to modify and adapt the templates to the particularities of the arguments they are making, using such prefabricated formulas as learning tools need not result in writing and thinking that are themselves formulaic. Admittedly, no teaching tool can guarantee that students will engage in hard, rigorous thought. Our templates do, however, provide concrete prompts that can stimulate and shape such thought: What do "they say" about my topic? How would a naysayer respond to my argument? What is my evidence? Do I need to qualify my point? Who cares?

In fact, templates have a long and rich history. Public orators from ancient Greece and Rome through the European Renaissance studied rhetorical *topoi* or "commonplaces," model passages and formulas that represented the different strategies available to public speakers. In many respects, our templates echo this classical rhetorical tradition of imitating established models.

The journal *Nature* requires aspiring contributors to follow a guideline that is like a template on the opening page of their manuscript: "Two or three sentences explaining what the main result [of their study] reveals in direct comparison with what was thought to be the case previously, or how the main result adds to previous knowledge." In the field of education, a form designed by the education theorist Howard Gardner asks postdoctoral fellowship applicants to complete the following template: "Most scholars in the field believe _________. As a result of my study, _________." That these two examples are geared toward post-doctoral fellows and veteran researchers shows that it is not only struggling undergraduates who can use help making these key rhetorical moves but experienced academics as well.

Templates have even been used in the teaching of personal narrative. The literary and educational theorist Jane Tompkins devised the following template to help student writers make the often difficult move from telling a story to explaining what it means: "X tells a story about _________ to make the point that _________. My own experience with _________ yields a point that is similar / different / both similar and different. What I take away from my own experience with _________ is _________. As a result, I conclude _________." We especially like this template because it suggests that "they say / I say" argument need not be mechanical, impersonal, or dry and that telling a story and making an argument are more compatible activities than many think.

WHY IT'S OK TO USE "I"

But wait—doesn't the "I" part of "they say / I say" flagrantly encourage the use of the first-person pronoun? Aren't we aware that some teachers prohibit students from using "I" or "we" on the grounds that these pronouns encourage ill-considered, subjective opinions rather than objective and reasoned arguments? Yes, we are aware of this first-person prohibition, but we think it has serious flaws. First, expressing ill-considered, subjective opinions is not necessarily the worst sin beginning writers can commit; it might be a starting point from which they can move on to more reasoned, less self-indulgent perspectives. Second, prohibiting students from using "I" is simply not an effective way of curbing students' subjectivity, since one can offer poorly argued, ill-supported opinions just as easily without it. Third and most important, prohibiting the first person tends to hamper students' ability not only to take strong positions but also to differentiate their own positions from those of others, as we point out in Chapter 5. To be sure, writers can resort to various circumlocutions—"it will here be argued," "the evidence suggests," "the truth is"—and these may be useful for avoiding a monotonous series of "I believe" sentences. But except for avoiding such monotony, we see no good reason why "I" should be set aside in persuasive writing. Rather than prohibit "I," then, we think a better tactic is to give students practice at using it well and learning its use, both by supporting their claims with evidence and by attending closely to alternative perspectives—to what "they" are saying.

HOW THIS BOOK IS ORGANIZED

Because of its centrality, we have allowed the "they say / I say" format to dictate the structure of this book. So while Part 1 addresses the art of listening to others, Part 2 addresses how to offer one's own response. Part 1 opens with the chapter

"Starting with What Others Are Saying," which explains why it is generally advisable to begin a text by citing others rather than plunging directly into one's own views. Subsequent chapters take up the arts of summarizing and quoting what these others have to say. Part 2 begins with a chapter on different ways of responding, followed by chapters on marking the shift between what "they say" and what "I say," on introducing and answering objections, and on answering the all-important questions "so what?" and "who cares?" Part 3, "Tying It All Together," includes a chapter on connection and coherence; one on academic language, which encourages students to draw on their everyday voice as a tool for writing; and others on the art of metacommentary and using templates to revise a text. Part 4 offers guidance for entering conversations in specific academic contexts, with chapters on entering class discussions, writing online, reading, and writing in literature courses, the sciences, and social sciences. Finally, we provide five readings and an index of templates.

WHAT THIS BOOK DOESN'T DO

There are some things that this book does not try to do. We do not, for instance, cover logical principles of argument, such as syllogisms, warrants, logical fallacies, or the differences between inductive and deductive reasoning. Although such concepts can be useful, we believe most of us learn the ins and outs of argumentative writing not by studying logical principles in the abstract but by plunging into actual discussions and debates, trying out different patterns of response, and in this way getting a sense of what works to persuade different audiences and what doesn't. In our view, people learn more about arguing from hearing someone say, "You miss my point. What I'm saying is not ________ but ________," or "I agree with you that ________ and would even add that ________," than they do from studying the differences between inductive and deductive reasoning. Such formulas give students an immediate sense of what it feels like to enter a public conversation in a way that studying abstract warrants and logical fallacies does not.

ENGAGING WITH THE IDEAS OF OTHERS

One central goal of this book is to demystify academic writing by returning it to its social and conversational roots. Although writing may require some degree of quiet and solitude, the "they say / I say" model shows students that they can best develop their arguments not just by looking inward but by doing what they often do in a good conversation with friends and family—listening carefully to what others are saying and engaging with other views.

This approach to writing therefore has an ethical dimension, since it asks writers not simply to keep proving and reasserting what they already believe but also to stretch what they believe by putting it up against beliefs that differ, sometimes radically, from their own. In an increasingly diverse, global society, this ability to engage with the ideas of others is especially crucial to democratic citizenship.

Gerald Graff
Cathy Birkenstein

INTRODUCTION
Entering the Conversation

THINK ABOUT AN ACTIVITY that you do particularly well: cooking, playing the piano, shooting a basketball, even something as basic as driving a car. If you reflect on this activity, you'll realize that once you mastered it you no longer had to give much conscious thought to the various moves that go into doing it. Performing this activity, in other words, depends on your having learned a series of complicated moves—moves that may seem mysterious or difficult to those who haven't yet learned them.

The same applies to writing. Often without consciously realizing it, accomplished writers routinely rely on a stock of established moves that are crucial for communicating sophisticated ideas. What makes writers masters of their trade is not only their ability to express interesting thoughts but their mastery of an inventory of basic moves that they probably picked up by reading a wide range of other accomplished writers. Less experienced writers, by contrast, are often unfamiliar with these basic moves and unsure how to make them in their own writing. Hence this book, which is intended as a short, user-friendly guide to the basic moves of academic writing.

One of our key premises is that these basic moves are so common that they can be represented in *templates* that you can use right away to structure and even generate your own writing. Perhaps the most distinctive feature of this book is its presentation of many such templates, designed to help you successfully enter not only the world of academic thinking and writing but also the wider worlds of civic discourse and work.

Instead of focusing solely on abstract principles of writing, then, this book offers model templates that help you put those principles directly into practice. Working with these templates will give you an immediate sense of how to engage in the kinds of critical thinking you are required to do at the college level and in the vocational and public spheres beyond.

Some of these templates represent simple but crucial moves, like those used to summarize some widely held belief:

- **Many Americans assume that ________.**

Others are more complicated:

- **On the one hand, ________. On the other hand, ________.**
- **Author X contradicts herself. At the same time that she argues ________, she also implies ________.**
- **I agree that ________. However, ________.**
- **This is not to say that ________.**

It is true, of course, that critical thinking and writing go deeper than any set of linguistic formulas, requiring that you question assumptions, develop strong claims, offer supporting reasons and evidence, consider opposing arguments, and so on. But these deeper habits of thought cannot be put into practice unless you have a language for expressing them in clear, organized ways.

STATE YOUR OWN IDEAS AS A RESPONSE TO OTHERS

The single most important template that we focus on in this book is the "they say ________; I say ________" formula that gives our book its title. If there is any one point that we hope you will take away from this book, it is the importance not only of expressing your ideas ("I say") but of presenting those ideas as a *response to some other person or group* ("they say"). For us, the underlying structure of effective academic writing—and of responsible public discourse—resides not just in stating our own ideas but in listening closely to others around us, summarizing their views in a way that they will recognize, and responding with our own ideas in kind. Broadly speaking, academic writing is argumentative writing, and we believe that to argue well you need to do more than assert your own position. You need to enter a conversation, using what others say (or might say) as a launching pad or sounding board for your own views. For this reason, one of the main pieces of advice in this book is to write the voices of others into your text.

In our view, then, the best academic writing has one underlying feature: it is deeply engaged in some way with other people's views. Too often, however, academic writing is taught as a process of saying "true" or "smart" things in a vacuum, as if it were possible to argue effectively without being in conversation *with* someone else. If you have been taught to write a traditional five-paragraph essay, for example, you have learned how to develop a thesis and support it with evidence. This is good advice as far as it goes, but it leaves out the important fact that in the real world we don't make arguments without being provoked. Instead, we make arguments because someone has said or done something (or perhaps *not* said or done something) and we need to respond: "I can't see why you like the Lakers so much"; "I agree: it was a great film"; "That argument is contradictory." If it weren't for other people and our need to challenge, agree with, or otherwise respond to them, there would be no reason to argue at all.

"WHY ARE YOU TELLING ME THIS?"

To make an impact as a writer, then, you need to do more than make statements that are logical, well supported, and consistent. You must also find a way of entering into conversation with the views of others, with something "they say." The easiest and most common way writers do this is by *summarizing* what others say and then using it to set up what they want to say.

"But why," as a student of ours once asked, "do I always need to summarize the views of others to set up my own view? Why can't I just state my own view and be done with it?" Why indeed? After all, "they," whoever they may be, will have already had their say, so why do you have to *repeat* it? Furthermore, if they had their say in print, can't readers just go and read what was said themselves?

The answer is that if you don't identify the "they say" you're responding to, your own argument probably won't have a point. Readers will wonder what prompted you to say what you're saying and therefore motivated you to write. As the figure on the following page suggests, without a "they say," *what* you are saying may be clear to your audience, but *why* you are saying it won't be.

Even if we don't know what film he's referring to, it's easy to grasp what the speaker means here when he says that its characters are very complex. But it's hard to see why the speaker feels the need to say what he is saying. "Why," as one member

of his imagined audience wonders, "is he telling us this?" So the characters are complex—so what?

Now look at what happens to the same proposition when it is presented as a response to something "they say":

We hope you agree that the same claim—"the characters in the film are very complex"—becomes much stronger when presented as a response to a contrary view: that the film's characters "are sexist stereotypes." Unlike the speaker in the first cartoon, the speaker in the second has a clear goal or mission: to correct what he sees as a mistaken characterization.

THE AS-OPPOSED-TO-WHAT FACTOR

To put our point another way, framing your "I say" as a response to something "they say" gives your writing an element of contrast without which it won't make sense. It may be helpful to think of this crucial element as an "as-opposed-to-what factor" and, as you write, to continually ask yourself, "Who says otherwise?" and "Does anyone dispute it?" Behind the audience's "Yeah, so?" and "Why is he telling us this?" in the first cartoon above lie precisely these types of "As opposed to what?" questions. The speaker in the second cartoon, we think, is more satisfying because he answers these questions, helping us see his point that the film presents complex characters *rather than* simple sexist stereotypes.

HOW IT'S DONE

Many accomplished writers make explicit "they say" moves to set up and motivate their own arguments. One famous example is Martin Luther King Jr.'s "Letter from Birmingham Jail," which consists almost entirely of King's eloquent responses to a public statement by eight clergymen deploring the civil rights protests he was leading. The letter—which was written in 1963, while King was in prison for leading a demonstration against racial injustice in Birmingham—is structured almost entirely around a framework of summary and response, in which King summarizes and then answers their criticisms. In one typical passage, King writes as follows:

> You deplore the demonstrations taking place in Birmingham. But your statement, I am sorry to say, fails to express a similar concern for the conditions that brought about the demonstrations.
>
> MARTIN LUTHER KING JR., "Letter from Birmingham Jail"

King goes on to agree with his critics that "it is unfortunate that demonstrations are taking place in Birmingham," yet he hastens to add that "it is even more unfortunate that the city's white power structure left the Negro community with no alternative." King's letter is so thoroughly conversational, in fact, that it could be rewritten in the form of a dialogue or play.

> King's critics:
> King's response:
> Critics:
> Response:

Clearly, King would not have written his famous letter were it not for his critics, whose views he treats not as objections to his already-formed arguments but as the motivating source of those arguments, their central reason for being. He quotes not only what his critics have said ("Some have asked: 'Why didn't you give the new city administration time to act?'"), but also things they *might* have said ("One may well ask: 'How can you advocate breaking some laws and obeying others?'")—all to set the stage for what he himself wants to say.

A similar "they say / I say" exchange opens an essay about American patriotism by the social critic Katha Pollitt, who uses her own daughter's comment to represent the patriotic national fervor after the terrorist attacks of September 11, 2001.

> My daughter, who goes to Stuyvesant High School only blocks from the former World Trade Center, thinks we should fly the American flag out our window. Definitely not, I say: the flag stands for jingoism and vengeance and war. She tells me I'm wrong—the flag means standing together and honoring the dead and saying no to terrorism. In a way we're both right. . . .
>
> Katha Pollitt, "Put Out No Flags"

As Pollitt's example shows, the "they" you respond to in crafting an argument need not be a famous author or someone known to your audience. It can be a family member, like Pollitt's daughter, or a friend or classmate who has made a provocative claim. It can even be something an individual or a group might say—or a side of yourself, something you once believed but no longer do, or something you partly believe but also doubt. The important thing is that the "they" (or "you" or "she") represent some wider group with which readers might identify—in Pollitt's case, those who patriotically believe in flying the flag. Pollitt's example also shows that responding to the views of others need not always involve unqualified opposition. By agreeing and disagreeing with her daughter, Pollitt enacts what we call the "yes and no" response, reconciling apparently incompatible views.

See Chapter 4 for more on agreeing, but with a difference.

While King and Pollitt both identify the views they are responding to, some authors do not explicitly state their views but instead allow the reader to infer them. See, for instance, if you can identify the implied or unnamed "they say" that the following claim is responding to:

> I like to think I have a certain advantage as a teacher of literature because when I was growing up I disliked and feared books.
>
> GERALD GRAFF, "Disliking Books at an Early Age"

In case you haven't figured it out already, the phantom "they say" here is the common belief that in order to be a good teacher of literature, one must have grown up liking and enjoying books.

COURT CONTROVERSY, BUT...

As you can see from these examples, many writers use the "they say / I say" format to challenge standard ways of thinking and thus to stir up controversy. This point may come as a shock to you if you have always had the impression that in order to succeed academically you need to play it safe and avoid controversy in your writing, making statements that nobody can possibly disagree with. Though this view of writing may appear logical, it is actually a recipe for flat, lifeless writing and for writing that fails to answer what we call the "so what?" and "who cares?" questions. "William Shakespeare wrote many famous plays and sonnets" may be a perfectly true statement, but precisely because nobody is likely to disagree with it, it goes without saying and thus would seem pointless if said.

But just because controversy is important doesn't mean you have to become an attack dog who automatically disagrees with everything others say. We think this is an important point to underscore because some who are not familiar with this book have gotten the impression from the title that our goal is to train writers simply to disparage whatever "they say."

LISTEN BEFORE YOU LEAP

There certainly are occasions when strong critique is needed. It's hard to live in a deeply polarized society like our current one and not feel the need at times to criticize what others think. But even the most justified critiques fall flat, we submit, unless we really listen to and understand the views we are criticizing:

- **While I understand the impulse to __________, my own view is __________.**

Even the most sympathetic audiences, after all, tend to feel manipulated by arguments that scapegoat and caricature the other side.

Furthermore, genuinely listening to views we disagree with can have the salutary effect of helping us see that beliefs we'd initially disdained may not be as thoroughly reprehensible as we'd imagined. Thus the type of "they say / I say" argument that we promote in this book can take the form of agreeing up to a point or, as the Pollitt example above illustrates, of both agreeing and disagreeing simultaneously, as in:

- **While I agree with X that __________, I cannot accept her overall conclusion that __________.**
- **While X argues __________, and I argue __________, in a way we're both right.**

Agreement cannot be ruled out, however:

- I agree with __________ that __________.

THE TEMPLATE OF TEMPLATES

There are many ways, then, to enter a conversation and respond to what "they say." But our discussion of ways to do so would be incomplete were we not to mention the most comprehensive way that writers enter conversations, which incorporates all the major moves discussed in this book:

- In recent discussions of __________, a controversial issue has been whether __________. On the one hand, some argue that __________. From this perspective, __________. On the other hand, however, others argue that __________. In the words of X, one of this view's main proponents, "__________." According to this view, __________. In sum, then, the issue is whether __________ or __________.

  My own view is that __________. Though I concede that __________, I still maintain that __________. For example, __________. Although some might object that __________, I would reply that __________. The issue is important because __________.

This "template of templates," as we like to call it, represents the internal DNA of countless articles and even entire books. Writers commonly use a version of it not only to stake out their "they say" and "I say" at the start of their manuscript, but—just as important—to form the overarching blueprint that structures what they write over the entire length of their text.

Taking it line by line, this master template first helps you open your text by identifying an issue in some ongoing conversation or debate ("In recent discussions of ________, a controversial issue has been ________") and then map some of the voices in this controversy (by using the "on the one hand / on the other hand" structure). The template then helps you introduce a quotation ("In the words of X") and explain the quotation in your own words ("According to this view"). Then, in a new paragraph, it helps you state your own argument ("My own view is that"), qualify your argument ("Though I concede that"), and support your argument with evidence ("For example"). In addition, the template helps you make one of the most crucial moves in argumentative writing, what we call "planting a naysayer in your text," in which you summarize and then answer a likely objection to your own central claim ("Although it might be objected that ________, I reply ________"). Finally, this template helps you shift between general, overarching claims ("In sum, then") and smaller-scale, supporting claims ("For example").

Again, none of us is born knowing these moves, especially when it comes to academic writing—hence the need for this book.

BUT ISN'T THIS PLAGIARISM?

"But isn't this plagiarism?" at least one student each year will usually ask. "Well, is it?" we respond, turning the question around into one the entire class can profit from. "We are, after all, asking you to use language in your writing that isn't your own—language that you 'borrow' or, to put it less delicately, steal from other writers."

Often, a lively discussion ensues that raises important questions about authorial ownership and helps everyone better understand the frequently confusing line between plagiarism and the legitimate use of what others say and how they say it. Students are quick to see that no one person owns a conventional formula like "on the one hand / on the other hand." Phrases like "a controversial issue" are so commonly used and recycled that they are generic—community property that can be freely used without fear of committing plagiarism. It *is* plagiarism, however, if the words used to fill in the blanks of such formulas are borrowed from others without proper acknowledgment. In sum, then, while it is not plagiarism to recycle conventionally used formulas, it is a serious academic offense to take the substantive content from others' texts without citing the authors and giving them proper credit.

"OK—BUT TEMPLATES?"

Nevertheless, if you are like some of our students, your initial response to templates may be skepticism. At first, many of our students complain that using templates will take away their originality and creativity and make them all sound the same. "They'll turn us into writing robots," one of our students insisted. "I'm in college now," another student asserted. "This is third-grade-level stuff."

In our view, however, the templates in this book, far from being "third-grade-level stuff," represent the stock-in-trade of sophisticated thinking and writing, and they often require a great deal of practice and instruction to use successfully. As for the belief that preestablished forms undermine creativity, we think it rests on a very limited vision of what creativity is all about. In our view, the templates in this book will actually help your writing become *more* original and creative, not less. After all, even the most creative forms of expression depend on established patterns and structures. Most songwriters, for instance, rely on a time-honored verse-chorus-verse pattern, and few people would call Shakespeare uncreative because he didn't invent the sonnet or the dramatic forms that he used to such dazzling effect. Even the most avant-garde, cutting-edge artists like improvisational jazz musicians need to master the basic forms that their work improvises on, departs from, and goes beyond, or else their work will come across as uneducated child's play. Ultimately, then, creativity and originality lie not in the avoidance of established forms but in the imaginative use of them.

Furthermore, these templates do not dictate the *content* of what you say, which can be as original as you can make it, but only suggest a way of formatting *how* you say it. In addition, once you begin to feel comfortable with the templates in this book, you will be able to improvise creatively on them to fit new situations and purposes and find others in your reading. In other words, the templates offered here are learning tools to get you started, not structures set in stone. Once you get used to using them, you can even dispense with them altogether, for the rhetorical moves they model will be at your fingertips in an unconscious, instinctive way.

But if you still need proof that writing templates need not make you sound stiff and artificial, consider the following opening to an essay on the fast-food industry that we've included in Chapter 14:

> If ever there were a newspaper headline custom-made for Jay Leno's monologue, this was it. Kids taking on McDonald's this week, suing the company for making them fat. Isn't that like middle-aged men suing Porsche for making them get speeding tickets? Whatever happened to personal responsibility?
>
> I tend to sympathize with these portly fast-food patrons, though. Maybe that's because I used to be one of them.
>
> David Zinczenko, "Don't Blame the Eater"

Although Zinczenko relies on a version of the "they say / I say" formula, his writing is anything but dry, robotic, or uncreative. While Zinczenko does not explicitly use the words "they say" and "I say," the template still gives the passage its underlying structure: "*They say* that kids suing fast-food companies for making them fat is a joke; but *I say* such lawsuits are justified."

PUTTING IN YOUR OAR

Though the immediate goal of this book is to help you become a better writer, at a deeper level it invites you to become a certain type of person: a critical, intellectual thinker who, instead of sitting passively on the sidelines, can participate in the debates and conversations of your world in an active and empowered way. Ultimately, this book invites you to become a critical thinker who can enter the types of conversations described eloquently by the philosopher Kenneth Burke in the following widely cited passage. Likening the world of intellectual exchange to a never-ending conversation at a party, Burke writes:

> You come late. When you arrive, others have long preceded you, and they are engaged in a heated discussion, a discussion too heated for them to pause and tell you exactly what it is about. . . . You listen for a while, until you decide that you have caught the tenor of the argument; then you put in your oar. Someone answers; you answer him; another comes to your defense; another aligns himself against you. . . . The hour grows late, you must depart. And you do depart, with the discussion still vigorously in progress.
>
> KENNETH BURKE, *The Philosophy of Literary Form*

What we like about this passage is its suggestion that stating an argument (putting in your oar) can only be done in conversation with others; that entering the dynamic world of ideas must be done not as isolated individuals but as social beings deeply connected to others.

This ability to enter complex, many-sided conversations has taken on a special urgency in today's polarized red state / blue state America, where the future for all of us may depend on our ability to put ourselves in the shoes of those who think very differently from us. The central piece of advice in this book—that we listen carefully to others, including those who disagree with us, and then engage with them thoughtfully and respectfully—can help us see beyond our own pet beliefs, which may not be shared by everyone. The mere act of crafting a sentence that begins "Of course, someone might object that ________" may not seem like a way to change the world; but it does have the potential to jog us out of our comfort zones, to get us thinking critically about our own beliefs, and even to change minds, our own included.

Exercises

1. Write two paragraphs in which you first summarize our rationale for the templates in this book and then articulate your own position in response. If you want, you can use the template below to organize your paragraphs, expanding and modifying it as necessary to fit what you want to say:

   In the Introduction to "*They Say / I Say": The Moves That Matter in Academic Writing,* Gerald Graff and Cathy Birkenstein provide templates designed to ________. Specifically, Graff and Birkenstein argue that the types of writing templates they offer ________. As the authors themselves put it, "________." Although some people believe ________, Graff and Birkenstein insist that ________. In sum, then, their view is that ________.

   I [agree / disagree / have mixed feelings]. In my view, the types of templates that the authors recommend ________. For instance, ________. In addition, ________. Some might object, of course, on the grounds that ________. Yet I would argue that ________. Overall, then, I believe ________ —an important point to make given ________.

2. Read the following paragraph from an essay by Emily Poe, written when she was a student at Furman University. Disregarding for the moment what Poe says, focus your attention on the phrases she uses to structure what she says (italicized here). Then write a new paragraph using Poe's as a model but replacing her topic, vegetarianism, with one of your own.

INTRODUCTION

The term "vegetarian" tends to be synonymous with "tree-hugger" in many people's minds. *They see* vegetarianism as a cult that brainwashes its followers into eliminating an essential part of their daily diets for an abstract goal of "animal welfare." *However*, few vegetarians choose their lifestyle just to follow the crowd. *On the contrary*, many of these supposedly brainwashed people are actually independent thinkers, concerned citizens, and compassionate human beings. *For the truth is* that there are many very good reasons for giving up meat. Perhaps the best reasons are to improve the environment, to encourage humane treatment of livestock, or to enhance one's own health. *In this essay, then*, closely examining a vegetarian diet as compared to a meat-eater's diet will show that vegetarianism is clearly the better option for sustaining the Earth and all its inhabitants.

ONE

"THEY SAY"

Starting with What Others Are Saying

NOT LONG AGO we attended a talk at an academic conference where the speaker's central claim seemed to be that a certain sociologist—call him Dr. X—had done very good work in a number of areas of the discipline. The speaker proceeded to illustrate his thesis by referring extensively and in great detail to various books and articles by Dr. X and by quoting long passages from them. The speaker was obviously both learned and impassioned, but as we listened to his talk, we found ourselves somewhat puzzled: the argument—that Dr. X's work was very important—was clear enough, but why did the speaker need to make it in the first place? Did anyone dispute it? Were there commentators in the field who had argued against X's work or challenged its value? Was the speaker's interpretation of what X had done somehow novel or revolutionary? Since the speaker gave no hint of an answer to any of these questions, we could only wonder why he was going on and on about X. It was only after the speaker finished and took questions from the audience that we got a clue: in response to one questioner, he referred to several critics who had

The hypothetical audience in the figure on p. 5 reacts similarly.

vigorously questioned Dr. X's ideas and convinced many sociologists that Dr. X's work was unsound.

This story illustrates an important lesson: that to give writing the most important thing of all—namely, a point—writers need to indicate clearly not only what their thesis is but also what larger conversation that thesis is responding to. Because our speaker failed to mention what others had said about Dr. X's work, he left his audience unsure about why he felt the need to say what he was saying. Perhaps the point was clear to other sociologists in the audience who were more familiar with the debates over Dr. X's work than we were. But even they, we bet, would have understood the speaker's point better if he'd sketched in some of the larger conversation his own claims were a part of and reminded the audience about what "they say."

This story also illustrates an important lesson about the *order* in which things are said: to keep an audience engaged, writers need to explain what they are responding to—either before offering that response or, at least, very early in the discussion. Delaying this explanation for more than one or two paragraphs in a very short essay or blog entry, three or four pages in a longer work, or more than ten or so pages in a book reverses the natural order in which readers process material—and in which writers think and develop ideas. After all, it seems very unlikely that our conference speaker first developed his defense of Dr. X and only later came across Dr. X's critics. As someone knowledgeable in his field, the speaker surely encountered the criticisms first and only then was compelled to respond and, as he saw it, set the record straight.

Therefore, when it comes to constructing an argument (whether orally or in writing), we offer you the following advice: remember that you are entering a conversation and therefore need to start with "what others are saying," as the title of this chapter recommends, and then introduce your own ideas as a response. Specifically, we suggest that you summarize what "they say" as soon as you can in your text and remind readers of it at strategic points as your text unfolds. Though it's true that not all texts follow this practice, we think it's important for all writers to master it before they depart from it.

This is not to say that you must start with a detailed list of everyone who has written on your subject before you offer your own ideas. Had our conference speaker gone to the opposite extreme and spent most of his talk summarizing Dr. X's critics with no hint of what he himself had to say, the audience probably would have had the same frustrated "why is he going on like this?" reaction. What we suggest, then, is that as soon as possible you state your own position and the one it's responding to *together*, and that you think of the two as a unit. It is generally best to summarize the ideas you're responding to briefly, at the start of your text, and to delay detailed elaboration until later. The point is to give your readers a quick preview of what is motivating your argument, not to drown them in details right away.

Starting with a summary of others' views may seem to contradict the common advice that writers should lead with their own thesis or claim. Although we agree that you shouldn't keep readers in suspense too long about your central argument, we also believe that you need to present that argument as part of some larger conversation, indicating something about the arguments of others that you are supporting, opposing, amending, complicating, or qualifying. One added benefit of summarizing others' views as soon as you can: you let those others do some of the work of framing and clarifying the issue you're writing about.

Consider, for example, how George Orwell starts his famous essay "Politics and the English Language" with what others are saying:

> Most people who bother with the matter at all would admit that the English language is in a bad way, but it is generally assumed that we cannot by conscious action do anything about it. Our civilization is decadent and our language—so the argument runs—must inevitably share in the general collapse. . . .
>
> [But] the process is reversible. Modern English . . . is full of bad habits . . . which can be avoided if one is willing to take the necessary trouble.
>
> George Orwell, "Politics and the English Language"

Orwell is basically saying, "Most people assume that we cannot do anything about the bad state of the English language. But I say we can."

Of course, there are many other powerful ways to begin. Instead of opening with someone else's views, you could start with an illustrative quotation, a revealing fact or statistic, or—as we do in this chapter—a relevant anecdote. If you choose one of these formats, however, be sure that it in some way illustrates the view you're addressing or leads you to that view directly, with a minimum of steps.

In opening this chapter, for example, we devote the first paragraph to an anecdote about the conference speaker and then move quickly at the start of the second paragraph to the misconception about writing exemplified by the speaker. In the following opening, from an opinion piece in the *New York Times Book Review*, Christina Nehring also moves quickly from an anecdote illustrating something she dislikes to her own claim—that book lovers think too highly of themselves:

> "I'm a reader!" announced the yellow button. "How about you?" I looked at its bearer, a strapping young guy stalking my town's Festival of Books. "I'll bet you're a reader," he volunteered, as though we were

two geniuses well met. "No," I replied. "Absolutely not," I wanted to yell, and fling my Barnes & Noble bag at his feet. Instead, I mumbled something apologetic and melted into the crowd.

There's a new piety in the air: the self-congratulation of book lovers.

CHRISTINA NEHRING, "Books Make You a Boring Person"

Nehring's anecdote is really a kind of "they say": book lovers keep telling themselves how great they are.

TEMPLATES FOR INTRODUCING WHAT "THEY SAY"

There are lots of conventional ways to introduce what others are saying. Here are some standard templates that we would have recommended to our conference speaker:

- **A number of sociologists have recently suggested <u>that X's work has several fundamental problems</u>.**
- **It has become common today to dismiss ________.**
- **In their recent work, Y and Z have offered harsh critiques of ________ for ________.**

TEMPLATES FOR INTRODUCING "STANDARD VIEWS"

The following templates can help you make what we call the "standard view" move, in which you introduce a view that has become so widely accepted that by now it is essentially the conventional way of thinking about a topic:

- Americans have always believed that individual effort can triumph over circumstances.
- Conventional wisdom has it that ________.
- Common sense seems to dictate that ________.
- The standard way of thinking about topic X has it that ________.
- It is often said that ________.
- My whole life I have heard it said that ________.
- You would think that ________.
- Many people assume that ________.

These templates are popular because they provide a quick and efficient way to perform one of the most common moves that writers make: challenging widely accepted beliefs, placing them on the examining table, and analyzing their strengths and weaknesses.

TEMPLATES FOR MAKING WHAT "THEY SAY" SOMETHING *YOU* SAY

Another way to introduce the views you're responding to is to present them as your own. That is, the "they say" that you respond to need not be a view held by others; it can be one that you yourself once held or one that you are ambivalent about:

- I've always believed that museums are boring.
- When I was a child, I used to think that ________.

- ▸ Although I should know better by now, I cannot help thinking that ________.
- ▸ At the same time that I believe ________, I also believe ________.

TEMPLATES FOR INTRODUCING SOMETHING IMPLIED OR ASSUMED

Another sophisticated move a writer can make is to summarize a point that is not directly stated in what "they say" but is implied or assumed:

- ▸ Although none of them have ever said so directly, my teachers have often given me the impression that education will open doors.
- ▸ One implication of X's treatment of ________ is that ________.
- ▸ Although X does not say so directly, she apparently assumes that ________.
- ▸ While they rarely admit as much, ________ often take for granted that ________.

These are templates that can help you think analytically—to look beyond what others say explicitly and to consider their unstated assumptions, as well as the implications of their views.

TEMPLATES FOR INTRODUCING AN ONGOING DEBATE

Sometimes you'll want to open by summarizing a debate that presents two or more views. This kind of opening demonstrates your awareness that there are conflicting ways to look at your subject, the clear mark of someone who knows the subject and therefore is likely to be a reliable, trustworthy guide. Furthermore, opening with a summary of a debate can help you explore the issue you are writing about before declaring your own view. In this way, you can use the writing process itself to help you discover where you stand instead of having to commit to a position before you are ready to do so.

Here is a basic template for opening with a debate:

- **In discussions of X, one controversial issue has been ________. On the one hand, ________ argues ________. On the other hand, ________ contends ________. Others even maintain ________. My own view is ________.**

The cognitive scientist Mark Aronoff uses this kind of template in an essay on the workings of the human brain:

> Theories of how the mind/brain works have been dominated for centuries by two opposing views. One, rationalism, sees the human mind as coming into this world more or less fully formed—preprogrammed, in modern terms. The other, empiricism, sees the mind of the newborn as largely unstructured, a blank slate.
>
> MARK ARONOFF, "Washington Sleeped Here"

A student writer, Michaela Cullington, uses a version of this template near the beginning of an essay to frame a debate over online writing abbreviations like "LOL" ("laughing out loud") and to indicate her own position in this debate:

> Some people believe that using these abbreviations is hindering the writing abilities of students, and others argue that texting is

> actually having a positive effect on writing. In fact, it seems likely that texting has no significant effect on student writing.
>
> MICHAELA CULLINGTON, "Does Texting Affect Writing?"

Another way to open with a debate involves starting with a proposition many people agree with in order to highlight the point(s) on which they ultimately disagree:

- **When it comes to the topic of ________, most of us will readily agree that ________. Where this agreement usually ends, however, is on the question of ________. Whereas some are convinced that ________, others maintain that ________.**

The political writer Thomas Frank uses a variation on this move:

> That we are a nation divided is an almost universal lament of this bitter election year. However, the exact property that divides us—elemental though it is said to be—remains a matter of some controversy.
>
> THOMAS FRANK, "American Psyche"

KEEP WHAT "THEY SAY" IN VIEW

We can't urge you too strongly to keep in mind what "they say" as you move through the rest of your text. After summarizing the ideas you are responding to at the outset, it's very important to continue to keep those ideas in view. Readers won't be able to follow your unfolding response, much less any complications you may offer, unless you keep reminding them what claims you are responding to.

In other words, even when presenting your own claims, you should keep returning to the motivating "they say." The longer and more complicated your text, the greater the chance that readers will forget what ideas originally motivated it—no matter how clearly you lay them out at the beginning. At strategic moments throughout your text, we recommend that you include what we call "return sentences." Here is an example:

- **In conclusion, then, as I suggested earlier, defenders of ________ can't have it both ways. Their assertion that ________ is contradicted by their claim that ________.**

We ourselves use such return sentences at every opportunity in this book to remind you of the view of writing that our book questions—that good writing means making true or smart or logical statements about a given subject with little or no reference to what others say about it.

By reminding readers of the ideas you're responding to, return sentences ensure that your text maintains a sense of mission and urgency from start to finish. In short, they frame your argument as a genuine response to others' views rather than just a set of observations about a given subject. The difference is huge. To be responsive to others and the conversation you're entering, you need to start with what others are saying and continue keeping it in the readers' view.

Exercises

1. Following is a list of topics people have debated. Working by yourself or with a partner, compose a "they say" argument

for each of these topics, using any of the templates from this chapter.

Example:

Self-driving vehicles. "Many people think that self-driving cars will make roads safer by reducing accidents caused by unavoidable human errors."

a. Free college tuition at public universities
b. Social media use among teenagers
c. The value of studying the humanities in college
d. Public-funded clean needle exchanges
e. Assigning homework in elementary school

When you finish, read aloud and compare your "they say" arguments with a partner or a small group. Which template moves were more challenging than others to use? Why do you think so?

2. Read the following passage from Kenneth Goldsmith's 2016 *Los Angeles Times* op-ed, "Go Ahead: Waste Time on the Internet."

The notion that the Internet is bad for you seems premised on the idea that the Internet is one thing—a monolith. In reality it's a befuddling mix of the stupid and the sublime, a shattered, contradictory, and fragmented medium. Internet detractors seem to miss this simple fact, which is why so many of their criticisms disintegrate under observation.

The way Internet pundits tell it, you'd think we stare for three hours at clickbait—those articles with hypersensational headlines—the way we once sat down and watched three hours of cartoons on Saturday morning TV. But most of us don't do any one thing on the Internet. Instead, we do many things, some of it frivolous, some of it heavy. Our time spent in front of the computer is a mixed time, a time that reflects our desires—as opposed to the time spent sitting in front of the television where we were fed shows we didn't necessarily enjoy. TV gave us few choices. Many of us truly did feel like we wasted our time—as our parents so often chided us—"rotting away" in front of the TV.

I keep reading—on screens—that in the age of screens we've lost our ability to concentrate, that we've become distracted. But when I look around me and see people riveted to their devices, I notice a great wealth of concentration, focus, and engagement.

a. Where in this passage do you see Goldsmith introducing what others are saying about the internet and the amount of time we spend on screens? What do you notice about the different ways Goldsmith introduces "they say" arguments?
b. Summarize Goldsmith's argument by using the following template for introducing an ongoing debate (p. 26):

In discussions of <u>how the internet affects people</u>, one controversial issue has been ________. On one hand, ________ argues ________. On the other hand, ________ contends ________. Others even maintain ________. My own view is ________.

3. Read over something you've written for one of your classes—a paragraph, a short response, or an essay—and then respond to the following questions. You can do this exercise with a partner or by yourself.

a. Where do you introduce what others are saying? Underline or highlight where you include a "they say." If you can't find a "they say" in your writing, add one using one of the templates from this chapter.

b. How soon in your argument do you introduce these other views? Make sure that you include a "they say" early in your writing (in the first paragraph or two for a short response or essay). If the views you're responding to are buried later in your piece, revise your writing so that they appear earlier.

TWO

"HER POINT IS"

The Art of Summarizing

IF IT IS TRUE, as we claim in this book, that to argue persuasively you need to be in dialogue with others, then summarizing others' arguments is central to your arsenal of basic moves. Because writers who make strong claims need to map their claims relative to those of other people, it is important to know how to summarize effectively what those other people say. (We're using the word "summarizing" here to refer to any information from others that you present in your own words, including that which you paraphrase.)

Many writers shy away from summarizing—perhaps because they don't want to take the trouble to go back to the text in question and wrestle with what it says, or because they fear that devoting too much time to other people's ideas will take away from their own. When assigned to write a response to an article, such writers might offer their own views on the article's *topic* while hardly mentioning what the article itself argues or says. At the opposite extreme are those who do nothing *but* summarize. Lacking confidence, perhaps, in their own ideas, these writers so overload their texts with summaries of others' ideas that their own voice gets lost. And since these summaries are not animated by the writers' own interests, they often read like mere lists of things that X thinks or Y says—with no clear focus.

As a general rule, a good summary requires balancing what the original author is saying with the writer's own focus. Generally speaking, a summary must at once be true to what the original author says while also emphasizing those aspects of what the author says that interest you, the writer. Striking this delicate balance can be tricky, since it means facing two ways at once: both outward (toward the author being summarized) and inward (toward yourself). Ultimately, it means being respectful of others but simultaneously structuring how you summarize them in light of your own text's central argument.

ON THE ONE HAND, PUT YOURSELF IN *THEIR* SHOES

To write a really good summary, you must be able to suspend your own beliefs for a time and put yourself in the shoes of someone else. This means playing what the writing theorist Peter Elbow calls the "believing game," in which you try to inhabit the worldview of those whose conversation you are joining—and whom you are perhaps even disagreeing with—and try to see their argument from their perspective. This ability to temporarily suspend one's own convictions is a hallmark of good actors, who must convincingly "become" characters whom in real life they may detest. As a writer, when you play the believing game well, readers should not be able to tell whether you agree or disagree with the ideas you are summarizing.

If, as a writer, you cannot or will not suspend your own beliefs in this way, you are likely to produce summaries that are so obviously biased that they undermine your credibility with readers. Consider the following summary:

> David Zinczenko's article "Don't Blame the Eater" is nothing more than an angry rant in which he accuses the fast-food companies of an evil conspiracy to make people fat. I disagree because these companies have to make money. . . .

If you review what Zinczenko actually says (pp. 199–202), you should immediately see that this summary amounts to an unfair distortion. While Zinczenko does argue that the practices of the fast-food industry have the *effect* of making people fat, his tone is never "angry," and he never goes so far as to suggest that the fast-food industry conspires to make people fat with deliberately evil intent.

Another telltale sign of this writer's failure to give Zinczenko a fair hearing is the hasty way he abandons the summary after only one sentence and rushes on to his own response. So eager is this writer to disagree that he not only caricatures what Zinczenko says but also gives the article a hasty, superficial reading. Granted, there are many writing situations in which, because of matters of proportion, a one- or two-sentence summary is precisely what you want. Indeed, as writing professor Karen Lunsford (whose own research focuses on argument theory) points out, it is standard in the natural and social sciences to summarize the work of others quickly, in one pithy sentence or phrase, as in the following example:

> Several studies (Crackle, 2012; Pop, 2007; Snap, 2006) suggest that these policies are harmless; moreover, other studies (Dick, 2011; Harry, 2007; Tom, 2005) argue that they even have benefits.

But if your assignment is to respond in writing to a single author, like Zinczenko, you will need to tell your readers enough about the argument so they can assess its merits on their own, independent of you.

When summarizing something you've read, be sure to provide a rigorous and thoughtful summary of the author's words, or you may fall prey to what we call "the closest cliché syndrome," in which what gets summarized is not the view the author in question has actually expressed but a familiar cliché that the writer mistakes for the author's view (sometimes because the writer believes it and mistakenly assumes the author must too). So, for example, Martin Luther King Jr.'s passionate defense of civil disobedience in "Letter from Birmingham Jail" might be summarized not as the defense of political protest that it actually is but as a plea for everyone to "just get along." Similarly, Zinczenko's critique of the fast-food industry might be summarized as a call for overweight people to take responsibility for their weight.

Whenever you enter into a conversation with others in your writing, then, it is extremely important that you go back to what those others have said, that you study it very closely, and that you not confuse it with something you already believe. Writers who fail to do this end up essentially conversing with imaginary others who are really only the products of their own biases and preconceptions.

ON THE OTHER HAND, KNOW WHERE *YOU* ARE GOING

Even as writing an effective summary requires you to temporarily adopt the worldview of another person, it does not mean ignoring your own view altogether. Paradoxically, at the same time that summarizing another text requires you to represent fairly what it says, it also requires that your own response exert a quiet influence. A good summary, in other words, has a focus or spin that allows the summary to fit with your own agenda while still being true to the text you are summarizing.

Thus if you are writing in response to the essay by Zinczenko, you should be able to see that an essay on the fast-food industry in general will call for a very different summary than will an essay on parenting, corporate regulation, or warning labels. If you want your essay to encompass all three topics, you'll need to subordinate these three issues to one of Zinczenko's general claims and then make sure this general claim directly sets up your own argument.

For example, suppose you want to argue that it is parents, not fast-food companies, who are to blame for children's obesity. To set up this argument, you will probably want to compose a summary that highlights what Zinczenko says about the fast-food industry *and parents*. Consider this sample:

> In his article "Don't Blame the Eater," David Zinczenko blames the fast-food industry for fueling today's so-called obesity epidemic, not only by failing to provide adequate warning labels on its high-calorie foods but also by filling the nutritional void in children's lives left by their overtaxed working parents. With many parents working long hours and unable to supervise what their children eat, Zinczenko claims, children today are easily victimized by the low-cost, calorie-laden foods that the fast-food chains are all too eager to supply. When he was a young boy, for instance, and his single mother was away at work, he ate at Taco Bell, McDonald's, and other chains on a regular basis, and ended up overweight. Zinczenko's hope is that with the new spate of lawsuits against

> the food industry, other children with working parents will have healthier choices available to them, and that they will not, like him, become obese.
>
> In my view, however, it is the parents, and not the food chains, who are responsible for their children's obesity. While it is true that many of today's parents work long hours, there are still several things that parents can do to guarantee that their children eat healthy foods. . . .

The summary in the first paragraph succeeds because it points in two directions at once—both toward Zinczenko's own text *and* toward the second paragraph, where the writer begins to establish her own argument. The opening sentence gives a sense of Zinczenko's general argument (that the fast-food chains are to blame for obesity), including his two main supporting claims (about warning labels and parents), but it ends with an emphasis on the writer's main concern: parental responsibility. In this way, the summary does justice to Zinczenko's arguments while also setting up the ensuing critique.

This advice—to summarize authors in light of your own agenda—may seem painfully obvious. But writers often summarize a given author on one issue even though their text actually focuses on another. To avoid this problem, you need to make sure that your "they say" and "I say" are well matched. In fact, aligning what they say with what you say is a good thing to work on when revising what you've written.

Often writers who summarize without regard to their own agenda fall prey to what might be called "list summaries," summaries that simply inventory the original author's various points but fail to focus those points around any larger overall claim. If you've ever heard a talk in which the points were connected only by words like "and then," "also," and "in addition," you

THE EFFECT OF A TYPICAL LIST SUMMARY

know how such lists can put listeners to sleep—as shown in the figure above. A typical list summary sounds like this:

> The author says many different things about his subject. *First* he says . . . *Then* he makes the point that . . . *In addition* he says . . . *And then* he writes . . . *Also* he shows that . . . *And then* he says . . .

It may be boring list summaries like this that give summaries in general a bad name and even prompt some instructors to discourage their students from summarizing at all.

Not all lists are bad, however. A list can be an excellent way to organize material—but only if, instead of being a miscellaneous grab bag, it is organized around a larger argument that informs each item listed. Many well-written summaries, for instance, list various points made by an author, sometimes itemizing those points ("First, she argues . . . ," "Second, she argues . . . ," "Third . . ."), and sometimes even itemizing those points in bullet form.

Many well-written arguments are organized in a list format as well. In "The New Liberal Arts," Sanford J. Ungar lists what he sees as seven common misperceptions that discourage college students from majoring in the liberal arts, the first of which begin:

> Misperception No. 1: A liberal-arts degree is a luxury that most families can no longer afford. . . .
>
> Misperception No. 2: College graduates are finding it harder to get good jobs with liberal-arts degrees. . . .
>
> Misperception No. 3: The liberal arts are particularly irrelevant for low-income and first-generation college students. They, more than their more-affluent peers, must focus on something more practical and marketable.
>
> SANFORD J. UNGAR, "The New Liberal Arts"

What makes Ungar's list so effective, and makes it stand out in contrast to the type of disorganized lists our cartoon parodies, is that it has a clear, overarching goal: to defend the liberal arts. Had Ungar's article lacked such a unifying agenda and instead been a miscellaneous grab bag, it almost assuredly would have lost its readers, who wouldn't have known what to focus on or what the final "message" or "takeaway" should be.

In conclusion, writing a good summary means not just representing an author's view accurately but doing so in a way that fits what you want to say, the larger point you want to make. On the one hand, it means playing Peter Elbow's believing game and doing justice to the source; if the summary ignores or misrepresents the source, its bias and unfairness will show. On the other hand, even as it does justice to the source, a summary has to have a slant or spin that prepares the way for your own claims. Once a summary enters your text, you should think of it as joint property—reflecting not just the source you are summarizing but your own perspective or take on it as well.

SUMMARIZING SATIRICALLY

Thus far in this chapter we have argued that, as a general rule, good summaries require a balance between what someone else has said and your own interests as a writer. Now, however, we want to address one exception to this rule: the satiric summary, in which writers deliberately give their own spin to someone else's argument in order to reveal a glaring shortcoming in it. Despite our previous comments that well-crafted summaries generally strike a balance between heeding what someone else has said and your own independent interests, the satiric mode can at times be a very effective form of critique because it lets the summarized argument condemn itself without overt editorializing by you, the writer.

One such satiric summary can be found in Sanford J. Ungar's essay "The New Liberal Arts," which we just mentioned. In his discussion of the "misperception," as he sees it, that a liberal arts education is "particularly irrelevant for low-income and first-generation college students," who "must focus on something more practical and marketable," Ungar restates this view as "another way of saying, really, that the rich folks will do the important thinking, and the lower classes will simply carry out their ideas." Few who would dissuade disadvantaged students from the liberal arts would actually state their position in this insulting way. But in taking their position to its logical conclusion, Ungar's satire suggests that this is precisely what their position amounts to.

USE SIGNAL VERBS THAT FIT THE ACTION

In introducing summaries, try to avoid bland formulas like "she says" or "they believe." Though language like this is sometimes serviceable enough, it often fails to reflect accurately what's been said. Using these weaker verbs may lead you to summarize the topic instead of the argument. In some cases, "he says" may even drain the passion out of the ideas you're summarizing.

We suspect that the habit of ignoring the action when summarizing stems from the mistaken belief we mentioned earlier, that writing is about playing it safe and not making waves, a matter of piling up truths and bits of knowledge rather than a dynamic process of doing things to and with other people. People who wouldn't hesitate to *say* "X totally misrepresented," "attacked," or "loved" something when chatting with friends will in their writing often opt for far tamer and even less accurate phrases like "X said."

But the authors you summarize at the college level seldom simply "say" or "discuss" things; they "urge," "emphasize," and "complain about" them. David Zinczenko, for example, doesn't just *say* that fast-food companies contribute to obesity; he *complains* or *protests* that they do; he *challenges*, *chastises*, and *indicts* those companies. The Declaration of Independence doesn't just *talk about* the treatment of the colonies by the British; it *protests against* it. To do justice to the authors you cite, we recommend that when summarizing—

or when introducing a quotation—you use vivid and precise signal verbs as often as possible. Though "he says" or "she believes" will sometimes be the most appropriate language for the occasion, your text will often be more accurate and lively if you tailor your verbs to suit the precise actions you're describing.

TEMPLATES FOR WRITING SUMMARIES

To introduce a summary, use one of the signal verbs above in a template like these:

- ▸ **In her essay X, she advocates a radical revision of the juvenile justice system.**
- ▸ **They celebrate the fact that ________.**
- ▸ **________, he admits.**

When you tackle the summary itself, think about what else is important beyond the central claim of the argument. For example, what are the conversations the author is responding to? What kinds of evidence does the author's argument rely on? What are the implications of what the author says, both for your own argument and for the larger conversation?

Here is a template that you can use to develop your summary:

- ▸ **X and Y, in their article ________, argue that ________. Their research, which demonstrates that ______, challenges the idea that ________. They use ________ to show ________. X and Y's argument speaks to ________ about the larger issue of ________.**

VERBS FOR INTRODUCING SUMMARIES AND QUOTATIONS

VERBS FOR MAKING A CLAIM

argue
assert
believe
claim
emphasize
insist
observe
remind us
report
suggest

VERBS FOR EXPRESSING AGREEMENT

acknowledge
admire
admit
agree
celebrate
concede
corroborate
do not deny
endorse
extol
praise
reaffirm
support
verify

VERBS FOR QUESTIONING OR DISAGREEING

complain
complicate
contend
contradict
deny
deplore the tendency to
qualify
question
refute
reject
renounce
repudiate

VERBS FOR MAKING RECOMMENDATIONS

advocate
call for
demand
encourage
exhort
implore
plead
recommend
urge
warn

Exercises

1. To get a feel for Peter Elbow's believing game, think about a debate you've heard recently—perhaps in class, at your workplace, or at home. Write a summary of one of the arguments you heard. Then write a summary of another position in the same debate. Give both your summaries to a classmate or two. See if they can tell which position you endorse. If you've succeeded, they won't be able to tell.

2. Read the following passage from "Our Manifesto to Fix America's Gun Laws," an argument written by the editorial board of the *Eagle Eye*, the student newspaper at Marjory Stoneman Douglas High School in Parkland, Florida, in response to the mass shooting that occurred there on February 14, 2018.

   > We have a unique platform not only as student journalists but also as survivors of a mass shooting. We are firsthand witnesses to the kind of devastation that gross incompetence and political inaction can produce. We cannot stand idly by as the country continues to be infected by a plague of gun violence that seeps into community after community and does irreparable damage to the hearts and minds of the American people. . . .

The changes we propose:

Ban semi-automatic weapons that fire high-velocity rounds
Civilians shouldn't have access to the same weapons that soldiers do. That's a gross misuse of the second amendment ...

Ban accessories that simulate automatic weapons
High-capacity magazines played a huge role in the shooting at our school. In only 10 minutes, 17 people were killed, and 17 others were injured. This is unacceptable ...

Establish a database of gun sales and universal background checks
We believe that there should be a database recording which guns are sold in the United States, to whom, and of what caliber and capacity they are ...

Raise the firearm purchase age to 21
In a few months from now, many of us will be turning 18. We will not be able to drink; we will not be able to rent a car. Most of us will still be living with our parents. We will not be able to purchase a handgun. And yet we will be able to purchase an AR-15 ...

a. Do you think the list format is appropriate for this argument? Why or why not?
b. Write a one-sentence summary of this argument, using one of the verbs from the list on pages 43–44.
c. Compare your summary with a classmate's. What are the similarities and differences between them?

3. A student was asked to summarize an essay by writer Ben Adler, "Banning Plastic Bags Is Good for the World, Right?

Not So Fast." Here is the draft: "Ben Adler says that climate change is too big of a problem for any one person to solve."

a. How does this summary fall prey to the "closest cliché syndrome" (p. 35)?
b. What's a better verb to use than "say"? Why do you think so?

THREE

"AS HE HIMSELF PUTS IT"

The Art of Quoting

A KEY PREMISE OF THIS BOOK is that to launch an effective argument you need to write the arguments of others into your text. One of the best ways to do so is not only by summarizing what "they say," as suggested in Chapter 2, but also by quoting their exact words. Quoting someone else's words gives a tremendous amount of credibility to your summary and helps ensure that it is fair and accurate. In a sense, then, quotations function as a kind of proof of evidence, saying to readers: "Look, I'm not just making this up. She makes this claim, and here it is in her exact words."

Yet many writers make a host of mistakes when it comes to quoting, not the least of which is the failure to quote enough in the first place, if at all. Some writers quote too little—perhaps because they don't want to bother going back to the original text and looking up the author's exact words or because they think they can reconstruct the author's ideas from memory. At the opposite extreme are writers who so overquote that they end up with texts that are short on commentary of their own—maybe because they lack confidence in their ability to comment on the quotations, or because they don't fully understand what they've quoted and therefore have trouble explaining what the quotations mean.

But the main problem with quoting arises when writers assume that quotations speak for themselves. Because the meaning of a quotation is obvious to *them*, many writers assume that this meaning will also be obvious to their readers, when often it is not. Writers who make this mistake think that their job is done when they've chosen a quotation and inserted it into their text. They draft an essay, slap in a few quotations, and whammo, they're done. Such writers fail to see that quoting means more than simply enclosing what "they say" in quotation marks. In a way, quotations are orphans: words that have been taken from their original contexts and that need to be integrated into their new textual surroundings. This chapter offers two key ways to produce this sort of integration: (1) by choosing quotations wisely, with an eye to how well they support a particular part of your text, and (2) by surrounding every major quotation with a frame explaining whose words they are, what the quotation means, and how the quotation relates to your own text. The point we want to emphasize is that quoting what "they say" must always be connected with what *you* say.

QUOTE RELEVANT PASSAGES

Before you can select appropriate quotations, you need to have a sense of what you want to do with them—that is, how they will support your text at the particular point where you insert them. Be careful not to select quotations just for the sake of demonstrating that you've read the author's work; you need to make sure they support your own argument.

However, finding relevant quotations is not always easy. In fact, sometimes quotations that were initially relevant to your argument, or to a key point in it, become less so as your text changes during the process of writing and revising. Given the evolving and messy nature of writing, you may sometimes think that you've found the perfect quotation to support your argument, only to discover later on, as your text develops, that your focus has changed and the quotation no longer works. It can be somewhat misleading, then, to speak of finding your thesis and finding relevant quotations as two separate steps, one coming after the other. When you're deeply engaged in the writing and revising process, there is usually a great deal of back-and-forth between your argument and any quotations you select.

FRAME EVERY QUOTATION

Finding relevant quotations is only part of your job; you also need to present them in a way that makes their relevance and meaning clear to your readers. Since quotations do not speak for themselves, you need to build a frame around them in which you do that speaking for them.

Quotations that are inserted into a text without such a frame are sometimes called "dangling" quotations for the way they're left dangling without any explanation. One teacher we've worked with, Steve Benton, calls these "hit-and-run" quotations, likening them to car accidents in which the driver speeds away and avoids taking responsibility for the dent in your fender or the smashed taillights, as in the figure that follows.

What follows is a typical hit-and-run quotation by a student responding to an essay by Deborah Tannen, a linguistics professor and prominent author, who complains that academics value opposition over agreement:

> Deborah Tannen writes about academia. Academics believe "that intellectual inquiry is a metaphorical battle. Following from that is a second assumption that the best way to demonstrate intellectual prowess is to criticize, find fault, and attack."
>
> I agree with Tannen. Another point Tannen makes is that . . .

Since this student fails to introduce the quotation adequately or explain why he finds it worth quoting, readers will have a hard time reconstructing what Tannen argued. First, the student simply gives us the quotation from Tannen without telling us who Tannen is or even indicating that the quoted words are hers. In addition, the student does not explain what he takes Tannen to be saying or how her claims connect with his own. Instead, he simply abandons the quotation in his haste to zoom on to another point.

To adequately frame a quotation, you need to insert it into what we like to call a "quotation sandwich," with the statement introducing it serving as the top slice of bread and the explanation following it serving as the bottom slice. The introductory or lead-in claims should explain who is speaking and set up what the quotation says; the follow-up statements should explain why you consider the quotation to be important and what you take it to say.

TEMPLATES FOR INTRODUCING QUOTATIONS

- X states, "Not all steroids should be banned from sports."
- As the prominent philosopher X puts it, "_________."
- According to X, "_________."
- X himself writes, "_________."
- In her book, _________, X maintains that "_________."
- Writing in the journal _________, X complains that "_________."
- In X's view, "_________."
- X agrees when she writes, "_________."
- X disagrees when he writes, "_________."
- X complicates matters further when she writes, "_________."

TEMPLATES FOR EXPLAINING QUOTATIONS

The one piece of advice about quoting that our students say they find most helpful is to get in the habit of following every major quotation by explaining what it means, using a template like one of the ones below.

- **Basically, X is warning that the proposed solution will only make the problem worse.**
- **In other words, X believes ________.**
- **In making this comment, X urges us to ________.**
- **X is corroborating the age-old adage that ________.**
- **X's point is that ________.**
- **The essence of X's argument is that ________.**

When offering such explanations, it is important to use language that accurately reflects the spirit of the quoted passage. It is often serviceable enough in introducing a quotation to write "X states" or "X asserts," but in most cases you can add precision to your writing by introducing the quotation in more vivid terms. Since, in the example above, Tannen is clearly alarmed by the culture of "attack" that she describes, it would be more accurate to use language that reflects that alarm: "Tannen is alarmed that," "Tannen is disturbed by," "Tannen deplores," or (in our own formulation here) "Tannen complains."

See pp. 43–44 for a list of action verbs for summarizing what other say.

Consider, for example, how the earlier passage on Tannen might be revised using some of these moves:

> Deborah Tannen, a prominent linguistics professor, complains that academia is too combative. Rather than really listening to others, Tannen insists, academics habitually try to prove one another wrong. As Tannen herself puts it, "We are all driven by our ideological

> assumption that intellectual inquiry is a metaphorical battle," that "the best way to demonstrate intellectual prowess is to criticize, find fault, and attack." In short, Tannen objects that academic communication tends to be a competition for supremacy in which loftier values like truth and consensus get lost.
>
> Tannen's observations ring true to me because I have often felt that the academic pieces I read for class are negative and focus on proving another theorist wrong rather than stating a truth. . . .

This revision works, we think, because it frames or nests Tannen's words, integrating them and offering guidance about how they should be read. Instead of launching directly into the quoted words, as the previous draft had done, this revised version identifies Tannen ("a prominent linguistics professor") and clearly indicates that the quoted words are hers ("as Tannen herself puts it"). And instead of being presented without explanation as it was before, the quotation is now presented as an illustration of Tannen's point that, as the student helpfully puts it, "academics habitually try to prove one another wrong" and compete "for supremacy." In this way, the student explains the quotation while restating it in his own words, thereby making it clear that the quotation is being used purposefully instead of having been stuck in simply to pad the essay or the works-cited list.

BLEND THE AUTHOR'S WORDS WITH YOUR OWN

This new framing material also works well because it accurately represents Tannen's words while giving those words the student's own spin. Instead of simply repeating Tannen word for word, the follow-up sentences echo just enough of her language while still moving the discussion in the student's own direction. Tannen's "battle," "criticize," "find fault," and "attack," for instance, get translated by the student into claims about how "combative" Tannen thinks academics are and how she thinks they "habitually try to prove one another wrong." In this way, the framing creates a kind of hybrid mix of Tannen's words and those of the writer.

CAN YOU OVERANALYZE A QUOTATION?

But is it possible to overexplain a quotation? And how do you know when you've explained a quotation thoroughly enough? After all, not all quotations require the same amount of explanatory framing, and there are no hard-and-fast rules for knowing how much explanation any quotation needs. As a general rule, the most explanatory framing is needed for quotations that may be hard for readers to process: quotations that are long and complex, that are filled with details or jargon, or that contain hidden complexities.

And yet, though the particular situation usually dictates when and how much to explain a quotation, we will still offer one piece of advice: when in doubt, go for it. It is better to risk being overly explicit about what you take a quotation to mean than to leave the quotation dangling and your readers in doubt. Indeed, we encourage you to provide such explanatory framing even when writing to an audience that you know to be familiar with the author being quoted and able to interpret your quotations on their own. Even in such cases, readers need to see how *you* interpret the quotation, since words—especially those of controversial figures—can be interpreted in various ways and used to support different, sometimes opposing, agendas. Your readers need to see what you make of the material you've quoted, if only to be sure that your reading of the material and theirs are on the same page.

HOW *NOT* TO INTRODUCE QUOTATIONS

We want to conclude this chapter by surveying some ways *not* to introduce quotations. Although some writers do so, you should not introduce quotations by saying something like "Orwell asserts an idea that" or "A quote by Shakespeare says." Introductory phrases like these are both redundant and misleading. In the first example, you could write either "Orwell asserts that" or "Orwell's assertion is that" rather than redundantly combining the two. The second example misleads readers, since it is the writer who is doing the quoting, not Shakespeare (as "a quote by Shakespeare" implies).

The templates in this book will help you avoid such mistakes. Once you have mastered templates like "as X puts it" or "in X's own words," you probably won't even have to think about them—and will be free to focus on the challenging ideas that templates help you frame.

Exercises

1. Find an essay that is posted on **theysayiblog.com**. Read the essay, and look closely to see how the writer has integrated quotations in the argument. How has the writer introduced the quotations in the argument? What, if anything, has the writer said to explain the quotations? How has the writer tied the quotations to the essay? Based on what you read in this chapter about how to sandwich quotations, what revisions would you suggest?

2. Below is a passage from Christine Michel Carter's 2019 *Harper's Bazaar* essay, "How Feminism Is Stifling Our Sons." In this essay, Carter points out how gender stereotypes are harmful to both girls and boys, and she argues that popular media needs to present more positive models of masculinity. Read this passage and choose a phrase or sentence to quote as a "they say" for an argument of your own. Use the templates from this chapter to sandwich this quote: introduce the quote, explain what it means, and connect it to your own ideas. Your entire response (the introduction, quote, explanation, and connection to your ideas) should be three or four sentences long.

   We've committed so strongly to teaching girls they're equal to boys that we've forgotten to extend the message to the boys themselves in a healthy, inclusive way. Along with our focus on feminism, we need to embrace a new men's movement too—one that pays attention to the young boys who are discovering their manhood against a backdrop of hashtags and equality campaigns that tend to either overlook or vilify where masculinity fits in.

3. Read over something you've written for one of your classes. Have you quoted any sources? If so, highlight or underline all the quotations. How have you integrated each quotation into your own text? How have you introduced it? explained what it means? indicated how it relates to *your* text? If you haven't done all these things, revise your text to do so using the list of verbs for introducing summaries and quotations (pp. 43–44) and the templates for introducing quotations (p. 51) and explaining quotations (p. 51). If you haven't written anything with quotations, revise an academic text you've written so that it uses quotations.

FOUR

"YES / NO / OK, BUT"

Three Ways to Respond

THE FIRST THREE CHAPTERS of this book discuss the "they say" stage of writing, in which you devote your attention to the views of some other person or group. In this chapter, we move to the "I say" stage, in which you offer your own argument as a response to what "they" have said.

Moving to the "I say" stage can be daunting in academia, where it often may seem that you need to be an expert in a field to have an argument at all. Many students have told us that they have trouble entering some of the high-powered conversations that take place in college or graduate school because they do not know enough about the topic at hand or because, they say, they simply are not "smart enough." Yet often these same students, when given a chance to study in depth the contribution that some scholar has made in a given field, will turn around and say things like "I can see where she is coming from, how she makes her case by building on what other scholars have said. Perhaps if I had studied the situation longer, *I* could have come up with a similar argument." What these students come to realize is that good arguments are based not on knowledge that only a special class of experts has access to but on everyday habits of mind that can be isolated, identified, and used by almost anyone. Though there's certainly no substitute for expertise and for knowing as much as possible about one's topic, the arguments that finally win the day are built, as the title of this chapter suggests, on some very basic rhetorical patterns that most of us use on a daily basis.

There are a great many ways to respond to others' ideas, but this chapter concentrates on the three most common and recognizable ways: agreeing, disagreeing, or some combination of both. Although each way of responding is open to endless variation, we focus on these three because readers come to any text needing to learn fairly quickly where the writer stands, and they do this by placing the writer on a mental map consisting of a few familiar options: the writer agrees with those being responded to, disagrees with them, or presents some combination of both agreeing and disagreeing.

When writers take too long to declare their position relative to views they've summarized or quoted, readers get frustrated, wondering, "Is this guy agreeing or disagreeing? Is he *for* what this other person has said, *against* it, or what?" For this reason, this chapter's advice applies to reading as well as to writing. Especially with difficult texts, you need not only to find the position the writer is responding to—the "they say"—but also to determine whether the writer is agreeing with it, challenging it, or some mixture of the two.

ONLY *THREE* WAYS TO RESPOND?

Perhaps you'll worry that fitting your own response into one of these three categories will force you to oversimplify your argument or lessen its complexity, subtlety, or originality. This is certainly a serious concern for academics who are rightly skeptical of writing that is simplistic and reductive. We would argue, however, that the more complex and subtle your argument is, and the more it departs from the conventional ways people think, the more your readers will need to be able to place it on their mental map in order to process the complex details you present. That is, the complexity, subtlety, and originality of your response are more likely to stand out and be noticed if readers have a baseline sense of where you stand relative to any ideas you've cited. As you move through this chapter, we hope you'll agree that the forms of agreeing, disagreeing, and both agreeing and disagreeing that we discuss, far from being simplistic or one-dimensional, are able to accommodate a high degree of creative, complex thought.

It is always a good tactic to begin your response not by launching directly into a mass of details but by stating clearly whether you agree, disagree, or both, using a direct, no-nonsense formula such as: "I agree," "I disagree," or "I am of two minds. I agree that ___________, but I cannot agree that _________." Once you have offered one of these straightforward statements (or one of the many variations discussed below), readers will have a strong grasp of your position and then be able to appreciate the complications you go on to offer as your response unfolds.

See p. 21 for suggestions on previewing where you stand.

Still, you may object that these three basic ways of responding don't cover all the options—that they ignore interpretive or analytical responses, for example. In other words, you might think that when you interpret a literary work, you don't necessarily agree or disagree with anything but simply explain the work's meaning, style, or structure. Many essays about literature and the arts, it might be said, take this form—they interpret a work's meaning, thus rendering matters of agreeing or disagreeing irrelevant.

We would argue, however, that the most interesting interpretations tend to be those that agree, disagree, or both—that instead of being offered solo, the best interpretations take strong stands relative to other interpretations. In fact, there would be no reason to offer an interpretation of a work of literature or art unless you were responding to the interpretations or possible interpretations of others. Even when you point out features or qualities of an artistic work that others have not noticed, you are implicitly disagreeing with what those interpreters have said by pointing out that they missed or overlooked something that, in your view, is important. In any effective interpretation, then, you need not only to state what you yourself take the work of art to mean but also to do so relative to the interpretations of other readers—be they professional scholars, teachers, classmates, or even hypothetical readers (as in, "Although some readers might think that this poem is about ___________, it is in fact about ___________").

DISAGREE—AND EXPLAIN WHY

Disagreeing may seem like one of the simpler moves a writer can make, and it is often the first thing people associate with critical thinking. Disagreeing can also be the easiest way to generate an essay: find something you can disagree with in what has been said or might be said about your topic, summarize it, and argue with it. But disagreement in fact poses hidden challenges. You need to do more than simply assert that you disagree with a particular view; you also have to offer persuasive reasons *why* you disagree. After all, disagreeing means more than adding "not" to what someone else has said, more than just saying, "Although they say women's rights are improving, I say women's rights are *not* improving." Such a response merely contradicts the view it responds to and fails to add anything interesting or new. To turn it into an argument, you need to give reasons to support what you say: because another's argument fails to take relevant factors into account; because it is based on faulty or incomplete evidence; because it rests on questionable assumptions; or because it uses flawed logic, is contradictory, or overlooks what you take to be the real issue. To move the conversation forward (and, indeed, to justify your very act of writing), you need to demonstrate that you have something to contribute.

You can even disagree by making what we call the "duh" move, in which you disagree not with the position itself but with the assumption that it is a new or stunning revelation. Here is an example of such a move, used to open an essay on the state of American schools:

> According to a recent report by some researchers at Stanford University, high school students with college aspirations "often lack crucial information on applying to college and on succeeding academically once they get there."
>
> Well, duh. . . . It shouldn't take a Stanford research team to tell us that when it comes to "succeeding academically," many students don't have a clue.
>
> GERALD GRAFF, "Trickle-Down Obfuscation"

Like all the other moves discussed in this book, the "duh" move can be tailored to meet the needs of almost any writing situation. If you find the expression "duh" too brash to use with your intended audience, you can always dispense with the term itself and write something like "It is true that ________; but we already knew that."

TEMPLATES FOR DISAGREEING, WITH REASONS

- X is mistaken because she overlooks recent fossil discoveries in the South.
- X's claim that ___________ rests on the questionable assumption that __________.
- I disagree with X's view that _______ because, as recent research has shown, __________.
- X contradicts herself/can't have it both ways. On the one hand, she argues __________. On the other hand, she also says __________.
- By focusing on ____________, X overlooks the deeper problem of __________.

You can also disagree by making what we call the "twist it" move, in which you agree with the evidence that someone else has presented but show through a twist of logic that this evidence actually supports your own, contrary position. For example:

> X argues for stricter gun control legislation, saying that the crime rate is on the rise and that we need to restrict the circulation of guns. I agree that the crime rate is on the rise, but that's precisely why I oppose stricter gun control legislation. We need to own guns to protect ourselves against criminals.

In this example of the "twist it" move, the writer agrees with X's claim that the crime rate is on the rise but then argues that this increasing crime rate is in fact a valid reason for *opposing* gun control legislation.

At times you might be reluctant to express disagreement, for any number of reasons—not wanting to be unpleasant, to hurt someone's feelings, or to make yourself vulnerable to being disagreed with in return. One of these reasons may in fact explain why the conference speaker we described at the start of Chapter 1 avoided mentioning the disagreement he had with other scholars until he was provoked to do so in the discussion that followed his talk.

As much as we understand such fears of conflict and have experienced them ourselves, we nevertheless believe it is better to state our disagreements in frank yet considerate ways than to deny them. After all, suppressing disagreements doesn't make them go away; it only pushes them underground, where they can fester in private unchecked. Nevertheless, disagreements do not need to take the form of personal put-downs. Furthermore, there is usually no reason to take issue with *every* aspect of someone else's views. You can single out for criticism only those aspects of what someone else has said that are troubling and then agree with the rest—although such an approach, as we will see later in this chapter, leads to the somewhat more complicated terrain of both agreeing and disagreeing at the same time.

AGREE—BUT WITH A DIFFERENCE

Like disagreeing, agreeing is less simple than it may appear. Just as you need to avoid simply contradicting views you disagree with, you also need to do more than simply echo views you agree with. Even as you're agreeing, it's important to bring something new and fresh to the table, adding something that makes you a valuable participant in the conversation.

There are many moves that enable you to contribute something of your own to a conversation even as you agree with what someone else has said. You may point out some unnoticed evidence or line of reasoning that supports X's claims that X herself hadn't mentioned. You may cite some corroborating personal experience or a situation not mentioned by X that her views help readers understand. If X's views are particularly challenging or esoteric, what you bring to the table could be an accessible translation—an explanation for readers not already in the know. In other words, your text can usefully contribute to the conversation simply by pointing out unnoticed implications or explaining something that needs to be better understood.

Whatever mode of agreement you choose, the important thing is to open up some difference or contrast between your position and the one you're agreeing with rather than simply parroting what it says.

TEMPLATES FOR AGREEING

- **I agree that diversity in the student body is educationally valuable because my experience at Central University confirms it.**
- **X is surely right about ___ because, as she may not be aware, recent studies have shown that ___.**
- **X's theory of ___ is extremely useful because it sheds light on the difficult problem of ___.**
- **Those unfamiliar with this school of thought may be interested to know that it basically boils down to ___.**

Some writers avoid the practice of agreeing almost as much as others avoid disagreeing. In a culture like America's, which prizes originality, independence, and competitive individualism, writers sometimes don't like to admit that anyone else has made the same point, seemingly beating them to the punch. In our view, however, as long as you can support a position taken by someone else without merely restating what was said, there is no reason to worry about being "unoriginal." Indeed, there is good reason to rejoice when you agree with others since those others can lend credibility to your argument. While you don't want to present yourself as a mere copycat of someone else's views, you also need to avoid sounding like a lone voice in the wilderness.

But do be aware that whenever you agree with one person's view, you are likely disagreeing with someone else's. It is hard to align yourself with one position without at least implicitly positioning yourself against others. The psychologist Carol Gilligan does just that in an essay in which she agrees with scientists who argue that the human brain is "hard-wired" for cooperation but in so doing aligns herself against anyone who believes that the brain is wired for selfishness and competition:

> These findings join a growing convergence of evidence across the human sciences leading to a revolutionary shift in consciousness. . . . If cooperation, typically associated with altruism and self-sacrifice, sets off the same signals of delight as pleasures commonly associated with hedonism and self-indulgence; if the opposition between selfish and selfless, self vs. relationship biologically makes no sense, then a new paradigm is necessary to reframe the very terms of the conversation.
>
> CAROL GILLIGAN, "Sisterhood Is Pleasurable: A Quiet Revolution in Psychology"

In agreeing with some scientists that "the opposition between selfish and selfless . . . makes no sense," Gilligan implicitly disagrees with anyone who thinks the opposition *does* make sense. Basically, what Gilligan says could be boiled down to a template:

- **I agree that __________, a point that needs emphasizing since so many people still believe __________.**
- **If group X is right that __________, as I think they are, then we need to reassess the popular assumption that __________.**

What such templates allow you to do, then, is to agree with one view while challenging another—a move that leads into the domain of agreeing and disagreeing simultaneously.

AGREE AND DISAGREE SIMULTANEOUSLY

This last option is often our favorite way of responding. One thing we particularly like about agreeing and disagreeing simultaneously is that it helps us get beyond the kind of "is too" / "is not" exchanges that often characterize the disputes of young children and the more polarized shouting matches of talk radio and TV.

Sanford J. Ungar makes precisely this move in his essay "The New Liberal Arts" when, in critiquing seven common "misperceptions" of liberal arts education, he concedes that several contain a grain of truth. For example, after summarizing "Misperception No. 2," that "college graduates are finding it harder to get good jobs with liberal-arts degrees," that few employers want to hire those with an "irrelevant major like philosophy or French," Ungar writes: "Yes, recent graduates have had difficulty in the job market. . . ." But then, after making this concession, Ungar insists that this difficulty affects graduates in all fields, not just those from the liberal arts. In this way, we think, Ungar paradoxically strengthens his case. By admitting that the opposing argument has a point, Ungar bolsters his credibility, presenting himself as a writer willing to acknowledge facts as they present themselves rather than one determined to cheerlead only for his own side.

TEMPLATES FOR AGREEING AND DISAGREEING SIMULTANEOUSLY

"Yes and no." "Yes, but . . ." "Although I agree up to a point, I still insist . . ." These are just some of the ways you can make your argument complicated and nuanced while maintaining a clear, reader-friendly framework. The parallel structure—"yes and no"; "on the one hand I agree, on the other I disagree"—enables readers to place your argument on that map of positions we spoke of earlier in this chapter while still keeping your argument sufficiently complex.

Charles Murray's essay "Are Too Many People Going to College?" contains a good example of the "yes and no" move when, at the outset of his essay, Murray responds to what he sees as the prevailing wisdom about the liberal arts and college:

> We should not restrict the availability of a liberal education to a rarefied intellectual elite. More people should be going to college, not fewer.
>
> Yes and no. More people should be getting the basics of a liberal education. But for most students, the places to provide those basics are elementary and middle school.
>
> Charles Murray, "Are Too Many People Going to College?"

In other words, Murray is saying yes to more liberal arts but not to more college.

Another aspect we like about this "yes and no," "agree and disagree" option is that it can be tipped subtly toward agreement or disagreement, depending on where you lay your stress. If you want to emphasize the disagreement end of the spectrum, you would use a template like the one below:

- **Although I agree with X up to a point, I cannot accept his overriding assumption that religion is no longer a major force today.**

Conversely, if you want to stress your agreement more than your disagreement, you would use a template like this one:

- **Although I disagree with much that X says, I fully endorse his final conclusion that ______.**

The first template above might be called a "yes, but . . ." move, the second a "no, but . . ." move. Other versions include the following:

- **Though I concede that ______, I still insist that ______.**
- **X is right that ______, but she seems on more dubious ground when she claims that ______.**
- **While X is probably wrong when she claims that ______, she is right that ______.**
- **Whereas X provides ample evidence that ______, Y and Z's research on ______ and ______ convinces me that ______ instead.**

Another classic way to agree and disagree at the same time is to make what we call an "I'm of two minds" or a "mixed feelings" move:

- **I'm of two minds about X's claim that ___________. On the one hand, I agree that ___________. On the other hand, I'm not sure if __________.**
- **My feelings on the issue are mixed. I do support X's position that __________, but I find Y's argument about __________ and Z's research on ___________ to be equally persuasive.**

This move can be especially useful if you are responding to new or particularly challenging work and are as yet unsure where you stand. It also lends itself well to the kind of speculative investigation in which you weigh a position's pros and cons rather than come out decisively either for or against. But again, as we suggested earlier, whether you are agreeing, disagreeing, or both agreeing and disagreeing, you need to be as clear as possible, and making a frank statement that you are ambivalent is one way to be clear.

IS BEING UNDECIDED OK?

Nevertheless, writers often have as many concerns about expressing ambivalence as they do about expressing disagreement or agreement. Some worry that by expressing ambivalence they will come across as evasive, wishy-washy, or unsure of themselves. Others worry that their ambivalence will end up confusing readers who require decisive, clear-cut conclusions.

The truth is that in some cases these worries are legitimate. At times ambivalence can frustrate readers, leaving them with the feeling that you failed in your obligation to offer the guidance they expect from writers. At other times, however, acknowledging that a clear-cut resolution of an issue is impossible can demonstrate your sophistication as a writer. In an academic culture that values complex thought, forthrightly declaring that you have mixed feelings can be impressive, especially after having ruled out the one-dimensional positions on your issue taken by others in the conversation. Ultimately, then, how ambivalent you end up being comes down to a judgment call based on different readers' responses to your drafts, on your knowledge of your audience, and on the challenges of your particular argument and situation.

Exercises

1. Below is a passage from Chris Nowinski's 2019 *Vox* essay, "Youth Tackle Football Will Be Considered Unthinkable 50 Years from Now." In this essay, Nowinski (director of the Concussion Legacy Foundation and former college football player) argues that tackle football should be banned for kids under fourteen years old.

    a. Read the passage. Then respond to Nowinski's argument using one of the templates from this chapter: one that responds by agreeing and one that responds by disagreeing.
    b. Work with a partner to compare your responses. Which response do you think is the strongest, and why?

    The science is clearer than ever: Exposure data shows children as young as 9 are getting hit in the head more than 500 times in one season of youth tackle football. That should not feel normal to us. Think of the last time, outside of sports, you allowed your child to get hit hard in the head 25 times in a day. Better yet, when was the last time you were hit hard in the head?

Scientists are now beginning to understand the long-term consequences of all those hits. Chronic traumatic encephalopathy, or CTE, is a degenerative brain disease that was once thought to be confined only to "punch-drunk" boxers. Yet in the past decade, Boston University and Veterans Affairs researchers have diagnosed CTE in American football, soccer, ice hockey, and rugby players, along with other collision sport athletes....

Our society is committed to protecting children—that's why we ban smoking, remove children from homes with lead paint, and force parents to put their children in car seats. We should also protect children from unnecessary brain damage in youth sports.

2. Working together with a partner, write a response where you agree and disagree simultaneously—the "OK, but" move. You can write your response using the Nowinski passage above as your "they say," or you can respond to a reading posted on **theysayiblog.com**. Use the templates from this chapter to compose your response. Decide if you want to emphasize disagreement or agreement, and revise your response accordingly.

3. Read an essay that is posted on **theysayiblog.com**.
   a. Is the writer agreeing, disagreeing, or both? Where do you see the writer doing this? Point to a particular sentence or passage.
   b. How connected is the writer's argument ("I say") to the larger conversation ("they say")?
   c. If the writer is disagreeing, how considerate is the writer to the views being rebutted? Why do you think being considerate while disagreeing is important in academic writing?

FIVE

"AND YET"

Distinguishing What You *Say from What* They *Say*

IF GOOD ACADEMIC WRITING involves putting yourself into dialogue with others, it is extremely important that readers be able to tell at every point when you are expressing your own view and when you are stating someone else's. This chapter takes up the problem of moving from what *they* say to what *you* say without confusing readers about who is saying what.

DETERMINE WHO IS SAYING WHAT IN THE TEXTS YOU READ

Before examining how to signal who is saying what in your own writing, let's look at how to recognize such signals when they appear in the texts you read—an especially important skill when it comes to the challenging works assigned in school. Frequently, when students have trouble understanding difficult texts, it is not just because the texts contain unfamiliar ideas or words but also because the texts rely on subtle clues to let readers know when a particular view should be attributed to the writer or to someone else. Especially with texts that present a true dialogue of perspectives, readers need to be alert to the often subtle markers that indicate whose voice the writer is speaking in.

Consider how the social critic and educator Gregory Mantsios uses these "voice markers," as they might be called, to distinguish the different perspectives in his essay on America's class inequalities:

> "We are all middle-class," or so it would seem. Our national consciousness, as shaped in large part by the media and our political leadership, provides us with a picture of ourselves as a nation of prosperity and opportunity with an ever expanding middle-class life-style. As a result, our class differences are muted and our collective character is homogenized.
>
> Yet class divisions are real and arguably the most significant factor in determining both our very being in the world and the nature of the society we live in.
>
> GREGORY MANTSIOS, "Rewards and Opportunities: The Politics and Economics of Class in the U.S."

Although Mantsios makes it look easy, he is actually making several sophisticated rhetorical moves here that help him distinguish the common view he opposes from his own position.

In the opening sentence, for instance, the phrase "or so it would seem" shows that Mantsios does not necessarily agree with the view he is describing, since writers normally don't present views they themselves hold as ones that only "seem" to be true. Mantsios also places this opening view in quotation marks to signal that it is not his own. He then further distances himself from the belief being summarized in the opening paragraph by attributing it to "our national consciousness, as shaped in large part by the media and our political leadership," and then further attributing to this "consciousness" a negative, undesirable "result": one in which "our class differences" get "muted" and "our collective character" gets "homogenized," stripped of its diversity and distinctness. Hence, even before Mantsios has declared his own position in the second paragraph, readers can get a pretty solid sense of where he probably stands.

Furthermore, the second paragraph opens with the word "Yet," indicating that Mantsios is now shifting to his own view (as opposed to the common view he has thus far been describing). Even the parallelism he sets up between the first and second paragraphs—between the first paragraph's claim that class differences do not exist and the second paragraph's claim that they do—helps throw into sharp relief the differences between the two voices. Finally, Mantsios's use of a direct, authoritative, declarative tone in the second paragraph also suggests a switch in voice. Although he does not use the words "I say" or "I argue," he clearly identifies the view he holds by presenting it not as one that merely *seems* to be true or that *others tell us* is true but as a view that *is* true or, as Mantsios puts it, "real."

Paying attention to these voice markers is an important aspect of reading comprehension. Readers who fail to notice these markers often take an author's summaries of what someone else believes to be an expression of what the author himself or herself believes. Thus, when we teach Mantsios's essay, some students invariably come away thinking that the statement "we are all middle-class" is Mantsios's own position rather than the perspective he is opposing, failing to see that in writing these words Mantsios acts as a kind of ventriloquist, mimicking what others say rather than directly expressing what he himself is thinking.

To see how important such voice markers are, consider what the Mantsios passage looks like if we remove them:

> We are all middle-class. . . . We are a nation of prosperity and opportunity with an ever expanding middle-class life-style. . . .
>
> Class divisions are real and arguably the most significant factor in determining both our very being in the world and the nature of the society we live in.

In contrast to the careful delineation between voices in Mantsios's original text, this unmarked version leaves it hard to tell where his voice begins and the voices of others end. With the markers removed, readers cannot tell that "We are all middle-class" represents a view the author opposes and that "Class divisions are real" represents what the author himself believes. Indeed, without the markers, especially the "yet," readers might well miss the fact that the second paragraph's claim that "Class divisions are real" contradicts the first paragraph's claim that "We are all middle-class."

TEMPLATES FOR SIGNALING WHO IS SAYING WHAT IN YOUR OWN WRITING

To avoid confusion in your own writing, make sure that at every point your readers can clearly tell who is saying what. To do so, you can use as voice-identifying devices many of the templates presented in previous chapters.

- Although X makes the best possible case for universal, government-funded health care, I am not persuaded.
- My view, however, contrary to what X has argued, is that ________.
- Adding to X's argument, I would point out that ________.
- According to both X and Y, ________.
- Politicians, X argues, should ________.
- Most athletes will tell you that ________.

BUT I'VE BEEN TOLD NOT TO USE "I"

Notice that the first three templates above use the first-person, as do many of the templates in this book, thereby contradicting the common advice about avoiding the first person in academic writing. Although you may have been told that the "I" word encourages subjective, self-indulgent opinions rather than well-grounded arguments, we believe that texts using "I" can be just as well supported—or just as self-indulgent—as those that don't. For us, well-supported arguments are grounded in persuasive reasons and evidence, not in the use or nonuse of any particular pronouns.

Furthermore, if you consistently avoid the first person in your writing, you will probably have trouble making the key move addressed in this chapter: differentiating your views from those of others or even offering your own views in the first place. But don't just take our word for it. See for yourself how freely the first person is used by the writers quoted in this book and by the writers assigned in your courses.

Nevertheless, certain occasions may warrant avoiding the first person and writing, for example, that "she is correct" instead of "I think that she is correct." Since it can be monotonous to read an unvarying series of "I" statements ("I believe . . . I think . . . I argue . . . "), it is a good idea to mix first-person assertions with ones like the following:

- X is right that certain common patterns can be found in the communities.
- The evidence shows that ________.
- X's assertion that ________ does not fit the facts.
- Anyone familiar with ________ should agree that ________.

One might even follow Mantsios's lead, as in the following template:

- Yet ________ are real, and are arguably the most significant factor in ________.

On the whole, however, academic writing today, even in the sciences and social sciences, makes use of the first person fairly liberally.

ANOTHER TRICK FOR IDENTIFYING WHO IS SPEAKING

To alert readers about whose perspective you are describing at any given moment, you don't always have to use overt voice markers like "X argues" followed by a summary of the argument. Instead, you can alert readers about whose voice you're speaking in by *embedding* a reference to X's argument in your own sentences. Hence, instead of writing

> Liberals believe that cultural differences need to be respected. I have a problem with this view, however.

you might write

> I have a problem with *what liberals call cultural differences*.
>
> There is a major problem with the liberal doctrine of *so-called cultural differences*.

You can also embed references to something you yourself have previously said. So instead of writing two cumbersome sentences like

> Earlier in this chapter we coined the term "voice markers." We would argue that such markers are extremely important for reading comprehension.

you might write

> We would argue that "voice markers," as we identified them earlier, are extremely important for reading comprehension.

Embedded references like these allow you to economize your train of thought and refer to other perspectives without any major interruption.

TEMPLATES FOR EMBEDDING VOICE MARKERS

- ▶ **X overlooks what I consider an important point about cultural differences.**
- ▶ **My own view is that what X insists is a _____ is in fact a _______.**
- ▶ **I wholeheartedly endorse what X calls _________.**
- ▶ **These conclusions, which X discusses in _________, add weight to the argument that _________.**

When writers fail to use voice-marking devices like the ones discussed in this chapter, their summaries of others' views tend to become confused with their own ideas—and vice versa. When readers cannot tell if you are summarizing your own views or endorsing a certain phrase or label, they have to stop and think: "Wait. I thought the author disagreed with this claim. Has she actually been asserting this view all along?" or "Hmmm, I thought she would have objected to this kind of phrase. Is she actually endorsing it?" Getting in the habit of using voice markers will keep you from confusing your readers and help alert you to similar markers in the challenging texts you read.

Exercises

1. Look at the short passages below. Right now, it's unclear who is saying what. Use the templates from this chapter to revise these passages so they include voice markers that allow a reader to distinguish between the two voices.

Example:
Students who major in preprofessional programs like accounting or medical technology are trained for in-demand careers. Students who study the humanities learn valuable skills that prepare them for many jobs, including some that may not even exist today.

Revision:
Well-meaning advisers argue that students who major in preprofessional programs like accounting or medical technologies are trained for in-demand careers. However, they overlook what I consider an important point, that studying the humanities gives students valuable skills that prepare them for many jobs, including some that may not even exist today.

a. Fracking, or drilling deeply into the ground to reach natural gas, can contaminate drinking water in communities near the drilling operations. Natural gas is a cleaner form of energy than coal, and fracking is a cost-effective way to access the reserves of natural gas in the United States.
b. Charter schools give families in struggling school districts options to choose which schools their kids will attend. Charter schools, controlled by private individuals or corporations, divert essential funds away from the public education systems that serve all children.

2. To see how one writer signals when she is asserting her own views and when she is summarizing those of someone else, read the following passage from Anne-Marie Slaughter's essay "Why Women Still Can't Have It All." As you do so, identify those spots where Slaughter refers to the views of others and the signal phrases she uses to distinguish her views from theirs.

Seeking out a more balanced life is not a women's issue; balance would be better for us all. Bronnie Ware, an Australian blogger who worked for years in palliative care and is the author of the 2011 book *The Top Five Regrets of the Dying*, writes that the regret she heard most often was "I wish I'd had the courage to live a life true to myself, not the life others expected of me." The second-most common regret was "I wish I didn't work so hard." She writes: "This came from every male patient that I nursed. They missed their children's youth and their partner's companionship."

Juliette Kayyem, who several years ago left the Department of Homeland Security soon after her husband, David Barron, left a high position in the Justice Department, says their joint decision to leave Washington and return to Boston sprang from their desire to work on the "happiness project," meaning quality time with their three children. (She borrowed the term from her friend Gretchen Rubin, who wrote a best-selling book and now runs a blog with that name.)

It's time to embrace a national happiness project. As a daughter of Charlottesville, Virginia, the home of Thomas Jefferson and the university he founded, I grew up with the Declaration of Independence in my blood. Last I checked, he did not declare American independence in the name of life, liberty, and professional success. Let us rediscover the pursuit of happiness, and let us start at home.

3. Read over a draft of your own writing—a paragraph or an essay—and then respond to the following questions. How do you distinguish your own voice from the argument(s) you are summarizing, quoting, and responding to? How could you use a template from this chapter to clarify the distinction between *your* argument and *their* argument(s)? Where could you use first-person voice markers or embedded references in your writing?

SIX

"SKEPTICS MAY OBJECT"

Planting a Naysayer in Your Text

THE WRITER Jane Tompkins describes a pattern that repeats itself whenever she writes a book or an article. For the first couple of weeks when she sits down to write, things go relatively well. But then in the middle of the night, several weeks into the writing process, she'll wake up in a cold sweat, suddenly realizing that she has overlooked some major criticism that readers will surely make against her ideas. Her first thought, invariably, is that she will have to give up on the project or that she will have to throw out what she's written thus far and start over. Then she realizes that "this moment of doubt and panic is where my text really begins." She then revises what she's written in a way that incorporates the criticisms she's anticipated, and her text becomes stronger and more interesting as a result.

This little story contains an important lesson for all writers, experienced and inexperienced alike. It suggests that even though most of us are upset at the idea of someone criticizing our work, such criticisms can actually work to our advantage. Although it's naturally tempting to ignore criticism of our ideas, doing so may in fact be a big mistake, since our writing improves when we not only listen to these objections but also give them an explicit hearing in our writing. Indeed, no single device more quickly improves a piece of writing than planting a naysayer in the text—saying, for example, that "although some readers may object" to something in your argument, you "would reply that ______________."

ANTICIPATE OBJECTIONS

But wait, you say. Isn't the advice to incorporate critical views a recipe for destroying your credibility and undermining your argument? Here you are, trying to say something that will hold up, and we want you to tell readers all the negative things someone might say against you?

Exactly. We *are* urging you to tell readers what others might say against you, but our point is that doing so will actually *enhance* your credibility, not undermine it. As we argue throughout this book, writing well does not mean piling up uncontroversial truths in a vacuum; it means engaging others in a dialogue or debate—not only by opening your text with a summary of what others *have* said, as we suggest in Chapter 1, but also by imagining what others *might* say against your argument as it unfolds. Once you see writing as an act of entering a conversation, you should also see how opposing arguments can work for you rather than against you.

Paradoxically, the more you give voice to your critics' objections, the more you tend to disarm those critics, especially if you go on to answer their objections in convincing ways. When you entertain a counterargument, you make a kind of preemptive strike, identifying problems with your argument before others can point them out for you. Furthermore, by entertaining counterarguments, you show respect for your readers, treating them not as gullible dupes who will believe anything you say but as independent, critical thinkers who are aware that your view is not the only one in town. In addition, by imagining what others might say against your claims, you come across as a generous, broad-minded person who is confident enough to be open to debate—like the writer in the figure on the following page.

Conversely, if you don't entertain counterarguments, you may very likely come across as closed-minded, as if you think your beliefs are beyond dispute. You might also leave important questions hanging and concerns about your arguments unaddressed. Finally, if you fail to plant a naysayer in your text, you may find that you have very little to say. Our own students often say that entertaining counterarguments makes it easier to generate enough text to meet their assignment's page-length requirements.

Planting a naysayer in your text is a relatively simple move, as you can see by looking at the following passage from a book by the writer Kim Chernin. Having spent some thirty pages complaining about the pressure on American women to be thin, Chernin inserts a whole chapter titled "The Skeptic," opening it as follows:

> At this point I would like to raise certain objections that have been inspired by the skeptic in me. She feels that I have been ignoring some of the most common assumptions we all make about our bodies and these she wishes to see addressed. For example: "You know perfectly well," she says to me, "that you feel better when you lose weight. You buy new clothes. You look at yourself more eagerly in the mirror. When someone invites you to a party you don't stop and ask yourself whether you want to go. You feel sexier. Admit it. You like yourself better."
>
> KIM CHERNIN, *The Obsession: Reflections on the Tyranny of Slenderness*

OH, NO! THEY'RE GONNA SAY THAT I'VE MISREPRESENTED X'S WORK!
"YOU WILL PROBABLY OBJECT THAT I HAVE MISREPRESENTED X'S WORK HERE, AND I CONCEDE THAT X NEVER SAYS ________ IN SO MANY WORDS. NEVERTHELESS . . ."
GG

The remainder of Chernin's chapter consists of her answers to this inner skeptic. In the face of the skeptic's challenge to her book's central premise (that the pressure to diet seriously harms women's lives), Chernin responds neither by repressing the skeptic's critical voice nor by giving in to it and relinquishing her own position. Instead, she embraces that voice and writes it into her text. Note, too, that instead of dispatching this naysaying voice quickly, as many of us would be tempted to do, Chernin stays with it and devotes a full paragraph to it. By borrowing some of Chernin's language, we can come up with templates for entertaining virtually any objection.

TEMPLATES FOR ENTERTAINING OBJECTIONS

- **At this point I would like to raise some objections that have been inspired by the skeptic in me. She feels that I have been ignoring the complexities of the situation.**
- **Yet some readers may challenge my view by insisting that __________.**
- **Of course, many will probably disagree on the grounds that __________.**

Note that the objections in the above templates are attributed not to any specific person or group but to "skeptics," "readers," or "many." This kind of nameless, faceless naysayer is perfectly appropriate in many cases. But the ideas that motivate arguments and objections often can—and, where possible, should—be ascribed to a specific ideology or school of thought (for example, liberals, Christian fundamentalists, neopragmatists) rather than to anonymous anybodies. In other words, naysayers can be labeled, and you can add precision and impact to your writing by identifying what those labels are.

TEMPLATES FOR NAMING YOUR NAYSAYERS

- **Here many *feminists* would probably object that gender does influence language.**
- **But *social Darwinists* would certainly take issue with the argument that __________.**
- ***Biologists*, of course, may want to question whether __________.**
- **Nevertheless, both *followers and critics of Malcolm X* will probably suggest otherwise and argue that __________.**

To be sure, some people dislike such labels and may even resent having labels applied to themselves. Some feel that labels put individuals in boxes, stereotyping them and glossing over what makes each of us unique. And it's true that labels can be used inappropriately, in ways that ignore individuality and promote stereotypes. But since the life of ideas, including many of our most private thoughts, is conducted through groups and types rather than solitary individuals, intellectual exchange requires labels to give definition and serve as a convenient shorthand. If you categorically reject all labels, you give up an important resource and even mislead readers by presenting yourself and others as having no connection to anyone else. You also miss an opportunity to generalize the importance and relevance of your work to some larger conversation. When you attribute a position you are summarizing to liberalism, say, or historical materialism, your argument is no longer just about your own solitary views but also about the intersection of broad ideas and habits of mind that many readers may already have a stake in.

The way to minimize the problem of stereotyping, then, is not to categorically reject labels but to refine and qualify their use, as the following templates demonstrate:

- **Although not all *Christians* think alike, some of them will probably dispute my claim that ____________.**
- ***Non-native English speakers* are so diverse in their views that it's hard to generalize about them, but some are likely to object on the grounds that ____________.**

Another way to avoid needless stereotyping is to qualify labels carefully, substituting "pro bono lawyers" for "lawyers" in general, for example, or "quantitative sociologists" for all "social scientists," and so on.

TEMPLATES FOR INTRODUCING OBJECTIONS INFORMALLY

Objections can also be introduced in more informal ways. For instance, you can frame objections in the form of questions:

- **But is my proposal realistic? What are the chances of its actually being adopted?**
- **Yet is it necessarily true that ____________? Is it always the case, as I have been suggesting, that ____________?**
- **However, does the evidence I've cited prove conclusively that ____________?**

You can also let your naysayer speak directly:

- **"Impossible," some will say. "You must be reading the research selectively."**

Moves like this allow you to cut directly to the skeptical voice itself, as the singer-songwriter Joe Jackson does in the following excerpt from a *New York Times* article complaining about the restrictions on public smoking in New York City bars and restaurants:

> I like a couple of cigarettes or a cigar with a drink, and like many other people, I only smoke in bars or nightclubs. Now I can't go to any of my old haunts. Bartenders who were friends have turned into cops, forcing me outside to shiver in the cold and curse under my breath. . . . It's no fun. Smokers are being demonized and victimized all out of proportion.
>
> "Get over it," say the anti-smokers. "You're the minority." I thought a great city was a place where all kinds of minorities could thrive. . . . "Smoking kills," they say. As an occasional smoker with otherwise healthy habits, I'll take my chances. Health consciousness is important, but so are pleasure and freedom of choice.
>
> JOE JACKSON, "Want to Smoke? Go to Hamburg"

Jackson could have begun his second paragraph, in which he shifts from his own voice to that of his imagined naysayer, more formally, as follows: "Of course anti-smokers will object that since we smokers are in the minority, we should simply stop complaining and quietly make the sacrifices we are being called on to make for the larger social good." Or "Anti-smokers might insist, however, that the smoking minority should submit to the nonsmoking majority." We think, though, that Jackson gets the job done in a far more lively way with the more colloquial form he chooses. Borrowing a standard move of playwrights and novelists, Jackson cuts directly to the objectors' view and then to his own retort, then back to the objectors' view and then to his own retort again, thereby creating a kind of dialogue or miniature play within his own text. This move works well for Jackson but only because he uses quotation marks and other voice markers to make clear at every point whose voice he is in.

See Chapter 5 for more advice on using voice markers.

REPRESENT OBJECTIONS FAIRLY

Once you've decided to introduce a differing or opposing view into your writing, your work has only just begun, since you still need to represent and explain that view with fairness and generosity. Although it is tempting to give opposing views short shrift, to hurry past them, or even to mock them, doing so is usually counterproductive. When writers make the best case they can for their critics (playing Peter Elbow's "believing game"), they actually bolster their credibility with readers rather than undermine it. They make readers think, "This is a writer I can trust."

See pp. 33–34 for more on the believing game.

We recommend, then, that whenever you entertain objections in your writing, you stay with them for several sentences or even paragraphs and take them as seriously as possible. We also recommend that you read your summary of opposing views with an outsider's eye: put yourself in the shoes of someone who disagrees with you and ask if such a reader would recognize himself in your summary. Would that reader think you have taken his views seriously, as beliefs that reasonable people might hold? Or would he detect a mocking tone or an oversimplification of his views?

There will always be certain objections, to be sure, that you believe do not deserve to be represented, just as there will be objections that seem so unworthy of respect that they inspire ridicule. Remember, however, that if you do choose to mock a view that you oppose, you are likely to alienate those readers who don't already agree with you—likely the very readers you want to reach. Also be aware that in mocking another's view you may contribute to a hostile argument culture in which someone may ridicule you in return.

ANSWER OBJECTIONS

Do be aware that when you represent objections successfully, you still need to be able to answer those objections persuasively. After all, when you write objections into a text, you take the risk that readers will find those objections more convincing than the argument you yourself are advancing. In the editorial quoted above, for example, Joe Jackson takes the risk that readers will identify more with the anti-smoking view he summarizes than with the pro-smoking position he endorses.

This is precisely what Benjamin Franklin describes happening to himself in *The Autobiography of Benjamin Franklin* (1793), when he recalls being converted to Deism (a religion that exalts reason over spirituality) by reading *anti*-Deist books. When he encountered the views of Deists being negatively summarized by authors who opposed them, Franklin explains, he ended up finding the Deist position more persuasive. To avoid having this kind of unintentional reverse effect on readers, you need to do your best to make sure that any counter-arguments you address are not more convincing than your own claims. It is good to address objections in your writing but only if you are able to overcome them.

One surefire way to *fail* to overcome an objection is to dismiss it out of hand—saying, for example, "That's just wrong." The difference between such a response (which offers no supporting reasons whatsoever) and the types of nuanced responses we're promoting in this book is the difference between bullying your readers and genuinely persuading them.

Often the best way to overcome an objection is not to try to refute it completely but to agree with part of it while challenging only the part you dispute. In other words, in answering counterarguments, it is often best to say "yes, but" or "yes and no," treating the counterview as an opportunity to revise and refine your own position. Rather than build your argument into an impenetrable fortress, it is often best to make concessions while still standing your ground, as Kim Chernin does in the following response to the counter-argument quoted above. While in the voice of the "skeptic," Chernin writes: "Admit it. You like yourself better when you've lost weight." In response, Chernin replies as follows:

See pp. 63–66 for more on agreeing, with a difference.

> Can I deny these things? No woman who has managed to lose weight would wish to argue with this. Most people feel better about themselves when they become slender. And yet, upon reflection, it seems to me that there is something precarious about this well-being. After all, 98 percent of people who lose weight gain it back. Indeed, 90 percent of those who have dieted "successfully" gain back more than they ever lost. Then, of course, we can no longer bear to look at ourselves in the mirror.

In this way, Chernin shows how you can use a counterview to improve and refine your overall argument by making a concession. Even as she concedes that losing weight feels good in the short run, she argues that in the long run the weight always returns, making the dieter far more miserable.

TEMPLATES FOR MAKING CONCESSIONS WHILE STILL STANDING YOUR GROUND

- Although I grant that the book is poorly organized, I still maintain that it raises an important issue.
- Proponents of X are right to argue that ____________. But they exaggerate when they claim that ____________.
- While it is true that ____________, it does not necessarily follow that ____________.
- On the one hand, I agree with X that ____________. But on the other hand, I still insist that ____________.

Templates like these show that answering naysayers' objections does not have to be an all-or-nothing affair in which either you definitively refute your critics or they definitively refute you. Often the most productive engagements among differing views end with a combined vision that incorporates elements of each one.

But what if you've tried out all the possible answers you can think of to an objection you've anticipated and you *still* have a nagging feeling that the objection is more convincing than your argument itself? In that case, the best remedy is to go back and make some fundamental revisions to your argument, even reversing your position completely if need be. Although finding out late in the game that you aren't fully convinced by your own argument can be painful, it can actually make your final text more intellectually honest, challenging, and serious. After all, the goal of writing is not to keep proving that whatever you initially said is right, but to stretch the limits of your thinking. So if planting a strong naysayer in your text forces you to change your mind, that's not a bad thing. Some would argue that that is what the academic world is all about.

Exercises

1. Read the following passage from "A People's Democratic Platform" by the cultural critic Eric Schlosser. As you'll see, he hasn't planted any naysayers in this text. Do it for him. Insert a brief paragraph stating an objection to his argument and then responding to the objection as he might.

    The United States must declare an end to the war on drugs. This war has filled the nation's prisons with poor drug addicts and small-time drug dealers. It has created a multibillion-dollar black market, enriched organized crime groups and promoted the corruption of government officials throughout the world. And it has not stemmed the widespread use of illegal drugs. By any rational measure, this war has been a total failure.

    We must develop public policies on substance abuse that are guided not by moral righteousness or political expediency but by common sense. The United States should immediately decriminalize the cultivation and possession of small amounts of marijuana for personal use. Marijuana should no longer be classified as a Schedule I narcotic, and those who seek to use marijuana as medicine should no longer face criminal sanctions. We must shift our entire approach to drug abuse from the criminal justice system to the public health system. Congress should appoint an independent commission to study the harm-reduction policies that have been adopted in Switzerland, Spain, Portugal, and the Netherlands. The commission should recommend policies for the United States based on one important criterion: what works.

In a nation where pharmaceutical companies advertise powerful antidepressants on billboards and where alcohol companies run amusing beer ads during the Super Bowl, the idea of a "drug-free society" is absurd. Like the rest of American society, our drug policy would greatly benefit from less punishment and more compassion.

2. Think of a debate you recently had with a friend or classmate. Compose a one-sentence summary of your argument. Then, by yourself or with a partner, brainstorm a list of possible objections or alternative perspectives on the issue. Pick one, and use it to write a naysayer objection that responds to your argument. Use the templates in this chapter to introduce and respond to this naysayer fairly.

3. Read over something you've written that makes an argument. Work with a partner to review your draft to see if you've anticipated and responded to any objections. Use these questions to guide your review: Have you anticipated all the likely objections to your argument? Whom, if anyone, have you attributed the objections to? Have you represented the objections fairly? Have you answered them well enough, or do you think you now need to qualify your own argument? Does the introduction of the naysayer strengthen your argument? Why or why not?

SEVEN

"SO WHAT? WHO CARES?"

Saying Why It Matters

Baseball is the national pastime. Bernini was the best sculptor of the baroque period. All writing is conversational. So what? Who cares? Why does any of this matter?

How many times have you had reason to ask these questions? Regardless of how interesting a topic may be to you as a writer, readers always need to know what is at stake in a text and why they should care. All too often, however, these questions are left unanswered—mainly because writers and speakers assume that audiences will know the answers already or will figure them out on their own. As a result, students come away from lectures feeling like outsiders to what they've heard, just as many of us feel left hanging after talks we've attended. The problem is not necessarily that the speakers lack a clear, well-focused thesis or that the thesis is inadequately supported with evidence. Instead, the problem is that the speakers don't address the crucial question of why their arguments matter.

That this question is so often left unaddressed is unfortunate since the speakers generally *could* offer interesting, engaging answers. When pressed, for instance, most academics will tell you that their lectures and articles matter because they address some belief that needs to be corrected or updated—and because their arguments have important, real-world consequences. Yet many academics fail to identify these reasons and consequences explicitly in what they say and write. Rather than assume that audiences will know why their claims matter, all writers need to answer the "so what?" and "who cares?" questions up front. Not everyone can claim to have a cure for cancer or a solution to end poverty. But writers who fail to show that others *should* care or already *do* care about their claims will ultimately lose their audiences' interest.

This chapter focuses on various moves that you can make to answer the "who cares?" and "so what?" questions in your own writing. In one sense, the two questions get at the same thing: the relevance or importance of what you are saying. Yet they get at this significance in different ways. Whereas "who cares?" literally asks you to identify a person or group who cares about your claims, "so what?" asks about the real-world applications and consequences of those claims—what difference it would make if they were accepted. We'll look first at ways of making clear who cares.

"WHO CARES?"

To see how one writer answers the "who cares?" question, consider the following passage from the science writer Denise Grady. Writing in the *New York Times*, she explains some of the latest research into fat cells:

> Scientists used to think body fat and the cells it was made of were pretty much inert, just an oily storage compartment. But within the past decade research has shown that fat cells act like chemical factories and that body fat is potent stuff: a highly active

> tissue that secretes hormones and other substances with profound and sometimes harmful effects. . . .
>
> In recent years, biologists have begun calling fat an "endocrine organ," comparing it to glands like the thyroid and pituitary, which also release hormones straight into the bloodstream.
>
> DENISE GRADY, "The Secret Life of a Potent Cell"

Notice how Grady's writing reflects the central advice we give in this book, offering a clear claim and also framing that claim as a response to what someone else has said. In so doing, Grady immediately identifies at least one group with a stake in the new research that sees fat as "active," "potent stuff": namely, the scientific community, which formerly believed that body fat is inert. By referring to these scientists, Grady implicitly acknowledges that her text is part of a larger conversation and shows who besides herself has an interest in what she says.

Consider, however, how the passage would read had Grady left out what "scientists used to think" and simply explained the new findings in isolation:

> Within the past few decades research has shown that fat cells act like chemical factories and that body fat is potent stuff: a highly active tissue that secretes hormones and other substances. In recent years, biologists have begun calling fat an "endocrine organ," comparing it to glands like the thyroid and pituitary, which also release hormones straight into the bloodstream.

Though this statement is clear and easy to follow, it lacks any indication that anyone needs to hear it. OK, one thinks while reading this passage, fat is an active, potent thing. Sounds plausible enough; no reason to think it's not true. But does anyone really care? Who, if anyone, is interested?

TEMPLATES FOR INDICATING WHO CARES

To address "who cares?" questions in your own writing, we suggest using templates like the following, which echo Grady in refuting earlier thinking:

- **Parents used to think yelling at their kids was necessary. But recently experts suggest that it can be counterproductive.**
- **This interpretation challenges the work of those critics who have long assumed that __________.**
- **These findings challenge the work of earlier researchers, who tended to assume that __________.**
- **Recent studies like these shed new light on __________, which previous studies had not addressed.**

Grady might have been more explicit by writing the "who cares?" question directly into her text, as in the following template:

- **But who really cares? Who besides me and a handful of recent researchers has a stake in these claims? At the very least, the researchers who formerly believed __________ should care.**

To gain greater authority as a writer, it can help to name specific people or groups who have a stake in your claims and to go into some detail about their views:

- **Researchers have long assumed that __________. For instance, one eminent scholar of cell biology, __________, assumed in __________, her seminal work on cell structures and functions, that fat cells __________. As __________ herself put it, "__________" (2012). Another leading scientist, __________, argued that fat cells**

"__________" (2011). Ultimately, when it came to the nature of fat, the basic assumption was that __________.

But a new body of research shows that fat cells are far more complex and that __________.

In other cases, you might refer to certain people or groups who *should* care about your claims:

- If sports enthusiasts stopped to think about it, many of them might simply assume that the most successful athletes __________. However, new research shows __________.
- These findings challenge neoliberals' common assumption that __________.
- At first glance, teenagers might say __________. But on closer inspection __________.

As these templates suggest, answering the "who cares?" question involves establishing the type of contrast between what others say and what you say that is central to this book. Ultimately, such templates help you create a dramatic tension or clash of views in your writing that readers will feel invested in and want to see resolved.

"SO WHAT?"

Although answering the "who cares?" question is crucial, in many cases it is not enough, especially if you are writing for general readers who don't necessarily have a strong investment in the particular clash of views you are setting up. In the case of Grady's argument about fat cells, such readers may still wonder why it matters that some researchers think fat cells are active, while others think they're inert. Or, to move to a different field of study, American literature, *so what* if some scholars disagree about Huck Finn's relationship with the runaway slave Jim in Mark Twain's *Adventures of Huckleberry Finn*? Why should anyone besides a few specialists in the field care about such disputes? What, if anything, hinges on them?

The best way to answer such questions about the larger consequences of your claims is to appeal to something that your audience already figures to care about. Whereas the "who cares?" question asks you to identify an interested person or group, the "so what?" question asks you to link your argument to some larger matter that readers already deem important. Thus, in analyzing *Huckleberry Finn*, a writer could argue that seemingly narrow disputes about the hero's relationship with Jim actually shed light on whether Twain's canonical, widely read novel is a critique of racism in America or is itself marred by it.

Let's see how Grady invokes such broad, general concerns in her article on fat cells. Her first move is to link researchers' interest in fat cells to a general concern with obesity and health:

> Researchers trying to decipher the biology of fat cells hope to find new ways to help people get rid of excess fat or, at least, prevent obesity from destroying their health. In an increasingly obese world, their efforts have taken on added importance.

Further showing why readers should care, Grady's next move is to demonstrate the even broader relevance and urgency of her subject matter:

> Internationally, more than a billion people are overweight. Obesity and two illnesses linked to it, heart disease and high blood pressure, are on the World Health Organization's list of the top 10 global health risks. In the United States, 65 percent of adults weigh too much,

> compared with about 56 percent a decade ago, and government researchers blame obesity for at least 300,000 deaths a year.

What Grady implicitly says here is "Look, dear reader, you may think that these questions about the nature of fat cells I've been pursuing have little to do with everyday life. In fact, however, these questions are extremely important—particularly in our 'increasingly obese world' in which we need to prevent obesity from destroying our health."

Notice that Grady's phrase "in an increasingly ______ world" can be adapted as a strategic move to address the "so what?" question in other fields as well. For example, a sociologist analyzing back-to-nature movements of the past thirty years might make the following statement:

> In a world increasingly dominated by cell phones and sophisticated computer technologies, these attempts to return to nature appear futile.

This type of move can be readily applied to other disciplines because no matter how much disciplines may differ from one another, the need to justify the importance of one's concerns is common to them all.

TEMPLATES FOR ESTABLISHING WHY YOUR CLAIMS MATTER

- ***Huckleberry Finn* matters/is important because <u>it is one of the most widely taught novels in the American school system</u>.**
- **Although X may seem trivial, it is in fact crucial in terms of today's concern over ______.**

- ▸ Ultimately, what is at stake here is ________.
- ▸ These findings have important implications for the broader domain of ________.
- ▸ If we are right about ________, then major consequences follow for ________.
- ▸ These conclusions/This discovery will have significant applications in ________ as well as in ________.

Finally, you can also treat the "so what?" question as a related aspect of the "who cares?" question:

- ▸ Although X may seem of concern to only a small group of ________, it should in fact concern anyone who cares about ________.

All these templates help you hook your readers. By suggesting the real-world applications of your claims, the templates not only demonstrate that others care about your claims but also tell your readers why *they* should care. Again, it bears repeating that simply stating and proving your thesis isn't enough. You also need to frame it in a way that helps readers care about it.

WHAT ABOUT READERS WHO ALREADY KNOW WHY IT MATTERS?

At this point, you might wonder if you need to answer the "who cares?" and "so what?" questions in *everything* you write. Is it really necessary to address these questions if you're proposing something so obviously consequential as, say, a treatment for autism or a program to eliminate illiteracy? Isn't it obvious that everyone cares about such problems? Does it really need to be spelled out? And what about when you're writing for audiences who you know are already interested in your claims and who understand perfectly well why they're important? In other words, do you always need to address the "so what?" and "who cares?" questions?

As a rule, yes—although it's true that you can't keep answering them forever and at a certain point must say enough is enough. Although a determined skeptic can infinitely ask why something matters—"Why should I care about earning a salary? And why should I care about supporting a family?"—you have to stop answering at some point in your text. Nevertheless, we urge you to go as far as possible in answering such questions. If you take it for granted that readers will somehow intuit the answers to "so what?" and "who cares?" on their own, you may make your work seem less interesting than it actually is, and you run the risk that readers will dismiss your text as irrelevant and unimportant. By contrast, when you are careful to explain who cares and why, it's a little like bringing a cheerleading squad into your text. And though some expert readers might already know why your claims matter, even they need to be reminded. Thus the safest move is to be as explicit as possible in answering the "so what?" question, even for those already in the know. When you step back from the text and explain why it matters, you are urging your audience to keep reading, pay attention, and care.

Exercises

1. Below are two claims. Who might have a stake in these arguments? Use the templates in this chapter to answer in

one or two sentences the "who cares?" question for both arguments.

a. The benefits of online shopping don't justify the environmental consequences of shipping items purchased online.
b. The federal government should fund universal health care.

2. Here are two more claims. What are the possible real-world consequences of these arguments? Use the templates in this chapter to answer, in one or two sentences, the "so what?" question for both arguments.

   a. Violent video games do not cause mass shootings.
   b. Because all combat roles are now open to women, both men and women should be required to register for the Selective Service.

3. Read the following passage from Elizabeth Silkes's 2020 essay, "Cultural Heritage Reminds Us of Our Shared Humanity. That's Why Threats against Them Are So Dangerous," found on **theysayiblog.com**. Where do you see Silkes answering the "so what?" and "who cares?" questions? Who does she say should care about preserving cultural sites, and why should they?

   The destruction of cultural sites—from libraries to places of worship to museums—is ultimately about erasing a people's entire history. During the Bosnian war in the early 1990s, Serb and Croat forces destroyed or damaged hundreds of mosques in their efforts to rid the region of Muslims. In Zvornik, which had been a historic Muslim trading post on the Drina River, so many traces of the town's past had been eliminated that Brano Grujic, the Serb-installed mayor there, could falsely boast in 1993 that "there were never any mosques in Zvornik." As Helen Walasek, the author of *Bosnia and the Destruction of Cultural Heritage*, writes, sites such as archives and museums were targeted in part because they reflected Bosnia's pluralistic past. Such attacks were aimed at "eradicating any trace of Bosnia-Herzegovina's historic diversity and traditions of coexistence."...

The current conversation around preservation of cultural heritage in the Middle East comes at a critical time for the region, when conflict and atrocity have put a number of marginalized cultures at risk....

While cultural heritage is not the only way we form bonds with others, it is one of the most powerful and effective means of doing so across barriers. It is heartening to see the public outcry at this latest threat, but the risk to cultural sites during conflict remains extraordinarily high. This is especially so given the limited funding for multilateral organizations dedicated to their protection such as UNESCO, from which the United States formally withdrew a year ago. If our children and our children's children cannot access the most fundamental aspects of our own histories and those of others, they will never be able to identify the common threads that bind us all. And it is only through this binding that we can tap into—and act on—our shared humanity.

4. Read over the draft of an essay you are working on. Work with a partner to identify the answers to the "so what?" and "who cares?" questions for your argument. Then revise your draft to say why your argument matters by using the following template:

My point here, that __________, should interest those who __________. Beyond this limited audience, however, my point should speak to anyone who cares about the larger issue of __________.

EIGHT

"AS A RESULT"

Connecting the Parts

WE ONCE HAD A STUDENT named Billy, whose characteristic sentence pattern went something like this:

> Spot is a good dog. He has fleas.

"Connect your sentences," we urged in the margins of Billy's papers. "What does Spot's being good have to do with his fleas? These two statements seem unrelated. Can you connect them in some logical way?" When comments like these yielded no results, we tried inking in suggested connections for him:

> Spot is a good dog, *but* he has fleas.
> Spot is a good dog, *even though* he has fleas.

But our message failed to get across, and Billy's disconnected sentence pattern persisted to the end of the semester.

And yet Billy did focus well on his subjects. When he mentioned Spot the dog (or Plato or any other topic) in one sentence, we could count on Spot (or Plato) being the topic of the following sentence as well. This was not the case with some of Billy's classmates, who sometimes changed topic from sentence to sentence or even from clause to clause within a single sentence. But because Billy neglected to mark his connections, his writing was as frustrating to read as theirs. In all these cases, we had to struggle to figure out on our own how the sentences and paragraphs connected or failed to connect with one another.

What makes such writers so hard to read, in other words, is that they never gesture back to what they have just said or forward to what they plan to say. "Never look back" might be their motto, almost as if they see writing as a process of thinking of something to say about a topic and writing it down, then thinking of something else to say about the topic and writing that down, too, and on and on until they've filled the assigned number of pages and can hand the paper in. Each sentence basically starts a new thought rather than growing out of or extending the thought of the previous sentence.

When Billy talked about his writing habits, he acknowledged that he never went back and read what he had written. Indeed, he told us that, other than using his computer software to check for spelling errors and make sure that his tenses were all aligned, he never actually reread what he wrote before turning it in. As Billy seemed to picture it, writing was something one did while sitting at a computer, whereas reading was a separate activity generally reserved for an easy chair, book in hand. It had never occurred to Billy that to write a good sentence he had to think about how it connected to those that came before and after; that he had to think hard about how that sentence fit into the sentences that surrounded it. Each sentence for Billy existed in a sort of tunnel isolated from every other sentence on the page. He never bothered to fit all the parts of his essay together because he apparently thought of writing as a matter of piling up information or observations rather than building a sustained argument. What we suggest in this chapter, then, is that you converse not only with others in your writing but with yourself: that you establish clear relations between one statement and the next by connecting those statements.

This chapter addresses the issue of how to connect all the parts of your writing. The best compositions establish a sense of momentum and direction by making explicit connections among their different parts, so that what is said in one sentence (or paragraph) both sets up what is to come and is clearly informed by what has already been said. When you write a sentence, you create an expectation in the reader's mind that the next sentence will in some way echo and extend it, even if—*especially if*—that next sentence takes your argument in a new direction.

It may help to think of each sentence you write as having arms that reach backward and forward, as the figure below suggests. When your sentences reach outward like this, they establish connections that help your writing flow smoothly in a way readers appreciate. Conversely, when writing lacks such connections and moves in fits and starts, readers repeatedly have to go back over the sentences and guess at the connections on their own. To prevent such disconnection and make your writing flow, we advise

following a "do-it-yourself" principle, which means that it is your job as a writer to do the hard work of making the connections rather than, as Billy did, leaving this work to your readers.

This chapter offers several strategies you can use to put this principle into action: (1) using transition terms (like "therefore" and "as a result"); (2) adding pointing words (like "this" or "such"); (3) developing a set of key terms and phrases for each text you write; and (4) repeating yourself, but with a difference—a move that involves repeating what you've said, but with enough variation to avoid being redundant. All these moves require that you always look back and, in crafting any one sentence, think hard about those that precede it.

Notice how we ourselves have used such connecting devices thus far in this chapter. The second paragraph of this chapter, for example, opens with the transitional "And yet," signaling a change in direction, while the opening sentence of the third includes the phrase "in other words," telling you to expect a restatement of a point we've just made. If you look through this book, you should be able to find many sentences that contain some word or phrase that explicitly hooks them back to something said earlier, to something about to be said, or both. And many sentences in *this* chapter repeat key terms related to the idea of connection: "connect," "disconnect," "link," "relate," "forward," and "backward."

USE TRANSITIONS

For readers to follow your train of thought, you need not only to connect your sentences and paragraphs to each other but also to mark the kind of connection you are making. One of the easiest ways to make this move is to use *transitions* (from the Latin root *trans*, "across"), which help you cross from one point to another in your text. Transitions are usually placed at or near the start of sentences so they can signal to readers where your text is going: in the same direction it has been moving or in a new direction. More specifically, transitions tell readers whether your text is echoing a previous sentence or paragraph ("in other words"), adding something to it ("in addition"), offering an example of it ("for example"), generalizing from it ("as a result"), or modifying it ("and yet").

The following is a list of commonly used transitions, categorized according to their different functions:

ADDITION

also
and
besides
furthermore
in addition
in fact
indeed
moreover
so too

ELABORATION

actually
by extension
in other words
in short
that is
to put it another way
to put it bluntly
to put it succinctly
ultimately

EXAMPLE

after all
as an illustration
consider
for example
for instance
specifically
to take a case in point

CAUSE AND EFFECT

accordingly
as a result
consequently
hence
since
so
then
therefore
thus

COMPARISON

along the same lines
in the same way
likewise
similarly

CONTRAST

although
but
by contrast
conversely
despite
even though
however
in contrast
nevertheless
nonetheless
on the contrary
on the other hand
regardless
whereas
while
yet

CONCESSION

admittedly
although it is true
granted
naturally
of course
to be sure

CONCLUSION

as a result
consequently
hence
in conclusion
in short
in sum
therefore
thus
to sum up
to summarize

Ideally, transitions should operate so unobtrusively in a piece of writing that they recede into the background and readers do not even notice that they are there. It's a bit like what happens when drivers use their turn signals before turning right or left: just as other drivers recognize such signals almost unconsciously, readers should process transition terms with a minimum of thought. But even though such terms should function unobtrusively in your writing, they can be among the most powerful tools in your vocabulary. Think how your heart sinks when someone, immediately after praising you, begins a sentence with "but" or "however." No matter what follows, you know it won't be good.

Notice that some transitions can help you not only move from one sentence to another but also combine two or more sentences into one. Combining sentences in this way helps prevent the choppy, staccato effect that arises when too many short sentences are strung together, one after the other. For instance, to combine Billy's two choppy sentences ("Spot is a good dog. He has fleas.") into one, better-flowing sentence, we suggested that he rewrite them as "Spot is a good dog, *even though* he has fleas."

Transitions like these not only guide readers through the twists and turns of your argument but also help ensure that you *have* an argument in the first place. In fact, we think of words like "but," "yet," "nevertheless," "besides," and others as argument words, since it's hard to use them without making some kind of argument. The word "therefore," for instance, commits you to making sure that the claims preceding it lead logically to the conclusion that it introduces. "For example" also assumes an argument, since it requires the material you are introducing to stand as an instance or proof of some preceding generalization. As a result, the more you use transitions, the more you'll be able not only to connect the parts of your text but also to construct a strong argument in the first place. And if you draw on them frequently enough, using them should eventually become second nature.

To be sure, it is possible to overuse transitions, so take time to read over your drafts carefully and eliminate any transitions that are unnecessary. But following the maxim that you need to learn the basic moves of argument before you can deliberately depart from them, we advise you not to forgo explicit transition terms until you've first mastered their use. In all our years of teaching, we've read countless essays that suffered from having few or no transitions, but we cannot recall one in which the transitions were overused. Seasoned writers sometimes omit explicit transitions but only because they rely heavily on the other types of connecting devices that we turn to in the rest of this chapter.

Before doing so, however, let us warn you about inserting transitions without really thinking through their meanings—using "therefore," say, when your text's logic actually requires "nevertheless" or "however." So beware. Choosing transition terms should involve a bit of mental sweat, since the whole point of using them is to make your writing *more* reader-friendly, not less. The only thing more frustrating than reading Billy-style passages like "Spot is a good dog. He has fleas" is reading mis-connected sentences like "Spot is a good dog. For example, he has fleas."

USE POINTING WORDS

Another way to connect the parts of your argument is by using pointing words—which, as their name implies, point or refer backward to some concept in the previous sentence. The most common of these pointing words include "this," "these," "that," "those," "their," and "such" (as in "these pointing words" near the start of this sentence) and simple pronouns like "his," "he," "her," "she," "it," and "their." Such terms help you create the flow we spoke of earlier that enables readers to move effortlessly through your text. In a sense, these terms are like an invisible hand reaching out of your sentence, grabbing what's needed in the previous sentences and pulling it along.

Like transitions, however, pointing words need to be used carefully. It's dangerously easy to insert pointing words into your text that don't refer to a clearly defined object, assuming that because the object you have in mind is clear to you it will also be clear to your readers. For example, consider the use of "this" in the following passage:

> Alexis de Tocqueville was highly critical of democratic societies, which he saw as tending toward mob rule. At the same time, he accorded democratic societies grudging respect. *This* is seen in Tocqueville's statement that . . .

When "this" is used in such a way it becomes an ambiguous or free-floating pointer, since readers can't tell if it refers to Tocqueville's critical attitude toward democratic societies, his grudging respect for them, or some combination of both. "This what?" readers mutter as they go back over such passages and try to figure them out. It's also tempting to try to cheat with pointing words, hoping that they will conceal or make up for conceptual confusions that may lurk in your argument. By referring to a fuzzy idea as "this" or "that," you might hope the fuzziness will somehow come across as clearer than it is.

You can fix problems caused by a free-floating pointer by making sure there is one and only one possible object in the vicinity that the pointer could be referring to. It also often helps to name the object the pointer is referring to at the same time that you point to it, replacing the bald "this" in the example above with a more precise phrase like "this ambivalence toward democratic societies" or "this grudging respect."

REPEAT KEY TERMS AND PHRASES

A third strategy for connecting the parts of your argument is to develop a constellation of key terms and phrases, including their synonyms and antonyms, that you repeat throughout your text. When used effectively, your key terms should be items that readers could extract from your text in order to get a solid sense of your topic. Playing with key terms also can be a good way to come up with a title and appropriate section headings for your text.

Notice how often Martin Luther King Jr. uses the keywords "criticism," "statement," "answer," and "correspondence" in the opening paragraph of his famous "Letter from Birmingham Jail":

> Dear Fellow Clergymen:
>
> While confined here in the Birmingham city jail, I came across your recent *statement* calling my present activities "unwise and untimely." Seldom do I pause to *answer criticism* of my work and ideas. If I sought to *answer* all the *criticisms* that cross my desk, my secretaries would have little time for anything other than *such correspondence* in the course of the day, and I would have no time for constructive work. But since I feel that you are men of genuine good will and that your *criticisms* are sincerely set forth, I want to try to *answer* your *statement* in what I hope will be patient and reasonable terms.
>
> MARTIN LUTHER KING JR., "Letter from Birmingham Jail"

Even though King uses the terms "criticism" and "answer" three times each and "statement" twice, the effect is not overly repetitive. In fact, these key terms help build a sense of momentum in the paragraph and bind it together.

For another example of the effective use of key terms, consider the following passage, in which the historian Susan Douglas develops a constellation of sharply contrasting key terms around the concept of "cultural schizophrenics": women like herself who, Douglas claims, have mixed feelings about the images of ideal femininity with which they are constantly bombarded by the media:

> In a variety of ways, the mass media helped make us the cultural schizophrenics we are today, women who rebel against yet submit to prevailing images about what a desirable, worthwhile woman should be. . . . [T]he mass media has engendered in many women a kind of cultural identity crisis. We are ambivalent toward femininity on the one hand and feminism on the other. Pulled in opposite directions—told we were equal, yet told we were subordinate; told we could change history but told we were trapped by history—we got the bends at an early age, and we've never gotten rid of them.
>
> When I open *Vogue*, for example, I am simultaneously infuriated and seduced. . . . I adore the materialism; I despise the materialism. . . . I want to look beautiful; I think wanting to look beautiful is about the most dumb-ass goal you could have. The magazine stokes my desire; the magazine triggers my bile. And this doesn't only happen when I'm reading *Vogue*; it happens all the time. . . . On the one hand, on the other hand—that's not just me—that's what it means to be a woman in America.
>
> To explain this schizophrenia . . .
>
> SUSAN DOUGLAS, *Where the Girls Are: Growing Up Female with the Mass Media*

In this passage, Douglas establishes "schizophrenia" as a key concept and then echoes it through synonyms like "identity crisis," "ambivalent," "the bends"—and even demonstrates it through a series of contrasting words and phrases:

> rebel against / submit
> told we were equal / told we were subordinate
> told we could change history / told we were trapped by history
> infuriated / seduced
> I adore / I despise
> I want / I think wanting . . . is about the most dumb-ass goal
> stokes my desire / triggers my bile
> on the one hand / on the other hand

These contrasting phrases help flesh out Douglas's claim that women are being pulled in two directions at once. In so doing, they bind the passage together into a unified whole that, despite its complexity and sophistication, stays focused over its entire length.

REPEAT YOURSELF—BUT WITH A DIFFERENCE

The last technique we offer for connecting the parts of your text involves repeating yourself, but with a difference—which basically means saying the same thing you've just said but in a slightly different way that avoids sounding monotonous. To effectively connect the parts of your argument and keep it moving forward, be careful not to leap from one idea to a different idea or introduce new ideas cold. Instead, try to build bridges between your ideas by echoing what you've just said while simultaneously moving your text into new territory.

Several of the connecting devices discussed in this chapter are ways of repeating yourself in this special way. Key terms, pointing terms, and even many transitions can be used in a way that not only brings something forward from the previous sentence but in some way alters it, too. When Douglas, for instance, uses the key term "ambivalent" to echo her earlier reference to schizophrenics, she is repeating herself with a difference—repeating the same concept but with a different word that adds new associations.

In addition, when you use transition phrases like "in other words" and "to put it another way," you repeat yourself with a difference, since these phrases help you restate earlier claims but in a different register. When you open a sentence with "in other words," you are basically telling your readers that in case they didn't fully understand what you meant in the last sentence, you are now coming at it again from a slightly different angle, or that since you're presenting a very important idea, you're not going to skip over it quickly but will explore it further to make sure your readers grasp all its aspects.

We would even go so far as to suggest that after your first sentence, almost every sentence you write should refer back to previous statements in some way. Whether you are writing a "furthermore" comment that adds to what you have just said or a "for example" statement that illustrates it, each sentence should echo at least one element of the previous sentence in some discernible way. Even when your text changes direction and requires transitions like "in contrast," "however," or "but," you still need to mark that shift by linking the sentence to the one just before it, as in the following example:

> Cheyenne loved basketball. Nevertheless, she feared her height would put her at a disadvantage.

These sentences work because even though the second sentence changes course and qualifies the first, it still echoes key concepts from the first. Not only does "she" echo "Cheyenne," since both refer to the same person, but "feared" echoes "loved" by establishing the contrast mandated by the term "nevertheless." "Nevertheless," then, is not an excuse for changing subjects radically. It too requires repetition to help readers shift gears with you and follow your train of thought.

Repetition, in short, is the central means by which you can move from point A to point B in a text. To introduce one last analogy, think of the way experienced rock climbers move up a steep slope. Instead of jumping or lurching from one handhold to the next, good climbers get a secure handhold on the position they have established before reaching for the next ledge. The same thing applies to writing. To move smoothly from point to point in your argument, you need to firmly ground what you say in what you've already said. In this way, your writing remains focused while simultaneously moving forward.

"But hold on," you may be thinking. "Isn't repetition precisely what sophisticated writers should avoid, on the grounds that it will make their writing sound simplistic—as if they are belaboring the obvious?" Yes and no. On the one hand, writers certainly can run into trouble if they merely repeat themselves and nothing more. On the other hand, repetition is key to creating continuity in writing. It is impossible to stay on track in a piece of writing if you don't repeat your points throughout the length of the text. Furthermore, writers would never make an impact on readers if they didn't repeat their main points often enough to reinforce those points and make them stand out above subordinate points. The trick therefore is not to avoid repeating yourself but to repeat yourself in varied and interesting enough ways that you advance your argument without sounding tedious.

Exercises

1. The statements below aren't yet connected to each other. Use any of the transitions listed on pages 111 and 112 to connect them. You can combine the statements into one sentence, or you can keep them as two separate sentences, adding or deleting words. Once you're done, compare your responses with a partner's. How does your choice of transition words affect the meaning of the statements?

   a. Herd immunity is established when 93 percent of a population is vaccinated. Vaccinations can wear off in early adolescence.
   b. Writing can look like an individual pursuit. It requires other people. Other people help writers imagine how their audience will understand and respond to their claims.
   c. Some ski resorts have begun to diversify their operations to increase year-round profitability. Some have added zip lines that draw in people in the summer months.

2. Read the following passage from the MIT professor Sherry Turkle's essay "Stop Googling. Let's Talk." Annotate the connecting devices you see. Underline the transitions, circle the key terms, and put boxes around the pointing terms.

   > Across generations, technology is implicated in this assault on empathy. We've gotten used to being connected all the time, but we have found ways around conversation—at least from conversation that is open-ended and spontaneous, in which we play with ideas and allow ourselves to be fully present and vulnerable. But it is in this type of conversation—where we learn to make eye contact, to become aware of another person's posture and tone, to comfort

one another and respectfully challenge one another—that empathy and intimacy flourish. In these conversations, we learn who we are.

Of course, we can find empathic conversations today, but the trend line is clear. It's not only that we turn away from talking face to face to chat online. It's that we don't allow these conversations to happen in the first place because we keep our phones in the landscape.

In our hearts, we know this, and now research is catching up with our intuitions. We face a significant choice. It is not about giving up our phones but about using them with greater intention. Conversation is there for us to reclaim. For the failing connections of our digital world, it is the talking cure.

3. Read over something you've written with an eye for the devices you've used to connect the parts. Working either by yourself or with a partner, do the following:

   a. Underline all the transitions, pointing terms, key terms, and repetitions.
   b. Describe the patterns you see. Do you rely on certain devices more than others?
   c. Locate a passage that could use better connections. Revise it using the devices introduced in this chapter. Is it easier to read now?

NINE

"YOU MEAN I CAN JUST SAY IT THAT WAY?"

Academic Writing Doesn't Mean Setting Aside Your Own Voice

We wish we had a dollar for each time a student has asked us a version of the above question. It usually comes when the student is visiting us during our office hours, seeking advice about how to improve a draft of an essay. When we ask the student to tell us in simple words the point being made in the essay, the student will almost invariably produce a statement that is far clearer and more incisive than anything in the draft.

"Write that down," we will urge. "What you just said is sooo much better than anything you wrote in your draft. We suggest going home and revising your paper in a way that makes that claim the focal point of your essay."

"Really?" our student will ask, looking surprised. "You mean I can just say it that way?"

"Sure. Why not?"

"Well, saying it that way seems just so elementary—so obvious. I mean, I don't want to sound stupid."

The goal of this chapter is to counteract this common misconception: that relying in college on the straightforward, down-to-earth language you use every day will make you sound stupid; that to impress your teachers you need to set aside your everyday voice and write in a way that is hard to understand.

It's easy to see how this misconception took hold, since academic writing is notoriously obscure. Students can't be blamed for such obscurity when much of the writing they're assigned to read is so hard to understand—as we can see in the following sentence from a science paper that linguist Steven Pinker quotes in his essay "Why Academics Stink at Writing":

> Participants read assertions whose veracity was either affirmed or denied by the subsequent presentation of an assessment word.

After struggling to determine what the writer of this sentence was trying to say, Pinker finally decided it was probably something as simple as this:

> Participants read sentences, each followed by the word *true* or *false*.

Had the author revised the original statement by tapping into more relaxed, everyday language, as Pinker did in revising it, much of this struggle could have been avoided. In our view, then, mastering academic writing does not mean completely abandoning your normal voice for one that's stiff, convoluted, or pompous, as students often assume. Instead, it means creating a new voice that draws on the voice you already have.

This is not to suggest that any language you use among friends has a place in academic writing. Nor is it to suggest that you may fall back on your everyday voice as an excuse to remain in your comfort zone and avoid learning the rigorous forms and habits that characterize academic culture. After all, learning new words and rhetorical moves is a major part of getting an education. We do, however, wish to suggest that everyday language can often enliven such moves and even enhance your precision in using academic terminology. In our view, then, it is a mistake to assume that the academic and everyday are completely separate languages that can never be used together. Ultimately, we suggest, academic writing is often at its best when it combines what we call "everydayspeak" and "academicspeak."

BLEND ACADEMIC AND COLLOQUIAL STYLES

In fact, we would point out that many academics are highly successful writers who themselves blend everyday and academic styles. Note, for example, how Judith Fetterley, a prominent scholar in the field of literary studies, blends academic and everyday ways of talking in the following passage on the novelist Willa Cather:

> As Merrill Skaggs has put it, "[Cather] is neurotically controlling and self-conscious about her work, but she knows at all points what she is doing. Above all else, she is self-conscious."
>
> Without question, Cather was a control freak.
>
> JUDITH FETTERLEY, "Willa Cather and the Question of Sympathy: An Unofficial Story"

In this passage, Fetterley makes use of what is probably the most common technique for blending academic and everyday language: she puts them side by side, juxtaposing "neurotically controlling" and "self-conscious" from a quoted source with her own colloquial term, "control freak." In this way, Fetterley lightens a potentially dry subject and makes it more accessible and even entertaining.

A TRANSLATION RECIPE

But Fetterley does more than simply put academicspeak and everydayspeak side by side. She takes a step further by translating the one into the other. By translating Skaggs's polysyllabic description of Cather as "neurotically controlling and self-conscious" into the succinct, if blunt, "control freak," Fetterley shows how rarefied, academic ways of talking and more familiar language can not only coexist but can also actually enhance one another—her informal "control freak" serving to explain the formal language that precedes it.

To be sure, slangy, colloquial expressions like "control freak" may be far more common in the humanities than in the sciences, and even in the humanities such casual usages are a recent development. Fifty years ago academic writing in all disciplines was the linguistic equivalent of a black-tie affair. But as times have changed, so has the range of options open to academic writers—so much so that it is not surprising to find writers in all fields using colloquial expressions and referring to movies, music, and other forms of popular culture.

Indeed, Fetterley's passage offers a simple recipe for mixing styles that we encourage you to try out in your own writing: first state the point in academic language, and then translate the point into everyday language. Everyone knows that academic terms like "neurotically controlling" and "self-conscious"—and others you might encounter like "subject position" or "bifurcate"—can be hard to understand. But this translation recipe, we think, eases such difficulties by making the academic familiar. Here is one way you might translate academicspeak into everydayspeak:

- **Scholar X argues, "__________." In other words, __________.**

Instead of "In other words," you might try variations like the following:

- **Essentially, X argues __________.**
- **X's point, succinctly put, is that __________.**
- **Plainly put, __________.**

Following Fetterley's lead and making moves like these can help you not only demystify challenging academic material but also reinterpret it, showing you understand it (and helping readers understand it) by putting it into your own terms.

SELF-TRANSLATION

But this translation recipe need not be limited to clarifying the ideas of others. It can also be used to clarify your own complex ideas, as the following passage by the philosopher Rebecca Goldstein illustrates:

> We can hardly get through our lives—in fact, it's hard to get through a week—without considering what makes specific actions right and others wrong and debating with ourselves whether that is a difference that must compel the actions we choose. (Okay, it's wrong! I get it! But why should I care?)
>
> Rebecca Goldstein, *Plato at the Googleplex: Why Philosophy Won't Go Away*

Though Goldstein's first sentence may require several rereadings, it is one that most of us, with varying degrees of effort, can come to understand: that we all wrestle regularly with the challenging philosophical questions of what the ethics of a given situation are and whether those ethics should alter our behavior. But instead of leaving us entirely on our own to figure out what she is saying, Goldstein helps us out in her closing parenthetical remarks, which translate the abstractions of her first sentence into the kind of concrete everydayspeak that runs through our heads.

Yet another example of self-translation—one that actually uses the word "translation"—can be found on the opening page of a book by scholar Helen Sword:

> There is a massive gap between what most readers consider to be good writing and what academics typically produce and publish. I'm not talking about the kinds of formal strictures necessarily imposed

> by journal editors—article length, citation style, and the like—but about a deeper, duller kind of disciplinary monotony, a compulsive proclivity for discursive obscurantism and circumambulatory diction (translation: an addiction to big words and soggy syntax).
>
> Helen Sword, *Stylish Academic Writing*

In this passage, Sword gives her own unique twist to the translation technique we've been discussing. After a stream of difficult polysyllabic words—"a compulsive proclivity for discursive obscurantism and circumambulatory diction"—she then concludes by translating these words into everydayspeak: "an addiction to big words and soggy syntax." The effect is to dramatize her larger point: the "massive gap between what most readers consider to be good writing and what academics typically produce and publish."

FAMOUS EXAMPLES

Even notoriously difficult thinkers could be said to use the translation practice we have been advocating in this chapter, as the following famous and widely quoted claims illustrate:

> I think, therefore I am.
> —René Descartes

> The master's tools will never dismantle the master's house.
> —Audre Lorde

> The medium is the message.
> —Marshall McLuhan

> Form follows function.
> —Louis Sullivan

These sentences can be read almost as sound bites—short, catchy statements that express a more complex idea. Though the term "sound bite" is usually used to refer to mindless media simplifications, the succinct statements above show what valuable work they can do. These distillations are admittedly reductive in that they do not capture all the nuances of the more complex ideas they represent. But consider their power to stick in the minds of readers. Without these memorable translations, we wonder if these authors' ideas would have achieved such widespread circulation.

Consider Descartes' "I think, therefore I am," for example, which comes embedded in the following passage, in which Descartes is struggling to find a philosophical foundation for absolute truth in the face of skeptical doctrines that doubt that anything can be known for certain. After putting himself in the shoes of a radical skeptic and imagining what it would be like to believe all apparent truths to be false, Descartes "immediately . . . observed," he writes:

> whilst I thus wished to think that all was false, it was absolutely necessary that I, who thus thought, should be somewhat; and as I observed that this truth, I think, therefore I am (*cogito ergo sum*), was so certain and of such evidence that no ground of doubt, however extravagant, could be alleged by the sceptics capable of shaking it, I concluded that I might, without scruple, accept it as the first principle of the philosophy of which I was in search.
>
> René Descartes, "Discourse on the Method, Part IV"

Had Descartes been less probing and scrupulous, we speculate, he would have stopped writing and ended the passage after the statement "it was absolutely necessary that I, who thus thought, should be somewhat." After all, the passage up to this point contains all the basic ingredients that the rest of it goes on to explain, the simpler, more accessible formulation

"I think, therefore I am" being merely a reformulation of this earlier material. But just imagine if Descartes had decided that his job as a writer was finished after his initial claim and had failed to add the more accessible phrase "I think, therefore I am." We suspect this idea of his would not have become one of the most famous touchstones of Western philosophy.

EVERYDAY LANGUAGE AS A THINKING TOOL

As the examples in this chapter suggest, then, translating academic language into everydayspeak can be an indispensable tool for clarifying and underscoring ideas for readers. But at an even more basic level, such translation can be an indispensable means for you as a writer to clarify your ideas to yourself. In other words, translating academicspeak into everydayspeak can function as a thinking tool that enables you to discover what you are trying to say to begin with.

For as writing theorists often note, writing is generally not a process in which we start with a fully formed idea in our heads that we then simply transcribe in an unchanged state onto the page. On the contrary, writing is more often a means of discovery in which we use the writing process to figure out what our idea is. This is why writers are often surprised to find that what they end up with on the page is quite different from what they thought it would be when they started. What we are trying to say here is that everydayspeak is often crucial for this discovery process, that translating your ideas into more common, simpler terms can help you figure out what your ideas really are, as opposed to what you initially imagined they were. Even Descartes, for example, may not have had the formulation "I think, therefore I am" in mind before he wrote the passage above; instead, he may have arrived at it as he worked through the writing process.

We ourselves have been reminded of this point when engaged in our own writing. One major benefit of writing collaboratively, as the two of us do, is that it repeatedly forces us to explain in simpler terms our less-than-clear ideas when one of us doesn't already know what the other means. In the process of writing and revising this book, for instance, we were always turning to each other after reading something the other had written and asking a version of the "Can you explain that more simply?" question that we described asking our students in our office in this chapter's opening anecdote: "What do you mean?" "I don't get it—can you explain?" "Huh!?" Sometimes, when the idea is finally stated in plain, everyday terms, we realize that it doesn't make sense or that it amounts to nothing more than a cliché—or that we have something worth pursuing. It's as if using everyday language to talk through a draft—as any writer can do by asking others to critique a draft—shines a bright light on our writing to expose its strengths and weaknesses.

STILL NOT CONVINCED?

To be sure, not everyone will be as enthusiastic as we are about the benefits of everydayspeak. Many will insist that, while some fields in the humanities may be open to everyday language, colloquial expressions, and slang, most fields in the sciences are not. And some people in both the humanities and the sciences will argue that some ideas simply can't be done justice to in everyday language. "Theory X," they will say, "is just too complex to be explained in simple terms," or "You have to be in the field to understand it." Perhaps so. But at least one distinguished scientist, the celebrated atomic physicist Enrico Fermi, thought otherwise. Fermi, it is said, believed that all faculty in his field should teach basic physics to undergraduates, because having to explain the science in relatively plain English helped clarify their thinking. This last point can be stated as a rule of thumb: if you can't explain it to your aunt Franny, chances are you don't understand it yourself.

Furthermore, when writers tell themselves that their ideas are just too complex to be explained to nonspecialists, they risk fooling themselves into thinking that they are making more sense than they actually are. Translating academicspeak into everydayspeak functions as a kind of baloney detector, a way of keeping us honest when we're in danger of getting carried away by our own verbosity.

CODE-MESHING

"But come on," some may say. "Get real! Academic writing must, in many cases, mean setting aside our own voices." Sure, it may be fine to translate challenging academic ideas into plain everyday language, as Goldstein, Sword, and Descartes do above, when it's a language that your audience will understand and find acceptable. But what if your everyday language—the one you use when you're most relaxed, with family and friends—is filled with slang and questionable grammar? And what if your everyday language is an ethnic or regional dialect—or a different language altogether? Is there really a place for such language in academic, professional, or public writing?

Yes and no. On the one hand, there are many situations—like when you're applying for a job or submitting a proposal to be read by an official screening body—in which it's probably safest to write in "standard" English. On the other hand, the line between language that might confuse audiences and language that engages or challenges them is not always obvious. Nor is the line between foreign words that readers don't already know and those that readers might happily learn. After all, standard written English is more open and inclusive than it may at first appear. And readers often appreciate writers who take risks and mix things up.

Many prominent writers mix standard written English with other dialects or languages, employing a practice that cultural and linguistic theorists Vershawn Ashanti Young and Suresh Canagarajah call "code-meshing." For instance, in the titles of two of her books, *Talkin and Testifyin: The Language of Black America* and *Black Talk: Words and Phrases From the Hood to the Amen Corner*, the language scholar Geneva Smitherman mixes African American vernacular phrases with more scholarly language in order to suggest, as she explicitly argues in these books, that black vernacular English is as legitimate a variety of language as standard English. Here are three typical passages:

> In Black America, the oral tradition has served as a fundamental vehicle for gittin ovah. That tradition preserves the Afro-American heritage and reflects the collective spirit of the race.
>
> Blacks are quick to ridicule "educated fools," people who done gone to school and read all dem books and still don't know nothin!
>
> It is a socially approved verbal strategy for black rappers to talk about how bad they is.
>
> GENEVA SMITHERMAN, *Talkin and Testifyin: The Language of Black America*

In these examples, Smitherman blends the types of terms we expect in scholarly writing like "oral tradition" and "fundamental vehicle" with Black vernacular phrases like "gittin ovah." She even blends the standard English spelling of words with African American English variants like "dem" and "ovah" in a way that evokes how some speakers of African American English sound. Some might object to these unconventional practices, but this is precisely Smitherman's point: that our habitual language practices need to be opened up, and that the number of participants in the academic conversation needs to be expanded.

Along similar lines, the writer and activist Gloria Anzaldúa mixes standard English with what she calls Chicano Spanish to make a political point about the suppression of the Spanish language in the United States. In one typical passage, she writes:

> From this racial, ideological, cultural, and biological cross-pollinization, an "alien" consciousness is presently in the making—a new *mestiza* consciousness, *una conciencia de mujer*.
>
> GLORIA ANZALDÚA,
> *Borderlands / La Frontera: The New Mestiza*

Anzaldúa gets her point across not only through *what* she says but also through the *way* she says it, showing that the new hybrid, or "*mestiza* consciousness," that she celebrates is, as she puts it, "presently in the making." Ultimately, such code-meshing suggests that languages, like the people who speak them, are not distinct, separate islands.

Because there are so many options in writing, then, there is no need to ever feel limited in your choice of words. You can always experiment with your language and improve it. Depending on your audience and purpose, and how much risk you're willing to take, you can dress up your language, dress it down, or some combination of both. You could even recast the title of this book, "*They Say / I Say*," as a teenager might say it: "She Goes / I'm Like."

We hope you agree with us, then, that to succeed as a college writer, you need not always set aside your everyday voice, even when that voice may initially seem unwelcome in the academic world. It is by blending everyday language with standard written English that what counts as "standard" changes and the range of possibilities open to academic writers continues to grow.

Exercises

1. Take a paragraph from this book and dress it down, rewriting it in informal colloquial language. Then rewrite the same paragraph again by dressing it up, making it much more formal. Then rewrite the paragraph in a way that blends the two styles. Share your paragraphs with a classmate and discuss which versions are most effective and why.

2. Find something you've written for a course, and study it to see whether you've used any of your own everyday expressions, any words or structures that are not "academic." If by chance you don't find any, see if there's a place or two where shifting into more casual or unexpected language would help you make a point, get your reader's attention, or just add liveliness to your text. Be sure to keep your audience and purpose in mind, and use language that will be appropriate to both.

3. Below is a short passage from Stephanie Owen and Isabel Sawhill's report, "Should Everyone Go to College?" Use one of the translation templates on page 127 to translate the academic language in the underlined sentence into everyday language. Compare your response with a classmate.

   We all know that, on average, college graduates make significantly more money over their lifetimes than those with only a high school education. What gets less attention is the fact that not all college degrees or college graduates are equal. There is enormous variation in the so-called return to education depending on factors such as institution attended, field of study, whether a student graduates, and post-graduation occupation.

4. Find a reading on **theysayiblog.com** that blends academic and everyday styles, such as James Hatch's 2019 essay, "My Semester with the Snowflakes." Identify a sentence or passage where you see the author mixing everyday and academic language. Explain how this blending affects the overall argument. How did you react as a reader?

TEN

"BUT DON'T GET ME WRONG"

The Art of Metacommentary

When we tell people that we are writing a chapter on the art of metacommentary, they often give us a puzzled look and tell us that they have no idea what "metacommentary" is. "We know what commentary is," they'll sometimes say, "but what does it mean when it's *meta*?" Our answer is that whether or not they know the term, they practice the art of metacommentary on a daily basis whenever they make a point of explaining something they've said or written: "What I meant to say was ________," "My point was not ________, but ________," or "You're probably not going to like what I'm about to say, but ________." In such cases, they are not offering new points but telling an audience how to interpret what they have already said or are about to say. In short, then, metacommentary is a way of commenting on your claims and telling others how—and how not—to think about them.

It may help to think of metacommentary as being like the chorus in a Greek play that stands to the side of the drama unfolding on the stage and explains its meaning to the audience—or like a voice-over narrator who comments on and explains the action in a television show or movie. Think of metacommentary as a sort of second text that stands alongside your main text and explains what it means. In the main text you say something; in the metatext you guide your readers in interpreting and processing what you've said.

What we are suggesting, then, is that you think of your text as two texts joined at the hip: a main text in which you make your argument and another in which you "work" your ideas, distinguishing your views from others they may be confused with, anticipating and answering objections, connecting one point to another, explaining why your claim might be controversial, and so forth. The figure below demonstrates what we mean.

THE MAIN TEXT SAYS SOMETHING. THE METATEXT TELLS READERS HOW—AND HOW NOT—TO THINK ABOUT IT.

USE METACOMMENTARY TO CLARIFY AND ELABORATE

But why do you need metacommentary to tell readers what you mean and guide them through your text? Can't you just clearly say what you mean up front? The answer is that no matter how clear and precise your writing is, readers can still fail to understand it in any number of ways. Even the best writers can provoke reactions in readers that they didn't intend, and even good readers can get lost in a complicated argument or fail to see how one point connects with another. Readers may also fail to see what follows from your argument, or they may follow your reasoning and examples yet fail to see the larger conclusion you draw from them. They may fail to see your argument's overall significance or mistake what you are saying for a related argument that they have heard before but that you want to distance yourself from. As a result, no matter how straightforward a writer you are, readers still need you to help them grasp what you really mean. Because the written word is prone to so much mischief and can be interpreted in so many different ways, we need metacommentary to keep misinterpretations and other communication misfires at bay.

Another reason to master the art of metacommentary is that it will help you develop your ideas and generate more text. If you have ever had trouble producing the required number of pages for a writing project, metacommentary can help you add both length and depth to your writing. We've seen many students who try to produce a five-page paper sputter to a halt at two or three pages, complaining they've said everything they can think of about their topic. "I've stated my thesis and presented my reasons and evidence," students have told us. "What else is there to do?" It's almost as if such writers have generated a thesis and don't know what to do with it. When these students learn to use metacommentary, however, they get more out of their ideas and write longer, more substantial texts. In sum, metacommentary can help you extract the full potential from your ideas, drawing out important implications, explaining ideas from different perspectives, and so forth.

So even when you may think you've said everything possible in an argument, try inserting the following types of metacommentary:

- **In other words, she doesn't realize how right she is.**
- **What _______ really means is _______.**
- **My point is not _______ but _______.**
- **Ultimately, then, my goal is to demonstrate that _______.**

Ideally, such metacommentary should help you recognize some implications of your ideas that you didn't initially realize were there.

Let's look at how the cultural critic Neil Postman uses metacommentary in the following passage describing the shift in American culture when it began to move from print and reading to television and movies:

> *It is my intention in this book to show* that a great . . . shift has taken place in America, with the result that the content of much of our public discourse has become dangerous nonsense. *With this in view, my task in the chapters ahead is* straightforward. *I must, first, demonstrate* how, under the governance of the printing

press, discourse in America was different from what it is now—generally coherent, serious and rational; *and then* how, under the governance of television, it has become shriveled and absurd. *But to avoid the possibility that my analysis will be interpreted as* standard-brand academic whimpering, a kind of elitist complaint against "junk" on television, *I must first explain that* . . . I appreciate junk as much as the next fellow, *and I know full well that* the printing press has generated enough of it to fill the Grand Canyon to overflowing. Television is not old enough to have matched printing's output of junk.

NEIL POSTMAN, *Amusing Ourselves to Death: Public Discourse in the Age of Show Business*

To see what we mean by metacommentary, look at the phrases above that we have italicized. With these moves, Postman essentially stands apart from his main ideas to help readers follow and understand what he is arguing.

He previews what he will argue: *It is my intention in this book to show . . .*

He spells out how he will make his argument: *With this in view, my task in the chapters ahead is . . . I must, first, demonstrate . . . and then . . .*

He distinguishes his argument from other arguments it may easily be confused with: *But to avoid the possibility that my analysis will be interpreted as . . . I must first explain that . . .*

TITLES AS METACOMMENTARY

Even the title of Postman's book, *Amusing Ourselves to Death: Public Discourse in the Age of Show Business*, functions as a form of metacommentary since, like all titles, it stands apart from the text itself and tells readers the book's main point: that the very pleasure provided by contemporary show business is destructive.

Titles, in fact, are one of the most important forms of metacommentary, functioning rather like carnival barkers telling passersby what they can expect if they go inside. Subtitles, too, function as metacommentary, further explaining or elaborating on the main title. The subtitle of this book, for example, not only explains that it is about "the moves that matter in academic writing" but also indicates that "they say / I say" is one of these moves. Thinking of a title as metacommentary can actually help you develop sharper titles, ones that, like Postman's, give readers a hint of what your argument will be. Contrast such titles with unhelpfully open-ended ones, like "Shakespeare" or "Steroids" or "English Essay" or essays with no titles at all. Essays with vague titles (or no titles) send the message that the writer has simply not bothered to reflect on what is being said and is uninterested in guiding or orienting readers.

USE OTHER MOVES AS METACOMMENTARY

Many of the other moves covered in this book function as metacommentary: entertaining objections, adding transitions, framing quotations, answering "so what?" and "who cares?" When you entertain objections, you stand outside of your text and imagine what a critic might say; when you add transitions, you essentially explain the relationship between various claims. And when you answer the "so what?" and "who cares?" questions, you look beyond your central argument and explain who should be interested in it and why.

TEMPLATES FOR INTRODUCING METACOMMENTARY

TO WARD OFF POTENTIAL MISUNDERSTANDINGS

The following moves help you differentiate certain views from ones they might be mistaken for:

- Essentially, I am arguing not that we should give up the policy but that we should monitor effects far more closely.
- This is not to say ________, but rather ________.
- X is concerned less with ________ than with ________.

TO ELABORATE ON A PREVIOUS IDEA

The following moves elaborate on a previous point, saying to readers: "In case you didn't get it the first time, I'll try saying the same thing in a different way."

- In other words, ________.
- To put it another way, ________.
- What X is saying here is that ________.

TO PROVIDE A ROAD MAP TO YOUR TEXT

This move orients readers, clarifying where you have been and where you are going—and making it easier for them to process and follow your text:

- Chapter 2 explores ________, while Chapter 3 examines ________.
- Having just argued that ________, I want now to complicate the point by ________.

TO MOVE FROM A GENERAL CLAIM TO A SPECIFIC EXAMPLE

These moves help you explain a general point by providing a concrete example that illustrates what you're saying:

- For example, ________.
- ________, for instance, demonstrates ________.
- Consider ________, for example.
- To take a case in point, ________.

TO INDICATE THAT A CLAIM IS MORE, LESS, OR EQUALLY IMPORTANT

The following templates help you give relative emphasis to the claim that you are introducing, showing whether that claim is of more or less weight than the previous one or equal to it:

- Even more important, ________.
- But above all, ________.
- Incidentally, we will briefly note, ________.
- Just as important, ________.
- Equally, ________.
- Finally, ________.

TO EXPLAIN A CLAIM WHEN YOU ANTICIPATE OBJECTIONS

Here's a template to help you anticipate and respond to possible objections:

Chapter 6 has more templates for anticipating objections.

- Although some readers may object that _____, I would answer that ________.

TO GUIDE READERS TO YOUR MOST GENERAL POINT

These moves show that you are wrapping things up and tying up various subpoints previously made:

- **In sum, then, ________.**
- **My conclusion, then, is that ________.**
- **In short, ________.**

In this chapter we have tried to show that the most persuasive writing often doubles back and comments on its own claims in ways that help readers negotiate and process them. Instead of simply piling claim upon claim, effective writers are constantly "stage-managing" how their claims will be received. It's true, of course, that to be persuasive a text has to have strong claims to argue in the first place. But even the strongest arguments will flounder unless writers use metacommentary to prevent potential misreadings and make their arguments shine.

Exercises

1. Complete each of the following metacommentary templates in any way that makes sense:

   a. In making a case for raising the minimum wage, I am not saying that ________.
   b. But my argument will do more than prove that one particular industrial chemical has certain toxic properties. In this essay, I will also ________.
   c. My point about the national obsession with sports reinforces the belief held by many ________ that ________.

d. I believe, therefore, that the war is completely unjustified. But let me back up and explain how I arrived at this conclusion: ________. In this way, I came to believe that this war is a big mistake.

2. Read the following passage from Pau Gasol's 2018 essay, "An Open Letter about Female Coaches." You can find the link to the full essay on **theysayiblog.com**. Underline where Gasol uses the moves of metacommentary to guide his readers through the main text of his argument. Does the author use any of the chapter's templates (see p. 144)? How do you think the author's use of metacommentary enhances (or harms) his writing?

The reason I wanted to start by telling you about my parents, is that their story makes me think about today's NBA. Specifically about how, in the 72-year history of the league, there has never been a female head coach. Even more specifically, it makes me think of Becky Hammon: a coach who has been the topic of much conversation lately, and who I've had the opportunity to play for in San Antonio.

But if you think I'm writing this to argue why Becky is qualified to be an NBA head coach . . . well, you're mistaken. That part is obvious: One, she was an accomplished player—with an elite point guard's mind for the game. And two, she has been a successful assistant for arguably the greatest coach in the game. What more do you need? But like I said—I'm not here to make that argument. Arguing on Coach Hammon's behalf would feel patronizing. To me, it would be strange if NBA teams were not interested in her as a head coach.

3. Read over the draft of an essay, and try the following:

   a. Locate a passage that needs more clarification or elaboration. Revise it using the metacommentary templates included in this chapter.
   b. Add in "road map" metacommentary to help your reader follow your text, using the template on page 144.
   c. Compose a title and subtitle that function as metacommentary on your whole argument.

ELEVEN

"WHAT I REALLY WANT TO SAY IS"

Revising Substantially

ONE OF THE MOST common frustrations teachers have—we've had it, too—is that students do not revise in any substantial way. As one of our colleagues put it, "I ask my classes to do a substantial revision of an essay they've turned in, emphasis on the word 'substantial,' but invariably little is changed in what I get back. Students hand in the original essay with a word changed here and there, a few spelling errors corrected, and a comma or two added. . . . I feel like all my advice is for nothing." We suspect, however, that in most cases when students do merely superficial revisions, it's not because they are indifferent or lazy, as some teachers may assume, but because they aren't sure what a good revision looks like. Like even many seasoned writers, these students would *like* to revise more thoroughly, but when they reread what they've written, they have trouble seeing where it can be improved—and how. What they lack is not just a reliable picture in their head of what their draft *could* be but also reliable strategies for getting there. In this chapter, we supply ten such revision strategies and a revision checklist (see pp. 165–70) that are designed to work in virtually any academic setting, regardless of assignment, instructor, discipline, or course.

1. THINK GLOBALLY

Perhaps the best strategy for revising your writing in a substantial way is to think globally, as we might put it, about your draft. This involves stepping back from your writing and looking at the big picture, asking yourself what, finally, you are trying to say. You might ask: Do I have a central argument, or do I just ramble and talk *about* my subject? And if I do have a central argument, does that argument make sense? Is it coherent and unified, or do I go off on tangents or even contradict myself? Do I logically link the parts, tying them together with clear connections between them all, developing a continuous line of argument over my essay's entire length? Does my evidence match my central argument and, as we put it in our revision checklist, is it clear what is motivating my argument—why it needs to be made in the first place? That is, do I present my argument as an entry into some larger conversation or debate, as a response to something "they say"? Have I included the strongest possible objections that can be made against my argument or answered any counterarguments in a superficial way? In the end, might any such counterarguments I address be more convincing to readers—or even to me—than my own argument?

It was big questions like these that inspired a student several years ago to radically revise an essay she'd written on the Iraq War, transforming it from a series of disconnected observations about the war into a sharply focused critique of the view that the war promoted democracy. Her first draft had been a mere collection of scattered claims, all presented as if they were of equal importance: Iraq had no weapons of mass destruction. The United States has the strongest military. Saddam Hussein was evil. Many Americans and Iraqis were killed. The war increased terrorism. And so forth. But her final draft nicely subordinated all its points to a larger "they say/I say" thesis: though Saddam Hussein is an evil dictator, it makes no sense to wage war on Iraq's innocent people. The final version was virtually a different essay.

We open with this suggestion to think globally not just because it is perhaps the central way to substantially revise an essay but also because it is so frequently neglected. Because writing is often associated with local, sentence-level mechanics and grammar, some writers picture revision as a small-scale matter of dotting an occasional "i" and crossing an occasional "t." What often gets overlooked, as writing expert Nancy Sommers points out, are "strategies for handling the whole essay," ones that would help writers "reorder lines of reasoning or ask questions about their purposes and readers." It would be as if a jewelry appraiser were to assess a gem only by studying its smallest, microscopic details and never holding it back to form an overall impression.

Revising globally, then, may mean changing the way we think. It asks us to move beyond microlevel edits, beyond

The messiness of the revision process.

merely tweaking or refining an existing argument. At its best, revision is a messy process that often helps us discover what our argument is in the first place. In fact, a good way to test how substantial your revisions are is to ask how much you learned about your argument through the revision process.

2. BUT STILL SWEAT THE SMALL STUFF

But just because the global level is very important in revising, it doesn't mean that local, surface-level issues—word choice, sentence structure, grammar, style, and so forth—aren't very important too. After all, everything you write is composed of countless small-scale decisions, and if you improve enough of them your next draft has a chance of constituting a significant revision. Also, it is always possible that changing just a single word will help you radically resee your central argument and lead to major, global changes. So while we suggest you think of global revisions as more important than microlevel ones, in practice the two levels are deeply interdependent. Although writers are often told to start out by focusing on their big idea—getting that big idea down on paper and only at a later stage worrying about small-scale mechanics—seasoned writers often move back and forth between the two levels throughout the revision process.

To see how we sweat the small stuff, consider the photo on the facing page of revisions we made on our last paragraph, none of which significantly alter the paragraph's central point. The central point—about the importance of small edits and their connection to big edits—is recognizable from the one draft to the other. And yet we like to think that, taken together, these edits make the passage much more readable. The mere decision alone to move this section up in the chapter and make it the

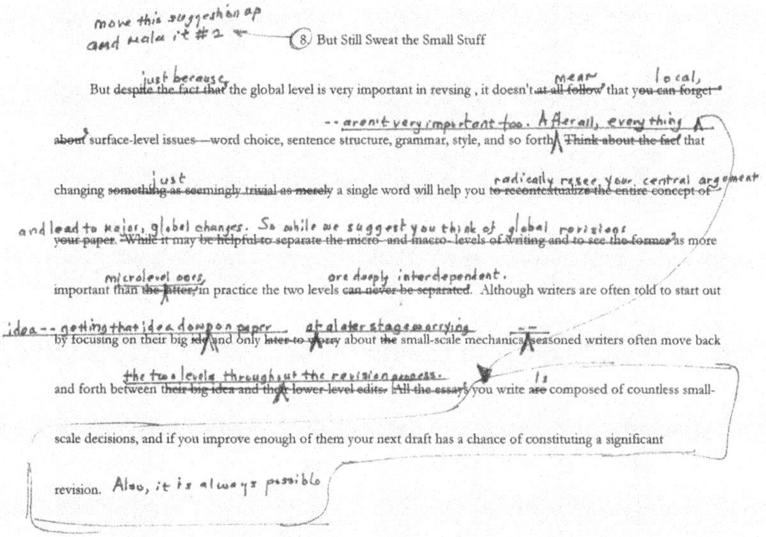

8. But Still Sweat the Small Stuff

But ~~despite the fact that~~ the global level is very important in revsing , it doesn't ~~at all follow~~ that ~~you can forget about~~ surface-level issues—word choice, sentence structure, grammar, style, and so forth. ~~Think about the fact~~ that changing ~~something as seemingly trivial as merely~~ a single word will help you ~~to recontextualize the entire concept of your paper. While it may be helpful to separate the micro- and macro- levels of writing and to see the former~~ as more important than ~~the latter,~~ in practice the two levels ~~can never be separated~~. Although writers are often told to start out by focusing on their big ~~idea~~ and only ~~later to worry~~ about ~~the~~ small-scale mechanics, seasoned writers often move back and forth between ~~their big idea and their lower-level edits. All the essays~~ you write ~~are~~ composed of countless small-scale decisions, and if you improve enough of them your next draft has a chance of constituting a significant revision.

second strategy listed has a big impact. The reader no longer needs to struggle to recall what we'd said several items back about thinking globally. We now have just said it.

3. READ YOUR OWN WRITING

But it is difficult to make any revisions, global or local, unless you do something even more fundamental, which is simply to read what you've written and then ideally reread and reread it again. It is very hard to set the revision process in motion if you don't do at least one initial read-through of your draft, and then do as many additional read-throughs as needed to get a solid grasp of the material with which you're dealing. As Donald Murray explains in *A Writer Teaches Writing*, "The writer reads and rereads and rereads, standing far back and reading quickly from a distance, moving in close and reading slowly line-by-line, reading again and again. . . ."

But why, you might wonder, should you read your own writing? You, after all, are the one who wrote it, so if anyone must know what your text says, shouldn't it be you? The answer is that, precisely because you're the author, you're too close to your text to know what it says. As writers, we tend to be so invested in what we've written that we need to find ways of stepping back from our text to gain some critical distance.

Perhaps the central way of gaining such distance is by reading the draft from an outsider's perspective—as if, instead of being the author, you were some other person who is on the lookout for logical glitches and inconsistencies, for better ways of stating a point, for parts that are hard to follow, for claims and subclaims that need more explanation, or for how your argument might be vulnerable to critique. You might also try reading your text aloud to yourself—or even try using text-to-speech technology on your computer or phone. And it never hurts, if you have time, to set your draft aside for a few days so that when you return to it you can reread it with fresh eyes.

4. AND HAVE OTHERS READ YOUR WRITING, TOO

Of course there are other ways to get critical distance on your work and see it from an outsider's perspective. One of the best ways is to show your work to someone who is willing to read it—a fellow student, family member, friend, or tutor—and ask for feedback. Teachers, in fact, may ask you to pair up with another student to comment on each other's work. It's a great way to get a sense of audience: how your text will be processed and received when it goes out into the world. In seeking out such readers, we often naturally gravitate toward those who share our opinions and predilections. But don't underestimate the value of readers who may know little about your subject or disagree with your position. Often, the more readers differ from you, the more likely they will be able to see things that you yourself could not have thought of.

5. GO BACK TO THE TEXT

While developing a deep familiarity with your own writing is essential in any revision process, developing a deep familiarity with your sources is also very important. It's surprising how often errors are introduced when we haven't read the text we're responding to carefully enough and start writing about it before we really understand it. It's also surprising how often errors are introduced when we fail to check and double-check our quotations against the originals and thus mistranscribe them in our texts. If we are right that the most persuasive writing responds to something that others have said, then writing that misquotes or misrepresents what those others say, as we suggested in Chapter 2 (see particularly our comments on the "closest cliché syndrome"), will be built on a false foundation.

If you're anything like us, however, you might not like going back to your source. At times we don't want to go back to a source because we don't want to take the time to unpack its difficult, challenging language. At other times, we don't want to return to a source because we fear, deep down, that it doesn't quite say what we want it to say. When this happens, there is always a danger of creating a straw man: distorting what an author says in order to pursue our own agenda, transforming the author into a mere projection of ourselves. In this respect, accurately representing what "they say" is not just an intellectual obligation but a moral one as well.

As an example, let's turn to Rosa, a student who wanted to write an essay defending the practice of meditation. In her first draft, Rosa made a strong case that meditation promotes democratic politics, but she misconstrued her essay's central source, a scholarly article by Dean Mathiowetz that reads:

Meditation Is Good for Nothing

> Does meditation bring political benefits in the sense of strengthening citizenship or democracy? Taking the Zen phrase "meditation doesn't work—it's good for nothing" as my point of departure . . . I argue that meditation can foster significant dimensions of democratic citizenship. . . .

Mathiowetz's argument here is that meditation can in fact "foster significant dimensions of democratic citizenship"—or, as he goes on to claim, that, paradoxically, because "meditation . . . is good for nothing," it can help citizens and politicians detach from their self-interested passions and biases and find common ground. Yet Rosa presented Mathiowetz as saying that meditation is literally "good for nothing" and has no political or civic benefits.

When Rosa realized her mistake, she was inspired to do a revision. And the following week, she produced a much improved draft that opens as follows:

> Many people think that meditation is a waste of time. According to these skeptics, meditation is a useless activity that is only for self-absorbed flakes who have no concern for the give-and-take of politics. But I disagree. As Dean Mathiowetz argues, the very uselessness of meditation makes it a valuable political tool. It can make us less polarized—better able to listen to one another and move beyond our rigid political views, and more committed to the common good.

In this way, Rosa was able to continue using Mathiowetz as a central source in her essay but without distorting his position. Instead of casting him as a naysayer in her essay who opposes meditation, she now presents Mathiowetz as the pro-meditation ally he really is.

6. DOES YOUR EXAMPLE SAY WHAT YOU SAY IT SAYS?

Offering an example to support your argument is such a natural, familiar part of writing that it may seem easy. And yet providing examples is often a challenge, largely because of the kind of disconnection issues we discussed in Chapter 8. When giving an example—which might take the form of a statistic, a quotation, evidence, or a story or anecdote—writers often discover that the example gets away from them. That is, the example they provide turns out not to support the point they want it to support and may even contradict it. So in revising your drafts, pay special attention to whether your example actually supports your argument, whether your example and what it is supposed to exemplify are united.

A student named Jacob needed help with this issue in an essay he'd written about how, as his title put it, "We All Need to Become More Green." In an attempt to provide a model example of someone who, in Jacob's words, has admirably "stopped using toxic, traditional household cleaners" that harm the environment, Jacob cites the case of his mother:

> My mother is a perfect example. She cares a lot about the environment and has always opposed chemicals. She frequently uses cleaning products in our house that are environmentally friendly but claims they never work. She once spent almost a hundred dollars on eco-friendly cleaners for our house but ended up throwing most of them out and returning to the toxic products she's always used. Nothing ever changes. She keeps using the old-fashioned cleaners but complaining about them.

Although each sentence here is admirably clear, Jacob ran into the classic problem of his thesis being out of sync with his example. Instead of showing that we should all stop using toxic cleaners, the story of his mother actually shows just how hard giving up such cleaners can be.

With Jacob's permission, his instructor circulated his essay to his class and asked how it might be revised. One student proposed that Jacob modify his thesis so that it asserts not just that we should all be more green, but that, to echo Kermit the Frog, "it's not easy being green," which, the student added, might be a fun new title for Jacob's essay. In his next draft, however, Jacob did decide to modify his argument, but in a different way by claiming that nobody, not even his deeply committed mother, will ever be able to become fully green if they don't lower their expectations about cleanliness.

7. KEEP ASKING "AS OPPOSED TO WHAT?"

Throughout this book we suggest that writers start "with what others are saying," as the subtitle of Chapter 1 puts it, and that they use this "they say" to motivate their "I say." But writers often neglect this important rhetorical move. They get so caught up in making their claims that they forget even the truest, most accurate, and well-supported claim will seem pointless if they fail to answer the all-important "as opposed to what?" or "who says otherwise?" question.

We sometimes forget to ask these questions ourselves. For example, it was only after years of writing and rewriting this very book that we realized there was an important "they say" or "as opposed to what?" contrast buried in our manuscript that we needed to draw out. At the end of a passage describing our templates as "one of the novel features of this book," we'd written:

> This book offers model templates to help you put key principles of writing directly into practice.

When we reread this sentence, we felt that it was missing something, that it sounded flat and uninspired. But why? After experimenting with different versions of the sentence, none of which seemed to help, we realized we weren't following our own advice. "There's no 'they say' here," Cathy announced. "Nothing we push off against, no 'as opposed to what.'" With this in mind, we embarked on another round of revisions and eventually came up with the following contrast, which now appears on page 2 of this edition:

> Instead of focusing solely on abstract principles of writing, then, this book offers model templates to help you put those principles directly into practice.

Why did we prefer this version? Because its new material, which we've underlined, not only establishes that we offer templates but also indicates why: to depart from and, we hope, improve upon writing instruction that focuses only on "abstract principles."

Had this sentence been all we changed, however, it would not have amounted to the type of "substantial" revision we've been saying is so important. But as often happens in the revision process, this one revision led to several others, setting in motion a series of revisions that significantly transformed our core argument. As we went back and reread the parts of the book we'd already written, we found several ways to extend the contrast we draw above between our templates and more abstract approaches. In the preface and introduction, we added two sections—"OK, but Templates?," and "What This Book Doesn't Do"—which help us further explain our template-based approach by contrasting it with what it isn't.

8. MOVE IT UP!

In her memoir *The Vanity Fair Diaries*, the magazine's former editor, Tina Brown, describes "the rewarding moment" in editing a manuscript

> when you see that the whole thing should start on page nine and flip the penultimate paragraph to the top of the piece, and all you want to do is call the writer immediately and tell him or her why. (73)

Brown's premise here is simple: *where* you say something matters, and the more important the point, the more it needs to be moved to "the top of the piece," where it will better get your reader's attention and infuse all you say that follows.

Imagine, after all, how frustrating it is for readers to have to slog through a lengthy text that doesn't state what its big point is until the very end, which is precisely what happens in Charles R. Morris's 333-page book, *A Rabble of Dead Money: The Great Crash and the Global Depression: 1929–1939*. Although Morris demonstrates impressive knowledge of the Great Depression and its historical era, he doesn't declare his central argument—that, contrary to what most people assume, "the 1929 stock market crash . . . did not cause the Depression"—until page 313. Had Morris foregrounded this point early in the book and used it to structure all that followed, readers wouldn't have been left wondering where he was going for the first three hundred pages: "Why is Morris telling us this?" "What's his big point?" "And this matters because . . . ?"

Delays of this kind are so common among writers that journalists long ago coined a term for it: "burying the lead" (or "lede," as it is sometimes spelled). Because writing is not a smoothly linear process of adding one perfectly polished paragraph on top of another until the last word is written, writers often don't know what their most important, or "lead," point will be until late in the writing process. As our cartoon on page 151 suggests, it is common for writers to start out thinking that their big idea will be one thing, only to realize later, just as they think their work is finished, that a different point needs to take center stage. When this happens, the best remedy, as Brown suggests, is to "flip" that point up "to the top of the piece," near the opening, and edit the rest so that your belatedly discovered argument informs your entire text from start to finish.

9. TAKE YOUR "UH-OH" MOMENTS SERIOUSLY

In our view, the best writers are always on the lookout for places in their writing that take their argument in the wrong direction. Especially when reading their work with a skeptical eye, as we suggested earlier, these self-critical writers keep looking for unanticipated implications in their writing that, for one reason or another, they are not comfortable with. As you reread your drafts, then, we suggest that you listen for any little voices in your head that say, "Uh-oh, what have I done? As I was arguing ________, I accidentally suggested ________." "Uh-oh" moments, as they might be called, can often be upsetting. But if you're willing to put in the time and to experiment with different solutions, you can head off such problems in your draft and possibly even turn them to your advantage.

Gerald had several such "uh-oh" moments as he was writing "Hidden Intellectualism," in which he makes the counterintuitive claim that schools should be organized like sports. One, for instance, came when he was arguing that the worlds of academic intellectual culture and of popular sports are more similar than one might assume. He had written:

> [T]he real intellectual world, the one that existed in the big world beyond school, is organized very much like the world of team sports, with rival texts, rival interpretations and evaluations of texts, . . . and elaborate team competitions in which "fans" of writers, intellectual systems, methodologies, and -isms contend against one another.

"Oh, no," Gerald thought to himself as he reread this passage. "Couldn't someone misunderstand me? Couldn't someone think that in saying schools should be organized like sports,

I'm promoting the ugly side of sports, the side that's filled with petty one-upmanship and, at times, even violence? How can I argue that schools should imitate the contentious domain of sports when schools already have too much small-minded and destructive competition?"

For a while, Gerald was disturbed enough by thoughts like these that he was tempted to simply eliminate the comparison he makes between sports and school. But after wrestling with the problem, he realized that he was defending sports not at their worst but at their best. As a result, the next chance he got, Gerald sat down with his manuscript and added the following new material, which explains that sports not only promote rivalry but

> also satisfy the thirst for community. When you entered sports debates, you became part of a community that was not limited to your family and friends, but was national and public.

In this way, Gerald was able to use his "uh-oh" moment to enhance his argument. What began as a serious problem ended up helping him discover an aspect of his own argument that he hadn't seen before: that schooling should emulate not the uglier side of sports but the side that encourages camaraderie and broad, public excitement.

10. DON'T LET THE MESS SHOW

At several points in this chapter we have suggested that revising your writing in a global, substantial way is often a messy undertaking. In this final section, however, we want to suggest that to create a coherent, unified, and reader-friendly text, you need to *hide* this very mess. In other words, when you find any problems in your text, you need to do what is often a lot of hard work to correct them and make it look as if they never existed. If, for instance, you find a problem with your thesis, you need to not only reframe your thesis but also make sure that all your supporting claims, evidence, and examples, as we suggested above, match that thesis, erasing any confusing disconnects between your thesis and the rest of your text. Along similar lines, if you find that a section of your text doesn't make sense, you need to revise it until it does or eliminate that section altogether, making sure that the material that had preceded and followed the deleted material is well stitched together. And for a final example, if you realize that your best argument is buried too far back in your essay, you need not only to "move it up," as we suggested above, but also revise your entire draft so that it looks as if that best argument is what you had originally planned to say.

Joseph M. Williams and Lawrence McEnerney, writing experts, make a version of this point:

> If you find that the sentence from your conclusion is more insightful than the one from your introduction, then you have to revise your introduction to make it seem that you had this sentence in mind all along (even though when you started drafting the paper you may have had no idea how you were going to end it).

This advice holds true, we think, not just for introductions and conclusions but for virtually every part of a text. Even if you discover that your best claim appears mid-essay, you need to engage in a little smoke and mirrors, revising in a way that makes "it seem that you had" this claim in mind from the very outset, even though you hadn't.

A REVISION CHECKLIST

The checklist that follows is keyed both to this chapter on revision and to the writing advice throughout this book. It is composed of a series of questions designed to help you when rereading and revising your drafts.

Is Your Revision Really Substantial?

Look over the revisions you've made to your draft before turning it in and ask yourself if you have made enough changes to seriously improve it. If you've merely changed a few words or phrases, then you probably haven't addressed these larger issues: How coherent is your argument? Does your argument enter in dialogue with a motivating "they say"? Does your argument address a naysayer's counterargument? Is your argument consistent or contradictory?

Did you reread your draft several times and perhaps show it to other readers for feedback? If so, do you adequately respond to any concerns these readers raised, including ones possibly expressed to you by your instructor or a classmate?

Are the parts of your composition in the most effective order, or do some need to be moved? If you rearranged any of your text, have you revised the remaining material to avoid letting the "mess" show? (See pp. 163–64)

How Well Do You Represent What Others Say?

Do you start with what "they say"? If not, try revising to do so. See pages 23–28 for templates that can help.

Is it clear what is motivating your argument—why it needs to be made in the first place? If not, see pages 23–26 for templates that can help.

Do you summarize what others have said? If so, have you represented their views accurately—and adequately? Can you improve your summaries, perhaps by going back to the text and rereading the source you're summarizing?

Do you quote others? Have you carefully checked your quotations against the original sources? Do you frame each quotation in a way that integrates it into your text, explaining the quotation in your own words, and have you carefully considered whether the quotation actually supports your argument? (See pp. 49–51 for tips on creating a "quotation sandwich.")

Look at the verbs you use to introduce summaries and quotations, and consider how well they fit the action you're describing. If you've used all-purpose signal verbs such as X "said" or "believes," are there other such phrases that might be more precise, such as X "complains" or "predicts"? (See pp. 43–44 for a list of such signal verbs.)

Have you documented all of the sources you mention, both in parenthetical notations in the body of your text and at the end in a works-cited or references list?

Do you remind readers of the "they say" you're responding to throughout your text, or do you get off track and inadvertently start responding to a different "they say"? Can you revise so as to respond more continuously throughout the entire length of your text? (See pp. 27–28 for advice on using return sentences to keep your argument focused.)

How Effective Is What *You* Say?

Is it clear how you are responding to your "they say"? Is it clear what your position is—*agree, disagree, or a combination of both*—or might readers be unsure and need clarification? Do you use signal verbs that fit your position and clear language ("I question whether . . ." or "I'm of two minds about . . .")? (See Chapter 4 for three ways to respond and Chapter 5 for help in distinguishing the "I say" from "they say.")

If you disagree with the "they say" you're responding to, do you give reasons why in a way that moves the conversation forward, or do you merely contradict the "they say"? If you agree with the "they say," do you "agree with a difference," adding something of your own to the conversation? (For help with this move, see pp. 63–64.) And finally, if you both agree and disagree with your "they say," do you do so without contradicting yourself or seeming evasive? (See Chapter 4 for help in responding in these three different ways.)

Are your "I say" and "they say" clearly connected? Do your argument and the argument you are responding to address the same issue, or does a switch occur that takes you on a tangent? Do you use the same key terms for explaining both? (See pp. 116 for our discussion of key terms.)

What reasons—evidence, data, or examples—do you offer to support your "I say"? Do your reasons actually support your position, or is there a mismatch between them? Could a naysayer use your reasons against you to support a contrary position, and if so, could you defend your reasoning by summarizing and answering this objection? (See Chapter 6 for tips on doing so).

Will readers be able to distinguish what you say from what others say? Do you use voice markers ("My own view, however, is . . ." or "Skeptics, however, would disagree . . .") to mark the shift from the views of others to your own view and back? (See Chapter 5 for advice about using voice markers to make that distinction clear.)

Have You Introduced Any Naysayers?

Have you acknowledged likely objections to your argument? If so, have you represented these objections fairly—and responded to them persuasively? *If not,* think about what other perspectives exist on your topic, and incorporate them into your draft. (See Chapter 6 for tips on planting and responding to naysayers in your text.)

Have You Used Metacommentary?

How well, if at all, do you stand back from your writing and clarify what you do and don't mean? Might your argument be improved if you did a better job of explaining what you mean—or *don't* mean—with phrases like "in other words," "don't get me wrong," or "what I'm really trying to say here is . . ." (See Chapter 10 for examples of how to reinforce your argument with metacommentary.)

Do you have a helpful title? Does your title merely identify your topic, or does it successfully point to the position you take on that topic? Is your title lively and engaging, and might a subtitle help indicate your position?

Have You Tied It All Together?

Can readers follow your argument from one sentence, paragraph, and section to the next? Can readers see how each successive point is joined together in service of your overall argument? Are there any tangents that need to be brought in line with your larger train of thought or perhaps eliminated altogether?

Do you use transition phrases like "however," "in addition," and "in other words," which clarify how your ideas relate to one another? Are these phrases the right ones for your purposes—or do you use "however," say, when you really mean "also" or "in addition"? (See pp. 111–12 for a list of transitions.)

Do you use pointing words like "this" and "that," which help you gesture backward in your text and lead readers from one point to the next? If so, is it always clear what "this" and "that" refer to, or do you need to add nouns (e.g., "this book" or "this tendency to exaggerate") to avoid ambiguity? (See pp. 114–16 for tips on using pointing words to connect parts of your argument.)

Have you used what we call "repetition with a difference" to help connect parts of your argument? That is, do you succeed in *saying the same thing but in a slightly different way each time, which helps you move your argument forward and avoid being monotonous?* (See pp. 118–20 for help with this move.)

Have You Shown Why Your Argument Matters?

Do you make clear why your argument is important—and why your readers should care? Might your draft be improved by using templates like "My critique here is important because___________" or "The stakes in how we answer this question are high, given that _____________"? (See Chapter 7 for advice on addressing the "so what? and "who cares?" questions.)

Exercises

1. Read over a draft of your writing, and think about it globally. Explain to yourself the "big picture" of your argument using the following template: "Aha! Now I see! What I'm really trying to say is not, as I initially thought, ________ but ________." Use your response to write yourself a revision plan. Name two important things you need to do so that your argument matches what you're "really trying to say."
2. Read over a draft of your writing, paying particular attention to how you use sources.
   a. Go back to your sources to check how accurately you are using them. Confirm that your summaries and paraphrases are fair representations of the sources' arguments. Have you transcribed your quotations correctly? Have you properly cited all your sources?
   b. Look critically at the examples—quotations, evidence, anecdotes, and so forth—that you use to support your claims. Ask yourself, "Does this example support my

argument?" Revise your writing to unify your argument and examples.

3. Read a draft of your writing out loud or listen to it using text-to-speech technology.

    a. As you read or listen, mark the places in the text that are hard to follow. Then go back to these places and revise them. Could you use better transitions? Might metacommentary help? Could you use more voice markers, such as "In Smith's opinion . . ." or "She argues . . ."?

    b. As you read or listen, also mark the places in the text where you find yourself saying "uh-oh" because your words or their implications don't reflect your underlying intentions. Then go back to these "uh-oh" moments to clarify your intentions. Consider using a template like "This is not to suggest . . . It is, however, to suggest . . ."

TWELVE

"I TAKE YOUR POINT"

Entering Class Discussions

HAVE YOU EVER been in a class discussion that feels less like a genuine meeting of the minds than like a series of discrete, disconnected monologues? You make a comment, say, that seems provocative to you, but the classmate who speaks after you makes no reference to what you said, instead going off in an entirely different direction. Then the classmate who speaks next makes no reference either to you or to anyone else, making it seem as if everyone in the conversation is more interested in their own ideas than in actually conversing with anyone else.

We like to think that the principles this book advances can help improve class discussions, which increasingly include various forms of online communication. Particularly important for class discussion is the point that our own ideas become more cogent and powerful the more responsive we are to others and the more we frame our claims not in isolation but as responses to what others before us have said. Ultimately, then, a good face-to-face classroom discussion (or online communication) doesn't just happen spontaneously. It requires the same sorts of disciplined moves and practices used in many writing situations, particularly that of identifying to what and to whom you are responding.

FRAME YOUR COMMENTS AS A RESPONSE TO SOMETHING THAT HAS ALREADY BEEN SAID

The single most important thing you need to do when joining a class discussion is to link what you are about to say to something that has already been said.

- **I really liked Aaron's point about the two sides being closer than they seem. I'd add that both seem rather moderate.**
- **I take your point, Nadia, that ________. Still . . .**
- **Though Kayla and Ryan seem to be at odds about ________, they may actually not be all that far apart.**

In framing your comments this way, it is usually best to name both the person and the idea you're responding to. If you name the person alone ("I agree with Aaron because ________"), it may not be clear to listeners what part of what Aaron said you are referring to. Conversely, if you only summarize what Aaron said without naming him, you'll probably leave your classmates wondering whose comments you're referring to.

But won't you sound stilted and deeply redundant in class if you try to restate the point your classmate just made? After all, in the case of the first template above, the entire class will have just heard Aaron's point about the two sides being closer than they seem. Why, then, would you need to restate it?

We agree that in oral situations it does often sound artificial to restate what others just said precisely because they just said it. It would be awkward if on being asked to pass the salt at lunch, one were to reply: "If I understand you correctly, you have asked me to pass the salt. Yes, I can, and here it is." But in oral discussions about complicated issues that are open to multiple interpretations, we usually do need to resummarize what others have said to make sure that everyone is on the same page. Since Aaron may have made several points when he spoke and may have been followed by other commentators, the class will probably need you to summarize which point of his you are referring to. And even if Aaron made only one point, restating that point is helpful not only to remind the group what his point was (since some may have missed or forgotten it) but also to make sure that he, you, and others have interpreted his point in the same way.

TO CHANGE THE SUBJECT, INDICATE EXPLICITLY THAT YOU ARE DOING SO

It is fine to try to change the conversation's direction. There's just one catch: you need to make clear to listeners that this is what you are doing. For example:

- **So far we have been talking about <u>the characters in the film</u>. But isn't the real issue here <u>the cinematography</u>?**
- **I'd like to change the subject to one that hasn't yet been addressed.**

You can try to change the subject without indicating that you are doing so. But you risk that your comment will come across as irrelevant rather than as a thoughtful contribution that moves the conversation forward.

BE EVEN MORE EXPLICIT THAN YOU WOULD BE IN WRITING

Because listeners in an oral discussion can't go back and reread what you just said, they are more easily overloaded than are readers of a print text. For this reason, in a class discussion you will do well to take some extra steps to help listeners follow your train of thought. (1) When you make a comment, limit yourself to one point only, though you can elaborate on this point, fleshing it out with examples and evidence. If you feel you must make two points, either unite them under one larger umbrella point, or make one point first and save the other for later. Trying to bundle two or more claims into one comment can result in neither getting the attention it deserves. (2) Use metacommentary to highlight your key point so that listeners can readily grasp it.

- **In other words, what I'm trying to get at here is ________.**
- **My point is this: ________.**
- **My point, though, is not ________ but ________.**
- **This distinction is important because ________.**

Exercises

1. Choose a text you've read in class, and discuss the text's argument in a small group. Use these questions to start your conversation:

   a. Whom (or what) is the writer responding to?

b. What perspectives does the writer include, and what perspectives are missing?

c. Why does this argument matter?

2. Listen carefully to a class discussion, either in this class or another one of your courses. Notice what moves from this chapter your classmates and your instructor make:

   a. How do they frame their comments to link their ideas to something that has already been said?

   b. How do they change the direction of the conversation?

   c. How do they use metacommentary to clarify their points?

   Reflect on the conversation as a whole. Were the people in the conversation responsive to one another's ideas, or did the conversation feel more like a series of unconnected points? Explain one strategy from this chapter that would improve class discussions.

3. In your next class discussion, try using use these strategies to help your classmates follow your ideas:

   a. Write down your thoughts before you say them.

   b. Limit yourself to just one point per comment.

   c. Use metacommentary to highlight your key idea.

   How did these strategies help clarify your ideas? How did they help you listen more attentively to others? How did they invite others to respond? What was challenging about this exercise?

THIRTEEN

DON'T MAKE THEM SCROLL UP

Entering Online Conversations

THE INTERNET HAS TRANSFORMED COMMUNICATION in more ways than we can count. With just a few taps on a keyboard, we can be connected with what others have said not only throughout history, but right now, in the most remote places. Almost instantaneously, communities can be created that are powerful enough to change the world. In addition, virtually the moment we voice an opinion online, we can get responses from supporters and critics alike, while any links we provide to sources can connect readers to voices they might otherwise never have known about and to conversations they might never have been able to join.

Because of this connectivity, the internet lends itself perfectly to the type of conversational writing at the core of this book. Just the other day, we were on a discussion board in which one of the participants wrote to another, let's call him X, in a form that could have provided a template for this textbook: "Fascinating point about ________, X. I'd never thought of it that way before. I'd always thought that _______, but if you're right, then that would explain why ________."

IDENTIFY WHAT YOU'RE RESPONDING TO

Unfortunately, not all online writers make clear who or what prompted them to write. As a result, too many online exchanges end up being not true conversations but a series of statements without clear relationships to one another. All too often, it's hard to tell if the writer is building on what someone else has said, challenging it, or trying to change the discussion topic altogether. So although the digital world may connect us far more rapidly and with far more people than ever, it doesn't always encourage a genuine meeting of minds.

We've seen this type of confusion in the writing our own students submit to online discussions. Even students who use the "they say / I say" framework routinely and effectively in the essays they write often neglect to make those same moves online. While our students engage enthusiastically in online discussions, their posts are often all "I say" with little or no "they say." As a result, they end up talking past rather than to one another.

What is happening here, we suspect, is that the easy accessibility made possible by the internet makes slowing down and summarizing or even identifying what others say seem unnecessary. Why repeat the views you are responding to, writers seem to assume, when readers can easily find them by simply scrolling up or clicking on a link?

The problem with this way of thinking is that readers won't always take the time to track down the comments you're responding to, assuming they can figure out what those comments are to begin with. And even when readers do make the effort to find the comments you're responding to, they may not be sure what aspect or part of those comments you're referring to

or how you interpret them. Ultimately, when you fail to identify your "they say," you leave readers guessing, like someone listening to one side of a phone conversation trying to piece together what's being said at the other end.

It's true, of course, that there are some situations online where summarizing what you're responding to would indeed be redundant. When, for instance, you're replying to a friend's text asking, "Meet in front of the theater at 7?" a mere "OK" suffices, whereas a more elaborate response—"With regard to your suggestion that we meet in front of the theater at 7, my answer is yes"—would be not only redundant but also downright bizarre. But in more complex academic conversations where the ideas are challenging, many people are involved, and there is therefore a greater chance of misunderstanding, you do need to clarify whom and what you're responding to.

To see how hard it can be to make sense of a post that fails to identify the "they say" it is responding to, consider the following example from an online class discussion devoted to Nicholas Carr's article "Is Google Making Us Stupid?":

Blogs and social media allow us to reach many people all at once. The internet makes us more efficient.

When we first read this post, we could see that this writer was making a claim about the efficiency of the internet, but we weren't sure what the claim had to do with Carr or with any of the other comments in the discussion. After all, the writer never names Carr or anyone else in the conversation. Nor does she use templates such as "Like Carr, I believe ________" or "What X overlooks is ________" to indicate whether she's agreeing or disagreeing with Carr or with one of her classmates. Indeed, we couldn't tell if the writer had even read Carr or any of the other posts, or if she was just expressing her own views on the topic.

We suspect, however, that in arguing that the internet is making us more efficient, this writer was probably trying to refute Carr's argument that the internet is, as Carr puts it in his title, "making us stupid." Then again, she could also have been criticizing someone who agreed with Carr—or, conversely, siding with someone else who disagreed with Carr.

It would have been better if she had used the "they say / I say" framework taught in this book, opening not with her own "I say," as she did but with the "they say" that's motivated her to respond, perhaps using one of the following templates:

- **X argues that ________.**
- **Like X, Y would have us believe that ________.**
- **In challenging X's argument that ____________, Y asserts that ________.**

It would also have helped if, in her "I say," she had identified the "they say" she is addressing, using a template like one of these:

- **But what X overlooks is that _________.**
- **What both X and Y fail to see is that _________.**
- **Z's point is well taken. Like him, I contend that _________ is not, as X insists, _________ but _________.**

Here's one way this writer might have responded:

> Carr argues that Google is undermining our ability to think and read deeply. But far from making people "stupid," as Carr puts it in his title, the internet, in my view, is making people more efficient. What Carr ignores is how blogs and social media allow us to reach many people at once.

This version makes clear that the writer is not just making a claim out of the blue but that she also had a reason for making her claim: to take a position in a conversation or debate.

TECHNOLOGY WON'T DO ALL THE WORK

But still, you might wonder, doesn't the internet enable writers to connect so directly with others that summarizing their claims is unnecessary? Granted, the internet does provide several unique ways of referring to what others are saying, like linking and embedding, that help us connect to what others are saying. But as the following examples show, these techniques don't mean that technology will do all the work for you.

LINKING TO WHAT "THEY SAY"

One way the internet makes it especially easy to connect directly with others is by allowing us to insert a link to what others have said into our own text. Anything with a URL can be linked to—blog posts, magazine articles, *Facebook* posts, and so forth. Readers can then click on the words to which you've attached the link and be taken directly to that page, as we can see in the following comment in another online class discussion about how the internet affects our brains:

> In his essay "Is Google Making Us Stupid?" Nicholas Carr argues that the kind of skimming we do when we read online destroys deep reading and thinking. But I would argue the opposite: that all the complex information we're exposed to online actually makes us read and think more deeply.

By including a link to Carr's essay, this writer gives her readers direct access to Carr's arguments, allowing them to assess how well she has summarized and responded to what he wrote. But the reason the writer's post succeeds is that she introduces the link to Carr's essay, summarizes what she takes Carr to be saying, and gives her response to it.

Here are a few templates for framing a link:

- **As X mentions in this article, "__________."**
- **In making this comment, X warns that __________.**
- **Economists often assume __________; however, new research by X suggests __________.**

JUXTAPOSING YOUR "THEY SAY" WITH YOUR "I SAY"

Another way that online forums enhance our ability to connect with others is by allowing readers to respond—not only to the original article or post but also to one another through what we might call "juxtaposition." On many online forums, when you reply to someone else's comment, your response appears below the original comment and indented slightly, so that it is visually clear whom you're responding to. This means that, in many cases, your "they say" and "I say" are presented almost as a single conversational unit, as the following example from the online discussion of Carr's article illustrates:

> Lee, 4/12/20, 3:02 PM
>
> Carr argues that the internet has harmed us by making it hard for us to read without breaks to look at other things. That might be true, but overall I think it has improved our lives by giving us access to so many different viewpoints.

>> Cody, 4/12/20, 5:15 PM
>>
>> Like Lee, I think the internet has improved our lives more than it's hurt them. I would add that it's enabled us to form and participate in political communities online that make people way more politically engaged.

Twitter also allows for this type of close proximity, by enabling you to embed someone else's tweet inside your own. For instance, consider the following tweet:

> **Jade T. Moore** @JadeTMoore
>
> @willwst I agree—access to books is a social justice issue.
>
> > **William West** @willwst
> >
> > Every child has the right to access to a school library.

Cody's response in the discussion board and Jade's on *Twitter* are effective not only because the platforms connect Cody and Jade to their "they say" but also because they take the time to make those connections clear. Cody connects his comment to his "they say" by including the words "Like Lee" and restating Lee's view, while Jade does so by including West's *Twitter* handle, @willwst, and the words "I agree." Sure, the technology does some of the work, by making the responses to comments directly available for readers to see—no scrolling or searching involved. But it can't do it all. Imagine if Cody, for instance, had merely written, "We're able to form and participate in political communities online that make people way more politically engaged." Or if Jade hadn't included an "I agree" with her comment. As readers, we'd have been left scratching our heads, unable to tell what Cody's claim had to do with Lee's claim, or what Jade's claim had to do with William's, despite how close together these claims are on the screen.

Digital communication, then, does shrink the world, as is often said, allowing us to connect with others in ways we couldn't before. But technology doesn't relieve writers of the need to use the "they say / I say" framework. A central premise of this book is that this framework is a rhetorical move that transcends the differences between all types of writing. Whether you're writing online or off, if you want others to listen to what you say, you'd better pay attention to what they think, and start with what they say. However limited your space, whatever your format, and whatever the technology, you can always find a way to identify and summarize your "they say."

Exercises

1. Look back at some of your old posts on a social media site, a class discussion board, or some other website. How well did you let other readers know whom and what you were responding to and what your own position was? What kinds of moves did you make? Does that site have any conventions or special features that you used? Revise one of your posts using the strategies described in this chapter so that your post more clearly follows the "they say / I say" format.

2. Choose an online forum (e.g., *Facebook*, *Twitter*, **theysayiblog.com**), and analyze how the site encourages users to enter conversations in response to others:

   a. Is it easy to tell whom and what people are responding to? Why or why not?

   b. What features, structures, or norms specific to that forum (e.g., embedding, hashtags, linking, etc.) influence how users formulate their "they say"?

c. Find a post that you think follows the "they say / I say" format. Describe how the writer uses the forum's specific features as well as templates from this book to clarify whom and what are being responded to.

3. Go to the blog that accompanies this book, **theysayiblog.com**. Examine some of the exchanges that appear there and evaluate the quality of the responses. For example, how well do the participants in these exchanges summarize one another's claims before making their own responses? How would you characterize the discussion? How well do people listen to one another? How do these online discussions compare with the face-to-face discussions you have in class? What advantages do each offer? Go to other blogs or forums on topics that interest you, and ask these same questions.

FOURTEEN

WHAT'S MOTIVATING THIS WRITER?

Reading for the Conversation

"WHAT IS THE AUTHOR'S ARGUMENT? What is the author trying to say?" For many years, these were the first questions we would ask our classes in a discussion of an assigned reading. The discussion that resulted was often halting, as our students struggled to get a handle on the argument, but eventually, after some awkward silences, the class would come up with something we could all agree was an accurate summary of the author's main thesis. Even after we'd gotten over that hurdle, however, the discussion would often still seem forced and would limp along as we all struggled with the question that naturally arose next: now that we had determined what the author was saying, what did we ourselves have to say?

For a long time we didn't worry much about these halting discussions, justifying them to ourselves as the predictable result of assigning difficult, challenging readings. Several years ago, however, as we started writing this book and began thinking about writing as the art of entering conversations, we latched on to the idea of leading with some different questions: "What other argument(s) is the writer responding to?" "Is the writer disagreeing or agreeing with something, and if so, what?" "What is motivating the writer's argument?" "Are there other ideas that you have encountered in this class or elsewhere that might be pertinent?" The results were often striking. The discussions that followed tended to be far livelier and to draw in a greater number of students. We were still asking students to look for the main argument, but we were now asking them to see that argument as a response to some other argument that provoked it, gave it a reason for being, and helped all of us see why we should care about it.

What had happened, we realized, was that by changing the opening question, we changed the way our students approached reading and perhaps the way they thought about academic work in general. Instead of thinking of the argument of a text as an isolated entity, they now thought of that argument as one that responded to and provoked other arguments. Since they were now dealing not with *one* argument but at least *two* (the author's argument and the one[s] being responded to), they now had alternative ways of seeing the topic at hand. This meant that instead of just trying to understand the view presented by the author, they were more able to question that view intelligently and engage in the type of discussion and debate that is the hallmark of a college education. In our discussions, animated debates often arose between students who found the author's argument convincing and others who were more convinced by the view it was challenging. In the best of these debates, the binary positions would be questioned by other students, who suggested each was too simple, that both might be right or that a third alternative was possible. Still other students might object that the discussion thus far had missed the author's real point and suggest that we all go back to the text and pay closer attention to what it actually said.

We eventually realized that the move from reading for the author's argument in isolation to reading for how the author's argument is in conversation with the arguments of others helps readers become active, critical readers rather than passive recipients of knowledge. On some level, reading for the conversation is more rigorous and demanding than reading for what one author says. It asks that you determine not only what the author thinks but also how what the author thinks fits with what others think and ultimately with what you yourself think. Yet on another level, reading this way is a lot simpler and more familiar than reading for the thesis alone, since it returns writing to the familiar, everyday act of communicating with other people about real issues.

DECIPHERING THE CONVERSATION

We suggest, then, that when assigned a reading, you imagine the author not as sitting alone in an empty room hunched over a desk or staring at a screen but as sitting in a crowded coffee shop talking to and engaging with others who are making claims. In other words, imagine an ongoing, multisided conversation in which all participants (including the author) are trying to persuade others to agree or at least to take their positions seriously.

The trick in reading for the conversation is to figure out *what views the author is responding to* and *what the author's own argument is*—or, to put it in the terms used in this book, to determine the "they say" and how the author responds to it. One of the challenges in reading for the "they say" and "I say" can be figuring out which is which, since it may not be obvious when writers are summarizing others and when they are speaking for themselves. Readers need to be alert for any changes in voice that a writer might make, since instead of using explicit road-mapping phrases like "although many believe," authors may simply summarize the view that they want to engage with and indicate only subtly that it is not their own.

Consider again the opening to the selection by David Zinczenko on page 199:

> If ever there were a newspaper headline custom-made for Jay Leno's monologue, this was it. Kids taking on McDonald's this week, suing the company for making them fat. Isn't that like middle-aged men suing Porsche for making them get speeding tickets? Whatever happened to personal responsibility?
>
> I tend to sympathize with these portly fast-food patrons, though. Maybe that's because I used to be one of them.
>
> DAVID ZINCZENKO, "Don't Blame the Eater"

See Chapter 6 for more discussion of naysayers.

Whenever we teach this passage, some students inevitably assume that Zinczenko must be espousing the view expressed in his first paragraph: that suing McDonald's is ridiculous. When their reading is challenged by their classmates, these students point to the page and reply, "Look. It's right here on the page. This is what Zinczenko wrote. These are his exact words." The assumption these students are making is that if something appears on the page, the author must endorse it. In fact, however, we ventriloquize views that we don't believe in, and may in fact passionately disagree with, all the time. The central clues that Zinczenko disagrees with the view expressed in his opening paragraph come in the second paragraph, when he finally offers a first-person declaration and uses a contrastive transition, "though," thereby resolving any questions about where he stands.

WHEN THE "THEY SAY" IS UNSTATED

Another challenge can be identifying the "they say" when it is not explicitly identified. Whereas Zinczenko offers an up-front summary of the view he is responding to, other writers assume that their readers are so familiar with these views that they need not name or summarize them. In such cases, you the reader have to reconstruct the unstated "they say" that is motivating the text through a process of inference.

See, for instance, if you can reconstruct the position that Tamara Draut is challenging in the opening paragraph of her essay "The Growing College Gap":

> "The first in her family to graduate from college." How many times have we heard that phrase, or one like it, used to describe a successful American with a modest background? In today's United States, a four-year degree has become the all-but-official ticket to middle-class security. But if your parents don't have much money or higher education in their own right, the road to college—and beyond—looks increasingly treacherous. Despite a sharp increase in the proportion of high school graduates going on to some form of postsecondary education, socio-economic status continues to exert a powerful influence on college admission and completion; in fact, gaps in enrollment by class and race, after declining in the 1960s and 1970s, are once again as wide as they were thirty years ago, and getting wider, even as college has become far more crucial to lifetime fortunes.
>
> TAMARA DRAUT, "The Growing College Gap"

You might think that the "they say" here is embedded in the third sentence: they say (or we all think) that a four-year degree is "the all-but-official ticket to middle-class security," and you might assume that Draut will go on to disagree.

If you read the passage this way, however, you would be mistaken. Draut is not questioning whether a college degree has become the "ticket to middle-class security" but whether most Americans can obtain that ticket, whether college is within the financial reach of most American families. You may have been thrown off by the "but" following the statement that college has become a prerequisite for middle-class security. However, unlike the "though" in Zinczenko's opening, this "but" does not signal that Draut will be disagreeing with the view she has just summarized, a view that in fact she takes as a given. What Draut disagrees with is that this ticket to middle-class security is still readily available to the middle and working classes.

Were one to imagine Draut in a room talking with others with strong views on this topic, one would need to picture her challenging not those who think college is a ticket to financial security (something she agrees with and takes for granted) but those who think the doors of college are open to anyone willing to put forth the effort to walk through them. The view that Draut is challenging, then, is not summarized in her opening. Instead, she assumes that readers are already so familiar with this view that it need not be stated.

Draut's example suggests that in texts where the central "they say" is not immediately identified, you have to construct it yourself based on the clues the text provides. You have to start by locating the writer's thesis and then imagine some of the arguments that might be made against it. What would it look like to disagree with this view? In Draut's case, it is relatively easy to construct a counterargument: it is the familiar faith in the

American Dream of equal opportunity when it comes to access to college. Figuring out the counterargument not only reveals what motivated Draut as a writer but also helps you respond to her essay as an active, critical reader. Constructing this counterargument can also help you recognize how Draut challenges your own views, questioning opinions that you previously took for granted.

WHEN THE "THEY SAY" IS ABOUT SOMETHING "NOBODY HAS TALKED ABOUT"

Another challenge in reading for the conversation is that writers sometimes build their arguments by responding to a *lack* of discussion. These writers build their case not by playing off views that can be identified (like faith in the American Dream or the idea that we are responsible for our body weight) but by pointing to something others have overlooked. As the writing theorists John M. Swales and Christine B. Feak point out, one effective way to "create a research space" and "establish a niche" in the academic world is "by indicating a gap in . . . previous research." Much research in the sciences and humanities takes this "Nobody has noticed X" form.

In such cases, the writer may be responding to scientists, for example, who have overlooked an obscure plant that offers insights into global warming or to literary critics who have been so busy focusing on the lead character in a play that they have overlooked something important about the minor characters.

READING PARTICULARLY CHALLENGING TEXTS

Sometimes it is difficult to figure out the views that writers are responding to, not because these writers do not identify those views but because their language and the concepts they are dealing with are particularly challenging. Consider, for instance, the first two sentences of *Gender Trouble: Feminism and the Subversion of Identity*, a book by the feminist philosopher and literary theorist Judith Butler, thought by many to be a particularly difficult academic writer:

> Contemporary feminist debates over the meaning of gender lead time and again to a certain sense of trouble, as if the indeterminacy of gender might eventually culminate in the failure of feminism. Perhaps trouble need not carry such a negative valence.
>
> JUDITH BUTLER, *Gender Trouble: Feminism and the Subversion of Identity*

There are many reasons readers may stumble over this relatively short passage, not the least of which is that Butler does not explicitly indicate where her own view begins and the view she is responding to ends. Unlike Zinczenko, Butler does not use the first-person "I" or a phrase such as "in my own view" to show that the position in the second sentence is her own. Nor does Butler offer a clear transition such as "but" or "however" at the start of the second sentence to indicate, as Zinczenko does with "though," that in the second sentence she is questioning the argument she has summarized in the first. And finally, like many academic writers, Butler uses abstract, challenging words that many readers may need to look up, like "indeterminacy" (the quality of being impossible to define or pin down), "culminate" (finally result in), and "negative valence" (a term borrowed from chemistry, roughly denoting "negative significance" or "meaning"). For all these reasons, we can imagine many readers feeling intimidated before they reach the third sentence of Butler's book.

But readers who break down this passage into its essential parts will find that it is actually a lucid piece of writing that conforms to the classic "they say / I say" pattern. Though it can be difficult to spot the clashing arguments in the two sentences, close analysis reveals that the first sentence offers a way of looking at a certain type of "trouble" in the realm of feminist politics that is being challenged in the second.

To understand difficult passages of this kind, you need to translate them into your own words—to build a bridge, in effect, between the passage's unfamiliar terms and ones more familiar to you. Building such a bridge should help you connect what you already know to what the author is saying—and will then help you move from reading to writing, providing you with some of the language you will need to summarize the text. One major challenge in translating the author's words into your own, however, is to stay true to what the author is actually saying, avoiding what we call "the closest cliché syndrome," in which one mistakes a commonplace idea for an author's more complex one (mistaking Butler's critique of the concept of "woman," for instance, for the common idea that women must have equal rights). The work of complex writers like Butler, who frequently challenge conventional thinking, cannot always be collapsed into the types of ideas most of us are already familiar with. Therefore, when you translate, do not try to fit the ideas of such writers into your preexisting beliefs, but instead allow your own views to be challenged. In building a bridge to the writers you read, it is often necessary to meet those writers more than halfway.

For more on translating, see Chapter 9.

For more on the closest cliché syndrome, see Chapter 2.

So what, then, does Butler's opening say? Translating Butler's words into terms that are easier to understand, we can see that the first sentence says that for many feminists today, "the indeterminacy of gender"—the inability to define the essence of sexual identity—spells the end of feminism; that for many feminists the inability to define "gender," presumably the building block of the feminist movement, means serious "trouble" for feminist politics. In contrast, the second sentence suggests that this same "trouble" need not be thought of in such "negative" terms, that the inability to define femininity, or "gender trouble" as Butler calls it in her book's title, may not be such a bad thing—and, as she goes on to argue in the pages that follow, may even be something that feminist activists can profit from. In other words, Butler suggests, highlighting uncertainties about masculinity and femininity can be a powerful feminist tool.

Pulling all these inferences together, then, the opening sentences can be translated as follows: "While many contemporary feminists believe that uncertainty about what it means to be a woman will undermine feminist politics, I, Judith Butler, believe that this uncertainty can actually help strengthen feminist politics." Translating Butler's point into our own book's basic move: "They say that if we cannot define 'woman,' feminism is in big trouble. But I say that this type of trouble is precisely what feminism needs." Despite its difficulty, then, we hope you agree that this initially intimidating passage does make sense if you stay with it.

We hope it is clear that critical reading is a two-way street. It is just as much about being open to the way that writers can challenge you, maybe even transform you, as it is about questioning those writers. And if you translate a writer's argument into your own words as you read, you should allow the text to take you outside the ideas that you already hold and to introduce you to new terms and concepts. Even if you end up disagreeing with an author, you first have to show that you have really listened to what is being said, have fully grasped the arguments, and can accurately summarize those arguments. Without such deep, attentive listening, any critique you make will be superficial and decidedly *uncritical*. It will be a critique that says more about you than about the writer or idea you're supposedly responding to.

In this chapter we have tried to show that reading for the conversation means looking not just for the thesis of a text in isolation but for the view or views that motivate that thesis—the "they say." We have also tried to show that reading for the conversation means being alert for the different strategies writers use to engage the view(s) that are motivating them, since not all writers engage other perspectives in the same way. Some writers explicitly identify and summarize a view they are responding to at the outset of their text and then return to it frequently as their text unfolds. Some refer only obliquely to a view that is motivating them, assuming that readers will be able to reconstruct that view on their own. Other writers may not explicitly distinguish their own view from the views they are questioning in ways that all of us find clear, leaving some readers to wonder whether a given view is the writer's own or one that is being challenged. And some writers push off against the "they say" that is motivating them in a challenging academic language that requires readers to translate what they are saying into more accessible, everyday terms. In sum, then, though most persuasive writers do follow a conversational "they say / I say" pattern, they do so in a great variety of ways. What this means for readers is that they need to be armed with various strategies for detecting the conversations in what they read, even when those conversations are not self-evident.

Don't Blame the Eater

DAVID ZINCZENKO

IF EVER THERE WERE a newspaper headline custom-made for Jay Leno's* monologue, this was it. Kids taking on McDonald's this week, suing the company for making them fat. Isn't that like middle-aged men suing Porsche for making them get speeding tickets? Whatever happened to personal responsibility?

I tend to sympathize with these portly fast-food patrons, though. Maybe that's because I used to be one of them.

I grew up as a typical mid-1980s latchkey kid. My parents were split up, my dad off trying to rebuild his life, my mom working long hours to make the monthly bills. Lunch and dinner, for me, was a daily choice between

---

DAVID ZINCZENKO, who was for many years the editor-in-chief of the fitness magazine *Men's Health*, is founder and CEO of Galvanized Brands, a global health and wellness media company. This piece was first published on the Op-Ed page of the *New York Times* on November 23, 2002.

*__Jay Leno__ Comedian and former host of NBC's *The Tonight Show*.

McDonald's, Taco Bell, Kentucky Fried Chicken, or Pizza Hut. Then as now, these were the only available options for an American kid to get an affordable meal. By age 15, I had packed 212 pounds of torpid teenage tallow on my once lanky 5-foot-10 frame.

Then I got lucky. I went to college, joined the Navy Reserves and got involved with a health magazine. I learned how to manage my diet. But most of the teenagers who live, as I once did, on a fast-food diet won't turn their lives around: they've crossed under the golden arches to a likely fate of lifetime obesity. And the problem isn't just theirs—it's all of ours.

Before 1994, diabetes in children was generally caused by a 5
genetic disorder—only about 5 percent of childhood cases were obesity-related, or Type 2, diabetes. Today, according to the National Institutes of Health, Type 2 diabetes accounts for at least 30 percent of all new childhood cases of diabetes in this country.

For tips on saying why it matters, see Chapter 7.

Not surprisingly, money spent to treat diabetes has skyrocketed, too. The Centers for Disease Control and Prevention estimate that diabetes accounted for $2.6 billion in health care costs in 1969. Today's number is an unbelievable $100 billion a year.

Shouldn't we know better than to eat two meals a day in fast-food restaurants? That's one argument. But where, exactly, are consumers—particularly teenagers—supposed to find alternatives? Drive down any thoroughfare in America, and I guarantee you'll see one of our country's more than 13,000 McDonald's restaurants. Now, drive back up the block and try to find someplace to buy a grapefruit.

Complicating the lack of alternatives is the lack of information about what, exactly, we're consuming. There are no calorie information charts on fast-food packaging, the way there are on grocery items. Advertisements don't carry warning labels the way tobacco ads do. Prepared foods aren't covered under Food and Drug Administration labeling laws. Some fast-food purveyors will provide calorie information on request, but even that can be hard to understand.

For example, one company's Web site lists its chicken salad as containing 150 calories; the almonds and noodles that come with it (an additional 190 calories) are listed separately. Add a serving of the 280-calorie dressing, and you've got a healthy lunch alternative that comes in at 620 calories. But that's not all. Read the small print on the back of the dressing packet and you'll realize it actually contains 2.5 servings. If you pour what you've been served, you're suddenly up around 1,040 calories, which is half of the government's recommended daily calorie intake. And that doesn't take into account that 450-calorie super-size Coke.

10 Make fun if you will of these kids launching lawsuits against the fast-food industry, but don't be surprised if you're the next plaintiff. As with the tobacco industry, it may be only a matter of time before state governments begin to see a direct line between the $1 billion that McDonald's and Burger King spend each year on advertising and their own swelling health care costs.

And I'd say the industry is vulnerable. Fast-food companies are marketing to children a product with proven health hazards and no warning labels. They would do well to protect themselves, and their customers, by providing the nutrition information people need to make informed choices about their products. Without such warnings, we'll see more sick, obese children and more angry, litigious parents. I say, let the deep-fried chips fall where they may.

part 5

Processes

To create anything, we generally break the work down into a series of steps. We follow a recipe (or the directions on a box) to bake a cake; we break a song down into different parts and the music into various chords to arrange a piece of music. So it is when we write. We rely on various processes to get from a blank screen or page to a finished product. The chapters that follow offer advice on some of these processes—from **WRITING AS INQUIRY** and **GENERATING IDEAS** to **DRAFTING** to **GETTING RESPONSE** to **EDITING** to **COMPILING A PORTFOLIO**, and more.

Processes

Writing as Inquiry 15

Sometimes we write to say what we think. Other times, however, we write in order to figure out what we think. Much of the writing you do in college will be the latter. Even as you learn to write, you will be writing to learn. This chapter is about writing with a spirit of inquiry—approaching writing projects with curiosity, moving beyond the familiar, keeping your eyes open, tackling issues that don't have easy answers. It's about starting with questions and going from there—and taking risks. As Mark Twain once said, "Sail away from the safe harbor. . . . Explore. Dream. Discover." This chapter offers strategies for doing just that with your writing.

Starting with Questions

The most important thing is to start with questions—with what you don't know rather than with what you do know. Your goal is to learn about your subject and then to learn more. If you're writing about a topic you know well, you want to expand on what you already know. In academic writing, good topics arise from important questions, issues, and problems that are already being discussed. As a writer, you need to find out what's being said about your topic and then see your writing as a way of entering that larger conversation.

So start with questions, and don't expect to find easy answers. If there were easy answers, there would be no reason for discussion—or for you to write. For purposes of inquiry, the best questions can't be answered by looking in a reference book. Instead, they are ones that help you explore what you think—and why. As it happens, many of the strategies in this book can help you ask questions of this kind. Following are some questions to get you started:

How can it be defined? What is it, and what does it do? Look it up in a dictionary; check *Wikipedia*. Remember, though, that these are only starting points. How *else* can it be defined? What more is there to know about it? If your topic is being debated, chances are that its very definition is subject to debate. If, for instance, you're writing about gay marriage, how you define marriage will affect how you approach the topic.

How can it be described? What details should you include? From what vantage point should you describe your topic? If, for example, your topic is the physiological effects of running a marathon, what are those effects—on the lungs, heart muscles, nerves, brain, and so on? How will you describe the physical experience of running over twenty-six miles from the runner's point of view?

How can it be explained? What does it do? How does it work? If you're investigating the use of performance-enhancing drugs by athletes, for example, what exactly are the effects of these drugs? What makes them dangerous—and are they always dangerous or only in certain conditions? Why are they illegal—and should they be illegal?

What can it be compared with? Again using performance-enhancing drugs by athletes as an example, how does taking such supplements compare with wearing high-tech footwear or uniforms? Does such a comparison make you see taking steroids or other performance-enhancing drugs in a new light?

What may have caused it? What might be its effects? Who or what does it affect? What causes cerebral palsy in children, for example? What are its symptoms? If children with cerebral palsy are not treated, what might be the consequences?

How can it be classified? Is it a topic or issue that can be placed into categories of similar topics or issues? What categories can it be placed into? Are there legal and illegal performance-enhancing supplements (human growth hormone and steroids, for instance), and what's the difference? Are some safe and others less safe? Classifying your topic in this way can help you consider its complexities.

How can it be analyzed? What parts can the topic be divided into? For example, if you are exploring the health effects of cell phone use, you might ask these questions: What evidence suggests that cell phone radiation causes cancer? What cancers are associated with cell phone use? What do medical experts and phone manufacturers say? How can cell phone users reduce their risk?

How can it be interpreted? What does it really mean? How do you interpret it, and how does your interpretation differ from others? What evidence supports your interpretation, and what argues against it? Imagine you're exploring the topic of sports injuries among young women. Do these injuries reflect a larger cultural preoccupation with competition? a desire to win college scholarships? something else?

What expectations does it raise? What will happen next? What makes you think so? If this happens, how will it affect those involved? For instance, will the governing bodies of professional sports require more testing of athletes' blood, urine, and hair than they do now? Will such tests be unfair to athletes taking drugs for legitimate medical needs?

What are the different positions on it? What controversies or disagreements exist, and what evidence is offered for the various positions? What else might be said? Are there any groups or individuals who seem especially authoritative? If so, you might want to explore what they have said.

What are your own feelings about it? What interests you about the topic? How much do you already know about it? For example, if you're an athlete, how do you feel about competing against others who may have taken supplements? If a friend has problems with drugs, do those problems affect your thinking about drugs in sports? How do you react to what others say about the topic? What else do you want to find out?

Are there other ways to think about it? Is what seems true in this case also true in others? How can you apply this subject in another situation? Will what works in another situation also work here? What do you have to do to adapt it? Imagine you are writing about traffic fatalities. If replacing stop signs with roundabouts or traffic circles reduced traffic fatalities in England, could doing so also reduce accidents in the United States?

216–17

You can also start with the journalist's **QUESTIONS**: *Who? What? When? Where? Why? How?* Asking questions from these various perspectives can help you deepen your understanding of your topic by leading you to see it from many angles.

Keeping a Journal

219–20

One way to get into the habit of using writing as a tool for inquiry is to keep a **JOURNAL**. You can use a journal to record your observations, reactions, whatever you wish. Some writers find journals especially useful places to articulate questions or speculations. You may be assigned by teachers to do certain work in a journal, but in general, you can use a journal to write for yourself. Note your ideas, speculate, digress—go wherever your thoughts lead you.

Keeping a Blog

You may also wish to explore issues or other ideas online in the form of a blog. Most blogs have a comments section that allows others to read and respond to what you write, leading to potentially fruitful discussions. You can also include links to other websites, helping you connect various strands of thought and research. The blogs of others, along with online discussion forums and groups, may also be useful sources of opinion on your topic, but keep in mind that they probably aren't authoritative research sources. There are a number of search engines that can help you find blog posts related to specific topics, including *Google Blog Search*, *Ask*, and *IceRocket*. You can create your own blog on sites such as *Blogger*, *Tumblr*, *Svbtle*, or *WordPress*.

Collaborating 16

Whether you're working in a face-to-face group, posting on an online discussion board, or exchanging drafts with a classmate, you likely spend a lot of time working with others on writing tasks. Even if you do much of your writing sitting alone at a computer, you probably get help from others at various stages in the writing process—and provide help as well. Two heads can be better than one—and learning to work well with a team is as important as anything else you'll learn in college. This chapter offers some guidelines for collaborating successfully with other writers.

Some Ground Rules for Face-to-Face Group Work

- Make sure everyone is facing everyone else and is physically part of the group. Doing that makes a real difference in the quality of the interactions—think how much better conversation works when you're sitting around a table than it does when you're sitting in a row.
- Thoughtfulness, respect, and tact are key, since most writers (as you know) are sensitive and need to be able to trust those commenting on their work. Respond to the contributions of others as you would like others to respond to yours.
- Each meeting needs an agenda—and careful attention paid to time. Appoint one person as timekeeper to make sure all necessary work gets done in the available time.
- Appoint another person to be group leader or facilitator. That person needs to make sure everyone gets a chance to speak, no one dominates the discussion, and the group stays on task.

288–89

- Appoint a member of the group to record the group's discussion, jotting down the major points as they come up and then writing a **SUMMARY** of the discussion that the group members then approve.

Online Collaboration

Sometimes you'll work with one or more people online. Working together online offers many advantages, including the ability to collaborate without being in the same place at the same time. Nonetheless, it also presents some challenges that differ from those of face-to-face group work. When sharing writing or collaborating with others online in other ways, consider the following suggestions:

- As with all online communication, remember that you need to choose your words carefully to avoid inadvertently hurting someone's feelings. Without facial expressions, gestures, and other forms of body language and without tone of voice, your words carry all the weight.
- Remember that the audience for what you write may well extend beyond your group—your work might be forwarded to others, so there is no telling who else might read it.
- Decide as a group how best to deal with the logistics of exchanging drafts and comments. You can cut and paste text directly into email, send it as an attachment to a message, or post it to your class course management system site or a file-sharing site like *Dropbox* or *Google Docs*. You may need to use a combination of methods, depending on each group member's access to equipment and software. In any case, name your files carefully so that everyone knows which version to use.

Writing Conferences

Conferences with instructors or writing tutors can be an especially helpful kind of collaboration. These one-on-one sessions often offer the most strongly focused assistance you can get—and truly valuable instruction. Here are some tips for making the most of conference time:

- *Come prepared.* Bring all necessary materials, including the draft you'll be discussing, your notes, any outlines—and, of course, any questions.
- *Be prompt.* Your instructor or tutor has set aside a block of time for you, and once that time is up, there's likely to be another student writer waiting.
- *Listen carefully, discuss your work seriously, and try not to be defensive.* Your instructor or tutor is only trying to help you produce the best piece possible. If you sense that your work is being misunderstood, explain what you're trying to say. Don't get angry! If a sympathetic reader who's trying to help can't understand what you mean, maybe you haven't conveyed your meaning well enough.
- *Take notes.* During the conference, jot down keywords and suggestions. Immediately afterward, flesh out your notes so you'll have a complete record of what was said.
- *Reflect on the conference.* Afterward, think about what you learned. What do you have to do now? Create a plan for revising or doing further work, and write out questions you will ask at your next conference.

Group Writing Projects

Creating a document with a team is common in business and professional work and in some academic fields as well. Here are some tips for making collaboration of this kind work well:

- *Define the task as clearly as possible.* Make sure everyone understands and agrees with the stated goals.
- *Divide the task into parts.* Decide which parts can be done by individuals, which can be done by a subgroup, and which need to be done by everyone together.
- *Assign each group member certain tasks.* Try to match tasks to each person's skills and interests and to divide the work equally.

- ***Establish a deadline for each task.*** Allow time for unforeseen problems before the project deadline.
- ***Try to accommodate everyone's style of working.*** Some people value discussion; others want to get right down to the writing. There's no best way to get work done; everyone needs to be conscious that their way is not the only way.
- ***Work for consensus—not necessarily total agreement.*** Everyone needs to agree that the plan to get the task done is doable and appropriate—if not exactly the way you would do it if you were working alone.
- ***Make sure everyone performs.*** Sometimes your instructor may help, but the group itself may have to develop a way to ensure that the work gets done well and fairly. During the course of the project, it's sometimes helpful for each group member to write an assessment both of the group's work and of individual members' contributions.

Generating Ideas and Text 17

All good writing revolves around ideas. Whether you're writing a job-application letter, a sonnet, or an essay, you'll always spend time and effort generating ideas. Some writers can come up with a topic, put their thoughts in order, and flesh out their arguments in their heads; but most of us need to write out our ideas, play with them, tease them out, and examine them from some distance and from multiple perspectives. This chapter offers activities that can help you do just that. *Freewriting*, *looping*, *listing*, and *clustering* can help you explore what you know about a subject; *cubing* and *questioning* nudge you to consider a subject in new ways; and *outlining*, *letter writing*, *journal keeping*, and *discovery drafting* offer ways to generate a text.

Freewriting

An informal method of exploring a subject by writing about it, freewriting ("writing freely") can help you generate ideas and come up with materials for your draft. Here's how to do it:

1. Write as quickly as you can without stopping for 5 to 10 minutes (or until you fill a screen or page).
2. If you have a subject to explore, write it at the top and then start writing about it, but if you stray, don't worry—just keep writing. If you don't have a subject yet, just start writing and don't stop until the time is up. If you can't think of anything to say, write that ("I can't think of anything to say") again and again until you do—and you will!
3. Once the time is up, read over what you've written, and underline or highlight passages that interest you.

4. Write some more, starting with one of those underlined or highlighted passages as your new topic. Repeat the process until you've come up with a usable topic.

Looping

Looping is a more focused version of freewriting; it can help you explore what you know about a subject. You stop, reflect on what you've written, and then write again, developing your understanding in the process. It's good for clarifying your knowledge and understanding of a subject and finding a focus. Here's what you do:

1. Write for 5 to 10 minutes on whatever you know about your subject. This is your first loop.
2. Read over what you wrote, and then write a single sentence summarizing the most important or interesting idea. You might try completing one of these sentences: "I guess what I was trying to say was . . . " or "What surprises me most in reading what I wrote is . . ." This will be the start of another loop.
3. Write again for 5 to 10 minutes, using your summary sentence as your beginning and your focus. Again, read what you've written, and then write a sentence capturing the most important idea—in a third loop.

Keep going until you have enough understanding of your topic to be able to decide on a tentative focus—something you can write about.

Listing

Some writers find it useful to keep lists of ideas that occur to them while they are thinking about a topic. Follow these steps:

1. Write a list of potential ideas about a topic. Don't try to limit your list—include anything that interests you.

2. Look for relationships among the items on your list: what patterns do you see? If other ideas occur to you, add them to the list.
3. Arrange the items in an order that makes sense for your purpose and can serve as the beginning of an outline for your writing.

Clustering or Mapping Ideas

Clustering (also called idea mapping) is a way of generating and connecting ideas visually. It's useful for seeing how various ideas relate to one another and for developing subtopics. The technique is simple:

1. Write your topic in the middle of a sheet of paper and circle it.
2. Write ideas relating to that topic around it, circle them, and connect them to the central circle.

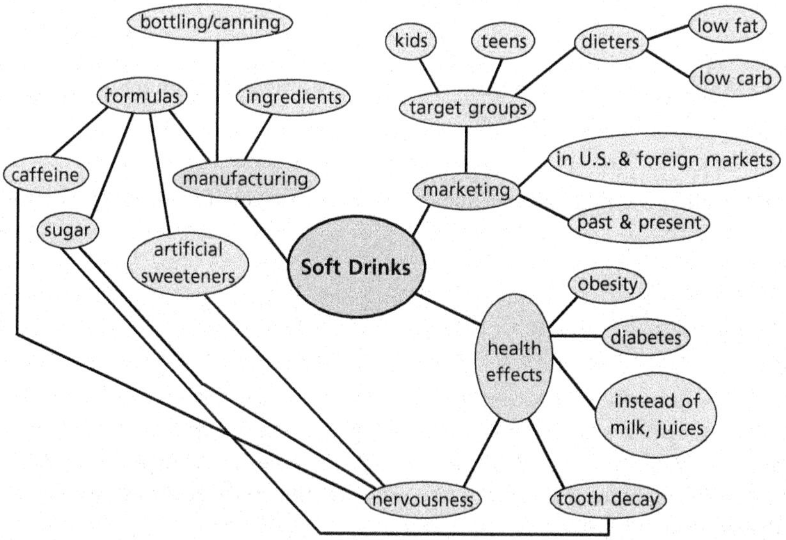

3. Write down examples, facts, or other details relating to each idea, and join them to the appropriate circles.
4. Keep going until you can't think of anything else relating to your topic.

You should end up with various ideas about your topic, and the clusters will allow you to see how they relate to one another. In the example cluster on the topic of "soft drinks" on the previous page, note how some ideas link not only to the main topic or related topics but also to other ideas.

Cubing

A cube has six sides. You can examine a topic as you might a cube, looking at it in these six ways:

- Describe it. What's its color? shape? age? size? What's it made of?
- Compare it to something else. What is it similar to or different from?
- Associate it with other things. What does it remind you of? What connections does it have to other things? How would you classify it?
- Analyze it. How is it made? Where did it come from? Where is it going? How are its parts related?
- Apply it. What is it used for? What can be done with it?
- Argue for or against it. Choose a position relating to your subject, and defend it.

Questioning

216–17

It's always useful to ask **QUESTIONS**. One way is to start with *What? Who? When? Where? How?* and *Why?* A particular method of exploring a topic is to ask questions as if the topic were a play. This method is especially useful for exploring literature, history, the arts, and the social sciences. Start with these questions:

- *What?* What happens? How is it similar to or different from other actions?
- *Who?* Who are the actors? Who are the participants, and who are the spectators? How do the actors affect the action, and how are they affected by it?
- *When?* When does the action take place? How often does it happen? What happens before, after, or at the same time? Would it be different at another time? Does the time have historical significance?
- *Where?* What is the setting? What is the situation, and what makes it significant?
- *How?* How does the action occur? What are the steps in the process? What techniques are required? What equipment is needed?
- *Why?* Why did this happen? What are the actors' motives? What end does the action serve?

Using Genre Features

Genres typically include particular kinds of information and organize it in particular ways. One way to generate ideas and text, then, is to identify the key features of the genre in which you're writing and use them to guide you as you write. Of course, you may alter the genre's features or combine two or more genres in order to achieve your purpose, but the overall shape and content of the genre can give you a way to develop and organize your ideas and research.

Outlining

You may create an *informal outline* by simply listing your ideas and numbering them in the order in which you want to write about them. You might prefer to make a *working outline*, to show the hierarchy of relationships among your ideas. While still informal, a working outline distinguishes your main ideas and your support, often through simple indentation:

First main idea
  Supporting evidence or detail
  Supporting evidence or detail

Second main idea
  Supporting evidence or detail
  Supporting evidence or detail

A *formal outline* shows the hierarchy of your ideas through a system of indenting, numbering, and lettering. Remember that when you divide a point into more specific subpoints, you should have at least two of them—you can't divide something into only one part. Also, try to keep items at each level parallel in structure. Formal outlines work this way:

Thesis statement

I. First reason
  A. Supporting evidence
    1. Detail of evidence
    2. Detail of evidence
  B. Supporting evidence
II. Another reason

Here is a formal outline of the first part of a research report by student Dylan Borchers, "Against the Odds: Harry S. Truman and the Election of 1948," that shows how he organized it:

I. Introduction: Outcome of 1948 election
II. Bad predictions by pollsters
  A. Pollsters stopped polling.
  B. Dewey supporters became overconfident.
  C. Truman supporters were either energized or stayed home.
III. Dewey's campaign overly cautious
  A. He was overconfident.
  B. His message was vague—he avoided taking stands.

IV. Dewey's public appearances poor
    A. He was seen as aloof, uncomfortable with crowds.
    B. He made blunders.
    C. His speeches were dull.

Writing out a formal outline can be helpful when you're dealing with a complex subject; as you revise your drafts, though, be flexible and ready to change your outline as your understanding of your topic develops.

Letter Writing

Sometimes the prospect of writing a report or essay can be intimidating. You may find that simply explaining your topic to someone will help you get started. In that case, write a letter or email to someone you know—your best friend, a parent or grandparent, a sibling—in which you discuss your subject. Explain it in terms that your reader can understand. Use the unsent letter to rehearse your topic; make it a kind of rough draft that you can then revise and develop to suit your actual audience.

Keeping a Journal

Some writers find that writing in a journal helps them generate ideas. Making note of your ideas, thoughts, feelings, or the events of your day can provide a wealth of topics, and a journal can also be a good place to explore what you think and why you think as you do.

Journals are private—you are the only audience—so you can feel free to write whatever comes to mind. And you can do more than write. If you choose a paper journal, doodle or draw in it, and keep clippings or scraps of paper between the pages; if you keep your journal on a computer, copy and paste interesting images or text you find online. Whatever form your journal takes, feel free to play with its contents, and don't worry about errors or grammar. The goal is to generate ideas; let yourself wander without censoring yourself or fretting that your writing is incorrect or incomplete or incoherent. That's okay.

One measure of the success of journaling and other personal writing is length: journal entries, **FREEWRITING**, **LISTING**, **CUBING**, and other types of informal writing are like warm-up exercises to limber you up and get you thinking. If you don't give them enough time and space, they may not do what you want them to. Often, students' best insights appear at the end of their journal entries. Had they stopped before that point, they would never have had those good ideas.

213–14
214–15
216

After you've written several journal entries, one way to study the ideas in them is to highlight useful patterns in different colors. For example, journal entries usually include some questioning and speculating, as well as summarizing and paraphrasing. Try color-coding each of these, sentence by sentence, phrase by phrase: yellow for summaries or paraphrases, green for questions, blue for speculations. Do any colors dominate? If, for example, your entries are mostly yellow, you may be restating the course content or quoting from the textbook too much and perhaps need to ask more questions. If you're generating ideas for an essay, you might assign colors to ideas or themes to see which ones are the most promising.

Discovery Drafting

Some writers do best by jumping in and writing. Here are the steps to take if you're ready to write a preliminary **DRAFT**:

222–24

1. Write your draft quickly, in one sitting if possible.
2. Assume that you are writing to discover what you want to say and how you need to say it—and that you will make substantial revisions in a later part of the process.

3. Don't worry about grammatical or factual correctness—if you can't think of a word, leave a blank space to fill in later. If you're unsure of a date or spelling, put a question mark in parentheses as a reminder to check it later. Just write.

18 Drafting

At some point, you need to write out a draft. By the time you begin drafting, you've probably written quite a bit—in the form of notes, lists, outlines, and other kinds of informal writing. This chapter offers some hints on how to write a draft—and reminds you that as you draft, you may well need to get more information, rethink some aspect of your work, or follow new ideas that occur to you as you write.

Establishing a Schedule with Deadlines

Don't wait until the last minute to write. Computers crash, printers jam. Life intervenes in unpredictable ways. You increase your chances of success immensely by setting and meeting **DEADLINES**: Research done by ____; rough draft done by ____; revisions done by ____; final draft edited, proofread, and submitted by ____. How much time you need varies with each writing task—but trying to compress everything into twenty-four or forty-eight hours before the deadline is asking for trouble.

233–34

Getting Comfortable

When are you at your best? When do you have your best ideas? For major writing projects, consider establishing a schedule that lets you write when you stand the best chance of doing good work. Schedule breaks for exercise and snacks. Find a good place to write, a place where you've got a good surface on which to spread out your materials, good lighting, a comfortable chair, and the right tools (computer, pen, paper) for the job. Often, however, we must make do: you may have to do your drafting in a busy computer lab or classroom. The trick is to make yourself as comfortable as you can manage. Sort out what you *need* from what you *prefer*.

Starting to Write

All of the above advice notwithstanding, don't worry so much about the trappings of your writing situation that you don't get around to writing. Write. Start by **FREEWRITING**, start with a first sentence, start with awful writing that you know you'll discard later—but write. That's what gets you warmed up and going.

213–14

Write quickly in spurts. Write quickly with the goal of writing a complete draft, or a complete section of a longer draft, in one sitting. If you need to stop in the middle, make some notes about where you were headed when you stopped so that you can easily pick up your train of thought when you begin again.

Break down your writing task into small segments. Big projects can be intimidating. But you can always write one section or, if need be, one paragraph or even a single sentence—and then another and another. It's a little like dieting. If I think I need to lose twenty pounds, I get discouraged and head for the doughnuts; but if I decide that I'll lose one pound and I lose it, well, I'll lose another—*that* I can do.

Expect surprises. Writing is a form of thinking; the words you write lead you down certain roads and away from others. You may end up somewhere you didn't anticipate. Sometimes that can be a good thing—but sometimes you can write yourself into a dead end or out onto a tangent. Just know that this is natural, part of every writer's experience, and it's okay to double back or follow a new path that opens up before you.

Expect to write more than one draft. A first sentence, first page, or first draft represents your attempt to organize into words your thoughts, ideas, feelings, research findings, and more. It's likely that some of that first try will not achieve your goals. That's okay—having writing on screen or on paper that you can change, add to, and cut means you're part of the way there. As you revise, you can fill in gaps and improve your writing and thinking.

Dealing with Writer's Block

You may sit down to write but find that you can't—nothing occurs to you; your mind is blank. Don't panic; here are some ways to get started writing again:

- Think of the assignment as a problem to be solved. Try to capture that problem in a single sentence: "How do I explain the context for my topic?" "What is the best way to organize my argument?" "What am I trying to do in the conclusion?"
- Start early and break the writing task into small segments drafted over several days. Waiting until the night before an assignment is due can create panic—and writer's block.
- Stop trying: take a walk, take a shower, do something else. Come back in a half hour, refreshed.
- Open a new document on your computer or get a fresh piece of paper and **FREEWRITE**, or try **LOOPING** or **LISTING**. What are you trying to say? Just let whatever comes come—you may write yourself out of your box.
- If you usually write on your computer, turn it off, get out paper and pencil, and write by hand.
- Try a graphic approach: try **CLUSTERING**, or draw a chart of what you want to say; draw a picture; doodle.
- Do some **RESEARCH** on your topic to see what others have said about it.
- Talk to someone about what you are trying to do. If there's a writing center at your school, talk to a tutor: get response. If there's no one to talk to, talk to yourself. It's the act of talking—using your mouth instead of your hands—that can free you up.

213–15
215–16
231

IF YOU NEED MORE HELP

See Chapter 17 on GENERATING IDEAS AND TEXT if you find you need more material.

213–21

Editing and Proofreading 19

Your ability to produce clear, error-free writing shows something about your ability as a writer and also leads readers to make assumptions about your intellect, your work habits, even your character. Readers of job-application letters and résumés, for example, may reject applications if they contain a single error, for no other reason than it's an easy way to narrow the field of potential candidates. In addition, they may well assume that applicants who present themselves sloppily in an application will do sloppy work on the job. This is all to say that you should edit and proofread your work carefully.

Editing

Editing is the stage where you work on the details of your paragraphs, sentences, words, and punctuation to make your writing as clear, precise, correct—and effective—as possible. Your goal is not to achieve "perfection" (whatever that may be) so much as to make your writing as effective as possible for your particular purpose and audience. Consult a good writing handbook for detailed advice, but use the following guidelines to help you check your drafts systematically for some common errors with paragraphs, sentences, and words:

Editing paragraphs

- Does each paragraph focus on one point? Does it have a topic sentence that announces that point, and if so, where is it located? If it's not the first sentence, should it be? If there's no clear topic sentence, should there be one?

- Does every sentence relate to the main point of the paragraph? If any sentences do not, should they be deleted, moved, or revised?
- Is there enough detail to develop the paragraph's main point? How is the point developed—with narrative? definition? some other strategy?
- Where have you placed the most important information—at the beginning? the end? in the middle? The most emphatic spot is at the end, so in general that's where to put information you want readers to remember. The second most emphatic spot is at the beginning.
- Are any paragraphs especially long or short? Consider breaking long paragraphs if there's a logical place to do so—maybe an extended example should be in its own paragraph, for instance. If you have paragraphs of only a sentence or two, see if you can add to them or combine them with another paragraph, unless you're using a brief paragraph to provide emphasis.
- Check the way your paragraphs fit together. Does each one follow smoothly from the one before? Do you need to add any transitions?
- Do the beginning paragraphs catch readers' attention? In what other ways might you begin your text?
- Do the final paragraphs provide a satisfactory ending? How else might you conclude your text?

Editing sentences

- Is each sentence complete? Does it have someone or something (the subject) performing some sort of action or expressing a state of being (the verb)? Does each sentence begin with a capital letter and end with a period, question mark, or exclamation point?
- Check your use of the passive voice. Although there are some rhetorical situations in which the passive voice ("The prince was killed by a rival") is more appropriate than the active voice ("A rival killed the prince") because you want to emphasize an action rather than who performed it, you'll do well to edit it out unless you have a good reason for using it.

- Check for parallelism. Items in a list or series should be parallel in form—all nouns (lions, tigers, bears), all verbs (hopped, skipped, jumped), all clauses (he came, he saw, he conquered), and so on.
- Do many of your sentences begin with *it* or *there*? Too often these words make your writing wordy and vague or even conceal needed information. Why write "There are reasons we voted for him" when you can say "We had reasons to vote for him"?
- Are your sentences varied? If they all start with the subject or are the same length, your writing might be dull and maybe even hard to read. Try varying your sentence openings by adding transitions, introductory phrases or clauses. Vary sentence lengths by adding detail to some or combining some sentences.
- Make sure you've used commas correctly. Is there a comma after each introductory element? ("After the lead singer quit, the group nearly disbanded. However, they then produced a string of hits.") Do commas set off nonrestrictive elements—parts that aren't needed to understand the sentence? ("The books I read in middle school, like the Harry Potter series, became longer and more challenging.") Are compound sentences connected with a comma? ("I'll eat broccoli steamed, but I prefer it roasted.")

Editing words

- Are you sure of the meaning of every word? Use a dictionary; be sure to look up words whose meanings you're not sure about. And remember your audience—do you use any terms they'll need to have defined?
- Is any of your language too general or vague? Why write that you competed in a race, for example, if you could say you ran the 4 × 200 relay?
- What about the tone? If your stance is serious (or humorous or critical or something else), make sure that your words all convey that attitude.
- Do any pronouns have vague or unclear antecedents? If you use "he" or "they" or "it" or "these," will readers know whom or what the words refer to?
- Have you used any clichés—expressions that are used so frequently that they are no longer fresh? "Live and let live," avoiding something

"like the plague," and similar expressions are so predictable that your writing will almost always be better off without them.

- Be careful with language that refers to others. Make sure that your words do not stereotype any individual or group. Mention age, gender, race, religion, sexual orientation, and so on only if they are relevant to your subject. When referring to an ethnic group, make every effort to use the terms members of the group prefer.
- Edit out language that might be considered sexist. Have you used words like *manpower* or *policemen* to refer to people who may be female? If so, substitute less gendered words such as *personnel* or *police officers*. Do your words reflect any gender stereotypes—for example, that all engineers are male, or all nurses female? If you mention someone's gender, is it even necessary? If not, eliminate the unneeded words.
- How many of your verbs are forms of *be* and *do*? If you rely too much on these words, try replacing them with more specific verbs. Why write "She did a proposal for" when you could say "She proposed"?
- Do you ever confuse *its* and *it's*? Use *it's* when you mean *it is* or *it has*. Use *its* when you mean *belonging to it*.

Proofreading

Proofreading is the final stage of the writing process, the point where you clean up your work to present it to your readers. Proofreading is like checking your appearance in a mirror before going into a job interview: being neat and well groomed looms large in creating a good first impression, and the same principle applies to writing. Misspelled words, missing pages, mixed-up fonts, and other lapses send a negative message about your work—and about you. Most readers excuse an occasional error, but by and large readers are an intolerant bunch: too many errors will lead them to declare your writing—and maybe your thinking—flawed. There goes your credibility. So proofread your final draft with care to ensure that your message is taken as seriously as you want it to be.

Up to this point, you've been told *not* to read individual words on the page and instead to read for meaning. Proofreading demands the opposite: you must slow down your reading so that you can see every word, every punctuation mark.

- Use your computer's grammar checker and spelling checker, but only as a first step, and know that they're not very reliable. Computer programs don't read writing; instead, they rely on formulas and banks of words, so what they flag (or don't flag) as mistakes may or may not be accurate. If you were to write, "My brother was diagnosed with a leaning disorder," *leaning* would not be flagged as misspelled because it is a word (and might even be a disorder), even though it's the wrong word in that sentence.
- To keep your eyes from jumping ahead, place a ruler or piece of paper under each line as you read. Use your finger or a pencil as a pointer.
- Some writers find it helpful to read the text one sentence at a time, beginning with the last sentence and working backward.
- Read your text out loud to yourself—or better, to others, who may *hear* problems you can't see. Alternatively, have someone else read your text aloud to you while you follow along on the screen or page.
- Ask someone else to read your text. The more important the writing is, the more important this step is.
- If you find a mistake after you've printed out your text and are unable to print out a corrected version, make the change as neatly as possible in pencil or pen.

part 6

Doing Research

We do research all the time, for many different reasons. We search the web for information about a new computer, ask friends about the best place to get coffee, try on several pairs of jeans before deciding which ones to buy. You have no doubt done your share of library research before now, and you probably have visited a number of schools' websites before deciding which college you wanted to attend. Research, in other words, is something you do every day. The following chapters offer advice on the kind of research you'll need to do for your academic work and, in particular, for research projects.

Doing Research

Getting a Start on Research 20

When you need to do research, it's sometimes tempting to jump in and start looking for information right away. However, doing research is complex and time-consuming. Research-based writing projects usually require you to follow several steps. You need to come up with a topic (or to analyze the requirements of an assigned topic) and come up with a research question to guide your research efforts. Once you do some serious, focused research to find the information you need, you'll be ready to turn your research question into a tentative thesis and sketch out a rough outline. After doing whatever additional research you need to fill in your outline, you'll write a draft—and get some response to that draft. You may then need to do additional research before revising. Once you revise, you'll need to edit and proofread. In other words, there's a lot to do. You need a schedule.

Establishing a Schedule and Getting Started

A good place to start a research project is by creating a time line for getting all this work done, perhaps using the form on the next page. Once you have a schedule, you can get started. The sections that follow offer advice on considering your rhetorical situation, coming up with a topic, and doing preliminary research; developing a research question, a tentative thesis, and a rough outline; and creating a working bibliography and keeping track of your sources. The chapters that follow offer guidelines for **FINDING SOURCES**, **EVALUATING SOURCES**, and **SYNTHESIZING IDEAS**.

243–64
265–72
273–79

Scheduling a Research Project

	Complete by:
Analyze your rhetorical situation.	________
Choose a possible topic or analyze the assignment.	________
Plan a research strategy and do preliminary research.	________
Come up with a research question.	________
Schedule interviews and other field research.	________
Find sources.	________
Read sources and take notes.	________
Do any field research.	________
Come up with a tentative thesis and outline.	________
Write a draft.	________
Get response.	________
Do any additional research.	________
Revise.	________
Prepare a list of works cited.	________
Edit.	________
Proofread the final draft.	________
Submit the final draft.	________

Considering the Rhetorical Situation

As with any writing task, you need to start by considering your purpose, your audience, and the rest of your rhetorical situation:

Purpose — Is this project part of an assignment—and if so, does it specify any one purpose? If not, what is your broad purpose? To inform? argue? analyze? A combination?

Audience — To whom are you writing? What does your audience likely know about your topic, and is there any back-

	ground information you'll need to provide? What opinions or attitudes do your readers likely hold? What kinds of evidence will they find persuasive? How do you want them to respond to your writing?
Genre	Are you writing to report on something? to compose a profile? to make a proposal? an argument? What are the requirements of your genre in terms of the number and kind of sources you must use?
Stance	What is your attitude toward your topic? What accounts for your attitude? How do you want to come across? Curious? Critical? Positive? Something else?
Media/Design	What medium or media will you use? Print? Spoken? Electronic? Will you need to create any charts, photographs, video, presentation software slides, or other visuals?

Coming Up with a Topic

If you need to choose a topic, consider your interests as they relate to the course for which you're writing. What do you want to learn about? What do you have questions about? What topics from the course have you found intriguing? What community, national, or global issues do you care about? Once you've thought of a potential topic, use the questions in Chapter 15, **WRITING AS INQUIRY**, to explore it and find an angle on it that you can write about—and want to. 205–8

If your topic is assigned, you need to make sure you understand exactly what it asks you to do. Read the assignment carefully, looking for keywords: does it ask you to analyze, compare, evaluate, **SUMMARIZE**, or argue? If the assignment offers broad guidelines but allows you to choose within them, identify the requirements and the range of possible topics and define your topic within those constraints. 288–89

For example, in an American history course, your instructor might ask you to "discuss social effects of the Civil War." Potential but broad topics might include poverty among Confederate soldiers or former slaveholders, the migration of members of those groups to Mexico or Northern cities, the establishment of independent African American churches, or the spread of the Ku Klux Klan—to name only a few of the possibilities.

Think about what you know about your topic. Chances are you already know something about your topic, and articulating that knowledge can help you see possible ways to focus your topic or come up with potential
213–16
sources of information. FREEWRITING, LISTING, CLUSTERING, and LOOPING are all good ways of tapping your knowledge of your topic. Consider where you might find information about it: Have you read about it in a textbook? heard stories about it on the news? visited websites focused on it? Do you know anyone who knows about this topic?

Narrow the topic. As you consider possible topics, look for ways to narrow your topic's focus to make it specific enough to discuss in depth. For example:

> **Too general:** fracking
>
> **Still too general:** fracking and the environment
>
> **Better:** the potential environmental effects of extracting natural gas through the process of hydraulic fracturing, or fracking

If you limit your topic, you can address it with specific information that you'll be more easily able to find and manage. In addition, a limited topic will be more likely to interest your audience than a broad topic that forces you to use abstract, general statements. For example, it's much harder to write well about "the environment" than it is to address a topic that explores a single environmental issue.

Consulting with Librarians and Doing Preliminary Research

Consulting with a reference librarian at your school and doing some preliminary research in the library can save you time in the long run. Reference librarians can direct you to the best scholarly sources for your topic and help you focus your topic by determining appropriate search terms and
249–52
KEYWORDS—significant words that appear in the title, abstract, or text of

potential sources and that you can use to search for information on your topic in library catalogs, in databases, and on the web. These librarians can also help you choose the most appropriate reference works, sources that provide general overviews of the scholarship in a field. General internet searches can be time-consuming, as they often result in thousands of possible sites—too many to weed out efficiently, either by revising your search terms or by going through the sites themselves, many of which are unreliable. Library databases, on the other hand, include only sources that already have been selected by experts, and searches in them usually present manageable numbers of results.

Wikipedia can often serve as a jumping-off point for preliminary research, but since its entries are written and edited by people who may not have expertise in the subject, it is not considered a reliable academic source. Specialized encyclopedias, however, usually present subjects in much greater depth and provide more scholarly references that might suggest starting points for your research. Even if you know a lot about a subject, doing preliminary research can open you to new ways of seeing and approaching it, increasing your options for developing and narrowing your topic.

Coming Up with a Research Question

Once you've surveyed the territory of your topic, you'll likely find that your understanding of the topic has become broader and deeper. You may find that your interests have changed and your research has led to surprises and additional research. That's okay: as a result of exploring avenues you hadn't anticipated, you may well come up with a better topic than the one you'd started with. At some point, though, you need to develop a research question—a specific question that you will then work to answer through your research.

To write a research question, review your analysis of the rhetorical situation, to remind yourself of any time constraints or length considerations. Generate a list of questions beginning with *What? When? Where? Who? How? Why? Would? Could?* and *Should?* Here, for example, are some questions about the tentative topic "the potential environmental effects of extracting natural gas through the process of hydraulic fracturing, or fracking":

> *What* are the environmental effects of fracking?
> *When* was fracking introduced as a way to produce natural gas?
> *Where* is fracking done, and how does this affect the surrounding people and environment?
> *Who* will benefit from increased fracking?
> *How* much energy does fracking use?
> *Why* do some environmental groups oppose fracking?
> *Would* other methods of extracting natural gas be safer?
> *Could* fracking cause earthquakes?
> *Should* fracking be expanded, regulated, or banned?

Select one question from your list that you find interesting and that suits your rhetorical situation. Use the question to guide your research.

Drafting a Tentative Thesis

Once your research has led you to a possible answer to your research question, try formulating that answer as a tentative thesis. You need not be committed to the thesis; in fact, you should not be. The object of your research should be to learn about your topic, not to find information that simply supports what you already think you believe. Your tentative thesis may (and probably will) change as you learn more about your subject, consider the many points of view on it, and reconsider your topic and, perhaps, your goal: what you originally planned to be an argument for considering other points of view may become a call to action. However tentative, a thesis allows you to move forward by clarifying your purpose for doing research. Here are some tentative thesis statements on the topic of fracking:

> Fracking is a likely cause of earthquakes in otherwise seismically stable regions of the country.
>
> The federal government should strictly regulate the production of natural gas by fracking.

Fracking can greatly increase our supplies of natural gas, but other methods of producing energy should still be pursued.

As with a research question, a tentative thesis should guide your research efforts—but be ready to revise it as you learn still more about your topic. Research should be a process of **INQUIRY** in which you approach your topic with an open mind, ready to learn and possibly change. If you hold too tightly to a tentative thesis, you risk focusing only on evidence that supports your view, making your writing biased and unconvincing. 205–8

Creating a Rough Outline

After you've created a tentative thesis, write out a rough **OUTLINE** for your research project. Your outline can be a simple list of topics you want to explore, something that will help you structure your research efforts and organize your notes and other materials. As you read your sources, you can use your outline to keep track of what you need to find and where the information you do find fits into your argument. Then you'll be able to see if you've covered all the ideas you intended to explore—or whether you need to rethink the categories on your outline. 217–19

Keeping a Working Bibliography

A working bibliography is a record of all the sources you consult. You should keep such a record so that you can find sources easily when you need them and then cite any that you use. Your library likely offers tools to store source information you find in its databases and catalog, and software such as *Zotero* or *EasyBib* can also help you save, manage, and cite your sources. You may find it helpful to print out bibliographical data you find useful or to keep your working bibliography on index cards or in a notebook. However you decide to compile your working bibliography, include all the information you'll need later to document any sources you use; follow the **DOCUMENTATION** style you'll use when you write so that 298–301

Information for a Working Bibliography

FOR A BOOK

Library call number
Author(s) or editor(s)
Title and subtitle
Publication information: city, publisher, year of publication
Other information: edition, volume number, translator, and so on
If your source is an essay in a collection, include its author, title, and page numbers.

FOR A SOURCE FROM A DATABASE

Publication information for the source, as listed above
Name of database
DOI (digital object identifier) or URL of original source, such as the periodical in which an article was published.
Stable URL or permalink for database
Date you accessed source

FOR AN ARTICLE IN A PRINT PERIODICAL

Author(s)
Title and subtitle
Name of periodical
Volume number, issue number, date
Page numbers

FOR A WEB SOURCE

URL
Author(s) or editor(s) if available
Name of site
Sponsor of site
Date site was first posted or last updated
Date you accessed site
If the source is an article or book reprinted on the web, include its title, the title and publication information of the periodical or book, where it was first published, and any page numbers.

you won't need to go back to your sources to find the information. Some databases make this step easy by preparing rough-draft citations in several styles that you can copy, paste, and edit.

On the previous page is most of the basic information you'll want to include for each source in your working bibliography. Go to digital.wwnorton.com/fieldguide5 for a worksheet you can use to keep track of this information.

Keeping Track of Your Sources

- ***Staple together photocopies and printouts.*** It's easy for individual pages to get shuffled or lost on a desk or in a backpack. Keep a stapler handy, and fasten pages together as soon as you copy them or print them out.
- ***Bookmark web sources*** or save them using a free bookmark management tool available through several library databases. For database sources, use the *DOI* or *stable URL*, *permalink*, or *document URL* (the terms used by databases vary)—not the URL in the "Address" or "Location" box in your browser, which will expire after you end your online session.
- ***Label everything.*** Label your copies with the source's author and title.
- ***Highlight sections you plan to use.*** When you sit down to draft, your goal will be to find what you need quickly, so as soon as you decide you might use a source, highlight the paragraphs or sentences that you think you'll use. If your instructor wants copies of your sources to see how you used them, you've got them ready. If you're using PDF copies, you can highlight or add notes using *Adobe Reader*.
- ***Use your rough outline to keep track of what you've got.*** In the margin of each highlighted section, write the number or letter of the outline division to which the section corresponds. (It's a good idea to write it in the same place consistently so you can flip through a stack of copies and easily see what you've got.) Alternatively, attach sticky notes to each copy, using a different color for each main heading in your outline.

- ***Keep everything in an online folder, file folder, or box.*** Keep everything related to your research in one place. If you create online subfolders or create folders that correspond to your rough outline, you'll be able to organize your material, at least tentatively. And if you highlight, label, and use sticky notes, your material will be even better organized, making writing a draft easier. The folder or box will also serve you well if you are required to create a portfolio that includes your research notes, copies of sources, and drafts.
- ***Use a reference manager.*** Web-based reference or citation management software allows you to create and organize a personal database of resources. You can import references from databases to a personal account, organize them, and draft citations in various formats. *RefWorks*, *EndNote*, *Mendeley*, and *Zotero* are four such systems; check with your librarian to see what system your library supports, or search online, as several of them are available for free. Be aware, though, that the citations generated are often inaccurate and need to be checked carefully for content and format. So treat them as rough drafts and plan to edit them.

243–64
265–72

IF YOU NEED MORE HELP

See the guidelines on FINDING SOURCES once you're ready to move on to in-depth research and those on EVALUATING SOURCES for help thinking critically about the sources you find.

Finding Sources 21

To analyze media coverage of the 2016 Democratic National Convention, you examine news stories and blogs published at the time. To write an essay interpreting a poem by Maya Angelou, you study the poem and read several critical interpretations in literary journals. To write a report on career opportunities in psychology, you interview a graduate of your university who is working in a psychology clinic. In each of these cases, you go beyond your own knowledge to consult additional sources of information.

This chapter offers guidelines for locating a range of sources—print and online, general and specialized, published and firsthand. Keep in mind that as you do research, finding and **EVALUATING SOURCES** are two activities that usually take place simultaneously. So this chapter and the next one go hand in hand. 265–72

Kinds of Sources

Primary and secondary sources. Your research will likely lead you to both primary and secondary sources. *Primary sources* include historical documents, literary works, eyewitness accounts, field reports, diaries, letters, and lab studies, as well as any original research you do through interviews, observation, experiments, or surveys. *Secondary sources* include scholarly books and articles, reviews, biographies, textbooks, and other works that interpret or discuss primary sources. Novels and films are primary sources; articles interpreting them are secondary sources. The Declaration of Independence is a primary historical document; a historian's description of the events surrounding the Declaration's writing is secondary. A published report of scientific findings is primary; a critique of that report is secondary.

Whether a work is considered primary or secondary sometimes depends on your topic and purpose. If you're analyzing a poem, a critic's article interpreting the poem is a secondary source—but if you're investigating that critic's work, the article would be a primary source for your own study and interpretation.

Secondary sources are often useful because they can help you understand and evaluate primary source material. Whenever possible, however, you should find and use primary sources, because secondary sources can distort or misrepresent the information in primary sources. For example, a seemingly reputable secondary source describing the 1948 presidential election asserted that the *New York Times* ran a headline reading, "Thomas E. Dewey's Election as President Is a Foregone Conclusion." But the actual article was titled "Talk Is Now Turning to the Dewey Cabinet," and it began by noting "[*the*] *popular view that* Gov. Thomas E. Dewey's election as President is a foregone conclusion." Here the secondary source got not only the headline wrong but also distorted the source's intended meaning by leaving out an important phrase. Your research should be as accurate and reliable as it can be; using primary sources whenever you can helps ensure that it is.

Scholarly and popular sources. Scholarly sources are written by academic experts or scholars in a particular discipline and are *peer-reviewed*—evaluated by other experts in the same discipline for their factual accuracy and lack of bias. They are also written largely *for* experts in a discipline, as a means of sharing research, insights, and in-depth analysis with one another; that's why they must meet high standards of accuracy and objectivity and adhere to the discipline's accepted research methods, including its style for documenting sources. Scholarly articles are usually published in academic journals; scholarly books may be published by university presses or by other academically focused publishers.

Popular sources include just about all other online and print publications, from websites to magazines to books written for nonspecialists. These sources generally explain or provide opinion on current events or topics of general interest; when they discuss scholarly research, they tend to simplify the concepts and facts, providing definitions, narratives, and examples to make them understandable to nonspecialist audiences. They are often written by journalists or other professional writers who may specialize in a particular area but who report or comment on the scholarship of others rather than doing any themselves. Their most important difference from scholarly sources is that popular sources are not reviewed by other experts in the field being discussed, although editors or fact-checkers review the writing before it's published.

In most of your college courses, you'll be expected to rely primarily on scholarly sources rather than popular ones. However, if you're writing about a very current topic or need to provide background information on a topic, a mix of scholarly and popular sources may be appropriate. To see how scholarly and popular sources differ in appearance, look closely at the scholarly source and popular source illustrations that appear on pages 246–47. Here's a guide to determining whether or not a potential source is scholarly:

IDENTIFYING SCHOLARLY SOURCES: WHAT TO LOOK FOR

- *Author.* Look for the author's scholarly credentials, including affiliations with academic or other research-oriented institutions.
- *Peer review.* Look for a list of reviewers at the front of the journal or on the journal's or publisher's website. If you don't find one, the source is probably not peer-reviewed.
- *Source citations.* Look for a detailed list of works cited or references at the end of the source and citations either parenthetically within the text or in footnotes or endnotes. (Popular sources may include a reference list but seldom cite sources within the text, except in signal phrases.)
- *Publisher.* Look for publishers that are professional scholarly organizations, such as the Modern Language Association or the Organization of American Historians, that are affiliated with universities or colleges, or that have a stated academic mission.
- *Language and content.* Look for abstracts (one-paragraph summaries of the contents) at the beginning of articles and for technical or specialized language and concepts that readers are assumed to be familiar with.
- *Other clues.* Look for little or no advertising on websites or within the journal; for a plain design with few or no illustrations, especially in print sources; and for listing in academic databases when you limit your search to *academic, peer-reviewed,* or *scholarly sources.*

Scholarly Source

Published in an academic journal.

Includes an abstract.

Cites academic research with consistent documentation style.

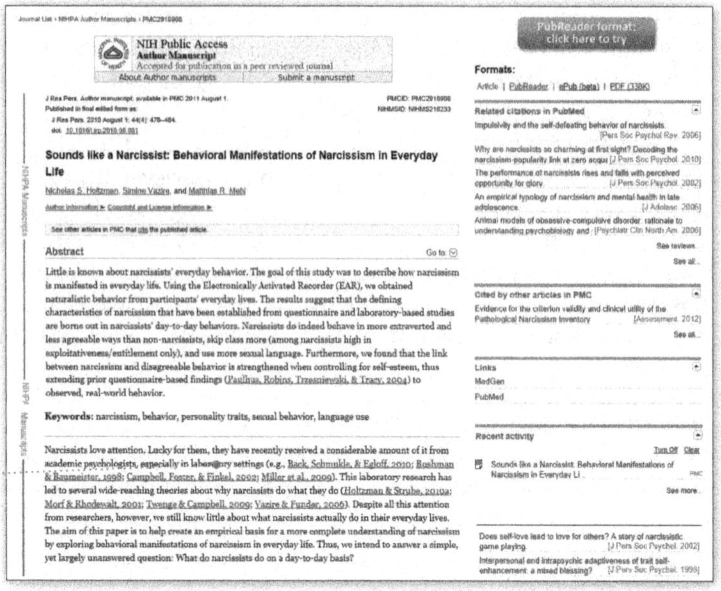

Journal List › NIHPA Author Manuscripts › PMC2918908

NIH Public Access
Author Manuscript
Accepted for publication in a peer reviewed journal
About Author manuscripts | Submit a manuscript

J Res Pers. Author manuscript; available in PMC 2011 August 1.
Published in final edited form as:
J Res Pers. 2010 August 1; 44(4): 478–484.
doi: 10.1016/j.jrp.2010.06.001
PMCID: PMC2918908
NIHMSID: NIHMS216233

Sounds like a Narcissist: Behavioral Manifestations of Narcissism in Everyday Life

Nicholas S. Holtzman, Simine Vazire, and Matthias R. Mehl

Author information ► Copyright and License information ►

See other articles in PMC that cite the published article.

Abstract Go to:

Little is known about narcissists' everyday behavior. The goal of this study was to describe how narcissism is manifested in everyday life. Using the Electronically Activated Recorder (EAR), we obtained naturalistic behavior from participants' everyday lives. The results suggest that the defining characteristics of narcissism that have been established from questionnaire and laboratory-based studies are borne out in narcissists' day-to-day behaviors. Narcissists do indeed behave in more extraverted and less agreeable ways than non-narcissists, skip class more (among narcissists high in exploitativeness/entitlement only), and use more sexual language. Furthermore, we found that the link between narcissism and disagreeable behavior is strengthened when controlling for self-esteem, thus extending prior questionnaire-based findings (Paulhus, Robins, Trzesniewski, & Tracy, 2004) to observed, real-world behavior.

Keywords: narcissism, behavior, personality traits, sexual behavior, language use

Narcissists love attention. Lucky for them, they have recently received a considerable amount of it from academic psychologists, especially in laboratory settings (e.g., Back, Schmukle, & Egloff, 2010; Bushman & Baumeister, 1998; Campbell, Foster, & Finkel, 2002; Miller et al., 2009). This laboratory research has led to several wide-reaching theories about why narcissists do what they do (Holtzman & Strube, 2010a; Morf & Rhodewalt, 2001; Twenge & Campbell, 2009; Vazire & Funder, 2006). Despite all this attention from researchers, however, we still know little about what narcissists actually do in their everyday lives. The aim of this paper is to help create an empirical basis for a more complete understanding of narcissism by exploring behavioral manifestations of narcissism in everyday life. Thus, we intend to answer a simple, yet largely unanswered question: What do narcissists do on a day-to-day basis?

PubReader format: click here to try

Formats:
Article | PubReader | ePub (beta) | PDF (338K)

Related citations in PubMed
Impulsivity and the self-defeating behavior of narcissists. [Pers Soc Psychol Rev. 2006]
Why are narcissists so charming at first sight? Decoding the narcissism-popularity link at zero acqua [J Pers Soc Psychol. 2010]
The performance of narcissists rises and falls with perceived opportunity for glory. [J Pers Soc Psychol. 2002]
An empirical typology of narcissism and mental health in late adolescence. [J Adolesc. 2006]
Animal models of obsessive-compulsive disorder: rationale to understanding psychobiology and [Psychiatr Clin North Am. 2006]
See reviews...
See all...

Cited by other articles in PMC
Evidence for the criterion validity and clinical utility of the Pathological Narcissism Inventory [Assessment. 2012]
See all...

Links
MedGen
PubMed

Recent activity
Turn Off Clear
Sounds like a Narcissist: Behavioral Manifestations of Narcissism in Everyday Li... PMC
See more...

Does self-love lead to love for others? A story of narcissistic game playing. [J Pers Soc Psychol. 2002]
Interpersonal and intrapsychic adaptiveness of trait self-enhancement: a mixed blessing? [J Pers Soc Psychol. 1998]

Describes research methods, includes numerical data.

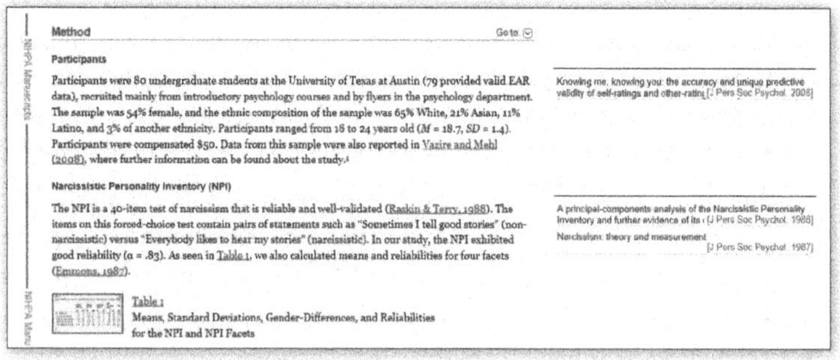

Method Go to:

Participants

Participants were 80 undergraduate students at the University of Texas at Austin (79 provided valid EAR data), recruited mainly from introductory psychology courses and by flyers in the psychology department. The sample was 54% female, and the ethnic composition of the sample was 65% White, 21% Asian, 11% Latino, and 3% of another ethnicity. Participants ranged from 18 to 24 years old ($M = 18.7$, $SD = 1.4$). Participants were compensated $50. Data from this sample were also reported in Vazire and Mehl (2008), where further information can be found about the study.[1]

Narcissistic Personality Inventory (NPI)

The NPI is a 40-item test of narcissism that is reliable and well-validated (Raskin & Terry, 1988). The items on this forced-choice test contain pairs of statements such as "Sometimes I tell good stories" (non-narcissistic) versus "Everybody likes to hear my stories" (narcissistic). In our study, the NPI exhibited good reliability ($\alpha = .83$). As seen in Table 1, we also calculated means and reliabilities for four facets (Emmons, 1987).

Table 1
Means, Standard Deviations, Gender-Differences, and Reliabilities for the NPI and NPI Facets

Knowing me, knowing you: the accuracy and unique predictive validity of self-ratings and other-ratin [J Pers Soc Psychol. 2008]

A principal-components analysis of the Narcissistic Personality Inventory and further evidence of its [J Pers Soc Psychol. 1988]
Narcissism: theory and measurement. [J Pers Soc Psychol. 1987]

Multiple authors who are academics.

Includes complete references list.

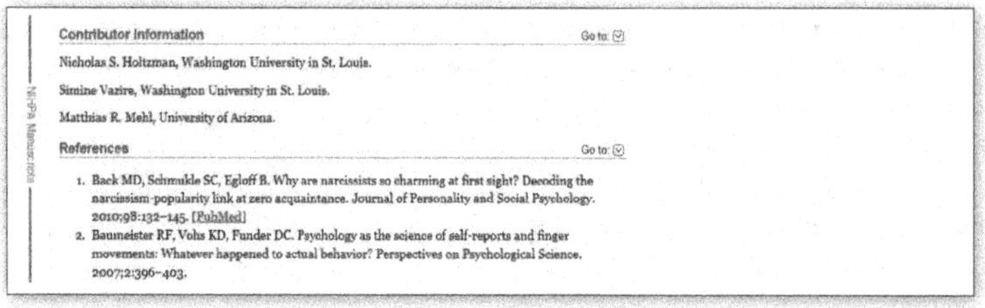

Contributor Information Go to:

Nicholas S. Holtzman, Washington University in St. Louis.

Simine Vazire, Washington University in St. Louis.

Matthias R. Mehl, University of Arizona.

References Go to:

1. Back MD, Schmukle SC, Egloff B. Why are narcissists so charming at first sight? Decoding the narcissism-popularity link at zero acquaintance. Journal of Personality and Social Psychology. 2010;98:132–145. [PubMed]
2. Baumeister RF, Vohs KD, Funder DC. Psychology as the science of self-reports and finger movements: Whatever happened to actual behavior? Perspectives on Psychological Science. 2007;2:396–403.

Popular Source

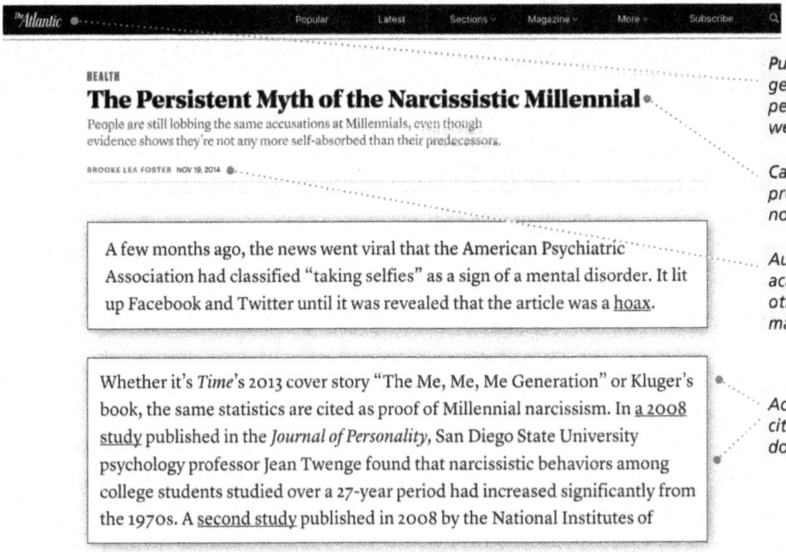
The Atlantic Popular Latest Sections Magazine More Subscribe

HEALTH

The Persistent Myth of the Narcissistic Millennial

People are still lobbing the same accusations at Millennials, even though evidence shows they're not any more self-absorbed than their predecessors.

BROOKE LEA FOSTER NOV 19, 2014

A few months ago, the news went viral that the American Psychiatric Association had classified "taking selfies" as a sign of a mental disorder. It lit up Facebook and Twitter until it was revealed that the article was a hoax.

Whether it's *Time*'s 2013 cover story "The Me, Me, Me Generation" or Kluger's book, the same statistics are cited as proof of Millennial narcissism. In a 2008 study published in the *Journal of Personality*, San Diego State University psychology professor Jean Twenge found that narcissistic behaviors among college students studied over a 27-year period had increased significantly from the 1970s. A second study published in 2008 by the National Institutes of

Print and online sources. Some sources are available only in print; some are available only online. But many print sources are also available on the web. You'll find print sources in your school's library, but chances are that many reference books and academic journal articles in your library will also be available online. In general, for academic writing it's best to try to find most of your online sources through the library's website rather than commercial search sites, which may lead you to unreliable sources and cause you to spend much more time sorting and narrowing search results.

Searching in Academic Libraries

College and university libraries typically offer several ways to search their holdings. Take a look at this search box, from the homepage of the Houston Community College libraries:

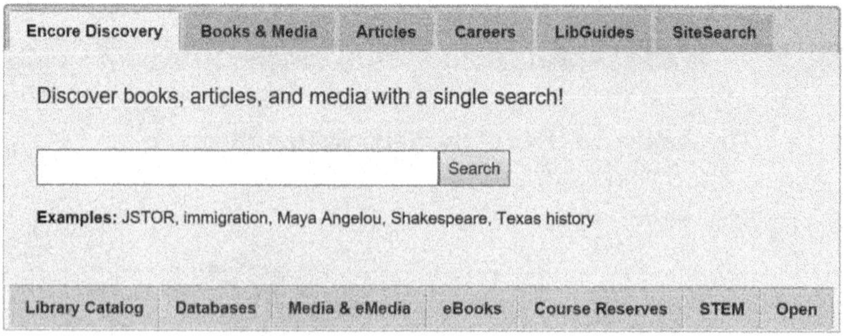

This box allows you to search through all the library's holdings at once an option that may be a good way to get started. You may already know, though, that you need to focus your search on one type of source, such as scholarly articles, leading you to choose the Articles search tab.

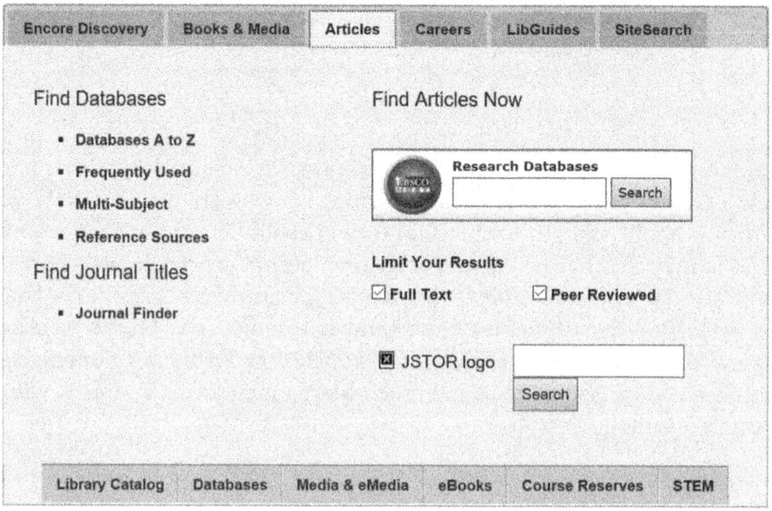

This box lets you shape and limit your search in several ways: by selecting a specific database, by choosing to search only for full-text articles and only peer-reviewed articles, and by searching within a specific journal. "Ask a Librarian" options can be very useful; many libraries offer email, texting, chat, and phone conversations with reference librarians when you need help but aren't working in the library.

Searching Effectively Using Keywords

Whether you're searching for books, articles in periodicals, or other material available on the web, chances are you'll conduct most of your search online. Most materials produced since the 1980s and most library catalogs are online, and most periodical articles can be found by searching electronic indexes and databases. In each case, you can search for authors, titles, or subjects.

To search online, you'll need to come up with keywords. Keywords are significant words that stand for an idea or concept. The key to searching efficiently is to use keywords and combinations of them that will focus your searches on the information you need—but not too much of it. Often you'll start out with one general keyword that will yield far too many results; then you'll need to switch to more specific terms or combinations (*homeopathy* instead of *medicine* or *secondary education Japan* instead of *education Japan*).

Other times your keyword search won't yield enough sources; then you'll need to use broader terms or combinations (*education Japan* instead of *secondary education Japan*) or substitute synonyms (*home remedy* instead of *folk medicine*). Sometimes you'll need to learn terms used in academic disciplines or earlier in history for things you know by other names, such as *myocardial infarction* rather than *heart attack* or *the Great War* instead of *World War I*. Or look through the sources that turn up in response to other terms to see what keywords you might use in subsequent searches. Searching requires flexibility, in the words you use and the methods you try.

Finding keywords using word clouds. One way to find keywords to help you narrow and focus your topic is to create a word cloud, a visual representation of words used in a text; the more often a word is used,

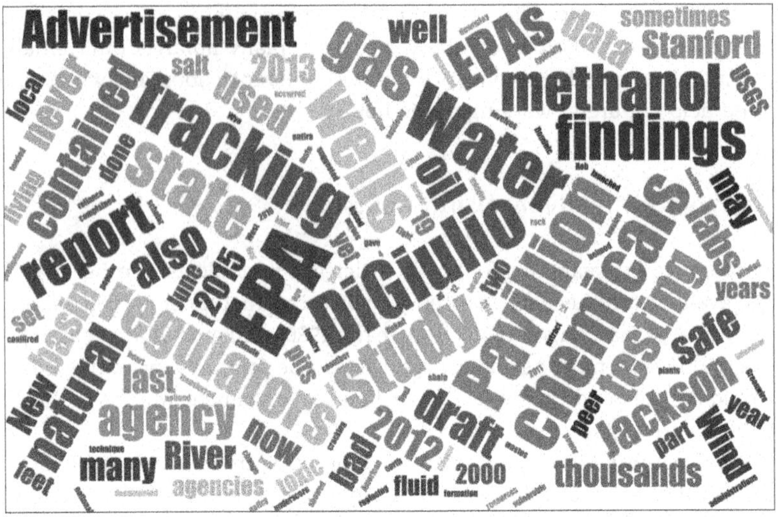

the larger it looks in the word cloud. Several websites, including *Tagxedo, Wordle,* and *TagCrowd,* let you create word clouds. Examining a word cloud created from an article in a reference work may help you see what terms are used to discuss your topic—and may help you see new possible ways to narrow it. Above, for example, is a word cloud derived from an article in *Scientific American* discussing fracking. Many of the terms—*fracking, water, gas, wells, drilling*—are just what you'd expect. However, some terms—*USGS, DiGiulio, coalfired*—may be unfamiliar and lead to additional possibilities for research. For instance, *DiGiulio* is the last name of an expert on fracking whose publications might be worth examining, while *USGS* is an acronym for the United States Geological Survey, a scientific government agency.

Finding keywords using databases. Once you've begun searching for and finding possible sources, you can expand your list of possible keywords by skimming the "detailed record" or "metadata" page for any scholarly articles you find, where full bibliographic information on the source may be found. A search for *fracking* resulted in this source:

Note the list of author-supplied keywords, which offers options for narrowing and focusing your topic. Each keyword is a link, so simply clicking on it will produce a new list of sources.

Advanced keyword searching. Most search sites have "advanced search" options that will help you focus your research. Some allow you to ask questions in conversational language: *What did Thomas Jefferson write about slavery?* Others allow you to focus your search by using specific words or symbols. Here are some of the most common ones:

- Type quotation marks around words to search for an exact phrase—"Thomas Jefferson."
- Type AND to specify that more than one keyword must appear in sources: Jefferson AND Adams. Some search engines require a plus sign instead: +Jefferson +Adams.
- Type OR if you're looking for sources that include any of several terms: Jefferson OR Adams OR Madison.
- Type NOT to find sources *without* a certain word: Jefferson NOT Adams. Some search engines call for a minus sign (actually, a hyphen) instead: +Jefferson –Adams.
- Type an asterisk to search for words in different form. For example, teach* will yield sources containing *teacher* and *teaching*.

Reference Works

The reference section of your school's library is the place to find encyclopedias, dictionaries, atlases, almanacs, bibliographies, and other reference works in print. Many of these sources are also online and can be accessed from any computer that is connected to the internet. Others are available only in the library. Remember, though, that whether in print or online, reference works are only a starting point, a place where you can get an overview of your topic.

General reference works. Consult encyclopedias for general background information on a subject, dictionaries for definitions of words, atlases for maps and geographic data, and almanacs for statistics and other data on current events. These are some works you might consult:

The New Encyclopaedia Britannica

The Columbia Encyclopedia

Webster's Third New International Dictionary

Oxford English Dictionary

National Geographic Atlas of the World

Statistical Abstract of the United States

The World Almanac and Book of Facts

Caution: *Wikipedia* is a popular online research tool, but since anyone can edit its entries, you can't be certain of its accuracy. Use it for general overviews, but look elsewhere—including *Wikipedia*'s own references and citations—for authoritative sources.

Specialized reference works. You can also go to specialized reference works, which provide in-depth information on a single field or topic. These may also include authoritative bibliographies, leading you to more specific works. A reference librarian can refer you to specialized encyclopedias in particular fields, but good places to start are online collections of many topic-specific reference works that offer overviews of a topic, place it in a larger context, and sometimes provide links to potential academic sources. Collections that are available through libraries include the following:

CQ Researcher offers in-depth reports on topics in education, health, the environment, criminal justice, international affairs, technology, the economy, and social trends. Each report gives an overview of a particular topic, outlines of the differing positions on it, and a bibliography of resources on it.

Gale Virtual Reference Library (*GVRL*) offers thousands of full-text specialized encyclopedias, almanacs, articles, and ebooks.

Oxford Reference contains hundreds of dictionaries, encyclopedias, and other reference works on a wide variety of subjects, as well as timelines with links to each item mentioned on each timeline.

SAGE Knowledge includes many encyclopedias and handbooks on topics in the social sciences.

Bibliographies. Bibliographies provide an overview of what has been published on a topic, listing published works along with the information you'll need to find each work. Some are annotated with brief summaries of each work's contents. You'll find bibliographies at the end of scholarly articles and books, and you can also find book-length bibliographies, both in the reference section of your library and online. Check with a reference librarian for bibliographies on your research topic.

Books / Searching the Library Catalog

The library catalog is your primary source for finding books. Almost all library catalogs are computerized and can be accessed through the library's website. You can search by author, title, subject, or keyword. The image below shows the result of a keyword search for material on looted art in Nazi Germany. This search of the library's catalog revealed six items—print books and ebooks—on the topic; to access information on each one, the researcher must simply click on the title or thumbnail image. The image on the next page shows detailed information for one source: bibliographic data about author, title, and publication;

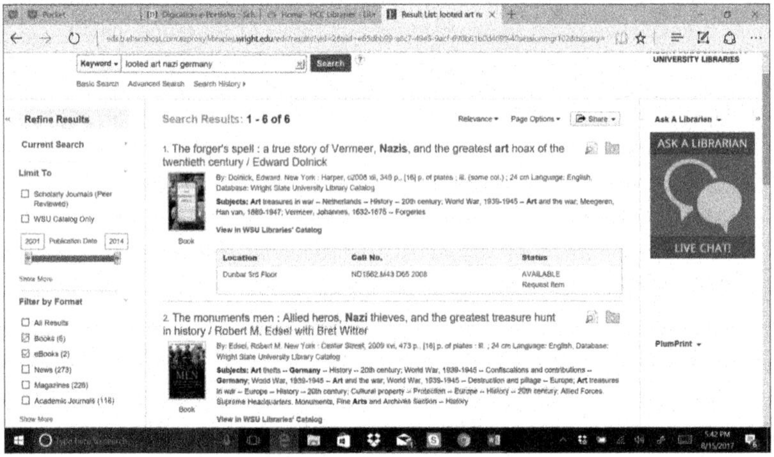

related subject headings (which may lead to other useful materials in the library)—and more. Library catalogs also supply a call number, which identifies the book's location on the library's shelves.

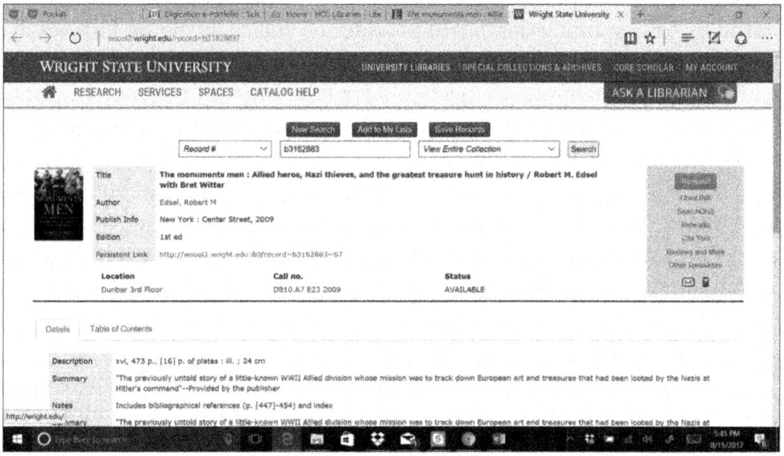

Ebooks / Finding Books Online

Many books in the library catalog are available online. Some may be downloaded to a tablet or mobile device. In addition, thousands of classic works that are in the public domain—no longer protected by copyright—may be read online. *Bartleby*, *Google Books*, *Open Library*, and *Project Gutenberg* are four collections of public-domain works. Here are some other sources of ebooks:

> *Hathi Trust Digital Library* offers access to millions of ebooks, about a third of them in the public domain, contributed by university libraries.
>
> *Internet Archive* includes millions of ebooks as well as audio, video, music, software, images, and the Way Back Machine, which archives historical webpages.
>
> The *Gale Virtual Reference Library (GVRL)*, *Oxford Reference*, and *SAGE Knowledge* all contain large ebook collections.

Periodicals / Searching Indexes and Databases

To find journal, magazine, and newspaper articles, you will need to search periodical indexes and databases. Indexes provide listings of articles organized by topics; many databases provide the full texts. Some indexes are in print and can be found in the reference section of the library; most are online. Some databases are available for free; most of the more authoritative ones, however, are available only by subscription and so must be accessed through a library.

Many databases now include not only scholarly articles but also dissertations, theses, book chapters, book reviews, and conference proceedings. Dissertations and theses are formal works of scholarship done as requirements for graduate degrees; book reviews offer critical evaluations of scholarly and popular books; and conference proceedings are papers presented, usually orally, at scholarly meetings.

When you access a source through a database, the URL or link address is different each time you log in, so if you want to return to a source, look for a *stable URL*, *permalink*, or *document URL* option and choose it to copy and paste into your list of sources.

General indexes and databases. A reference librarian can help you determine which databases will be most helpful to you, but here are some useful ones:

Academic Search Complete and *Academic Search Premier* are multidisciplinary indexes and databases containing the full text of articles in thousands of journals and indexing of even more, with abstracts of their articles.

FirstSearch offers access to millions of full-text, full-image articles in dozens of databases covering many disciplines.

InfoTrac offers millions of full-text articles in a broad spectrum of disciplines and on a wide variety of topics from thousands of scholarly and popular periodicals, including the *New York Times*.

JSTOR archives scanned copies of entire publication runs of scholarly journals in many disciplines, but it may not include current issues of the journals.

LexisNexis contains full-text publications and articles from a large number of newspapers and business and legal resources.

ProQuest Central provides access to full-text articles from thousands of books, scholarly journals, conference papers, magazines, newspapers, blogs, podcasts, and websites and a large collection of dissertations and theses.

Single-subject indexes and databases. The following are just a sample of what's available; check with a reference librarian for indexes and databases in the subject you're researching.

America: History and Life indexes scholarly literature on the history and culture of the United States and Canada.

BIOSIS Previews provides abstracts and indexes for thousands of sources on a wide variety of biological and medical topics.

ERIC is the U.S. Department of Education's Educational Resource Information Center database. It includes hundreds of journal titles as well as conference papers, technical reports, and other resources on education.

Historical Abstracts includes abstracts of articles on the history of the world, excluding the United States and Canada, since 1450.

Humanities International Index contains bibliographic references to more than 2,200 journals dealing with the humanities.

MLA International Bibliography indexes scholarly articles on modern languages, literature, folklore, and linguistics.

PsycINFO indexes scholarly literature in a number of disciplines relating to the behavioral and social sciences.

PubMed includes millions of citations for biomedical literature, many with links to full-text content.

Print indexes. You may need to consult print indexes to find articles published before the 1980s. Here are six useful ones:

The Readers' Guide to Periodical Literature (print, 1900–; online, 1983–)

InfoTrac Magazine Index (print, 1988–; online, 1973–)

The New York Times Index (print and online, 1851–)

Humanities Index (print, 1974–; online, 1984–)

Social Sciences Index (print, 1974–; online, 1983–)

General Science Index (print, 1978–; online, 1984–)

Images, Sound, and More

Your library likely subscribes to various databases that allow you to find and download video, audio, and image files. Here is a sampling:

AP Images provides access to photographs taken for the Associated Press, the cooperative agency of thousands of newspapers and radio and television stations worldwide.

ArtStor provides images in the arts, architecture, humanities, and sciences.

Dance in Video offers hundreds of videos of dance productions and documentaries on dance.

Education in Video includes thousands of videos of teaching demonstrations, lectures, documentaries, and footage of students and teachers in their classrooms.

Naxos Music Library contains more than 130,000 classical, jazz, and world music recordings, as well as libretti and synopses of hundreds of operas and other background information.

Theatre in Video provides videos of hundreds of performances of plays and film documentaries.

The following indexes and databases are freely available on the internet:

The WWW Virtual Library is a catalog of websites on a wide range of subjects, compiled by volunteers with expertise in particular subject areas.

CSA Discovery Guides provide comprehensive information on current issues in the arts and humanities, natural sciences, social sciences, and technology, with an overview of each subject, key citations with abstracts, and links to websites.

Voice of the Shuttle, or *VoS,* offers information on subjects in the humanities, arranged to mirror "the way the humanities are organized for research and teaching as well as the way they are adapting to social, cultural, and technological changes."

The Library of Congress offers online access to information on a wide range of subjects, including academic subjects, as well as prints, photographs, and government documents.

JURIST is a university-based online gateway to authoritative legal instruction, information, scholarship, and news.

Searching the Web

The web provides access to countless sites containing information posted by governments, educational institutions, organizations, businesses, and individuals. Such websites are different from other sources—including the kinds of online sources you access through indexes and databases—in two key ways: (1) their content varies greatly in its reliability and (2) they are not stable, which means that what you see on a site today may be different (or gone) tomorrow. Anyone who wants to can post material on the web, so you need to evaluate carefully what you find there to eliminate sources that are not current, lack credibility, or are primarily advertisements or promotional in nature.

Because it is so vast and dynamic, finding what you need on the web for academic writing can be a challenge. The primary way of finding information on the web is with a search site. You may find the most suitable results for academic writing by using *Google Scholar*, a search site that finds scholarly literature, including peer-reviewed papers, technical reports, and abstracts. Here are other ways of searching the web:

- ***Keyword searches.*** *Google*, *Yahoo!*, *Microsoft Edge*, and most other search sites all scan the web looking for keywords that you specify.
- ***Subject directories.*** *Google*, *Yahoo!*, and some other search sites offer directories that arrange information by topics, much like a library cataloging system. Such directories allow you to broaden or narrow your search if you need to—for example, a search for "birds" can be broadened to "animals" or narrowed to "blue-footed booby."
- ***Metasearches.*** *Yippy*, *Dogpile*, and *ZapMeta* are metasearch sites that allow you to use several search engines simultaneously. They are best for searching broadly; use a single search site for the most precise results.
- ***Twitter searches.*** In addition to *Twitter* Search, you can find *Twitter* content through search sites such as *Social Mention* and *Keyhole*.

Each search site and metasearch site has its own protocols for searching; most have an "advanced search" option that will help you search more productively. Remember, though, that you need to be careful about **EVALUATING SOURCES** that you find on the web because the web is unregulated and no one independently verifies the information posted on its sites. 265–72

Doing Field Research

Sometimes you'll need to do your own research, to go beyond the information you find in published sources and gather data by doing field research. Three kinds of field research you might want to consider are interviews, observations, and questionnaires.

Interviewing experts. Some kinds of writing—a profile of a living person, for instance—almost require that you conduct an interview. And sometimes you may just need to find information that you haven't been able to find in published sources. To get firsthand information on the experience of serving as a soldier in Afghanistan, you might interview your cousin who served a tour of duty there; to find current research on pesticide residues in food, you might need to interview a toxicologist. Whatever your goal, you can conduct interviews in person, using video-calling software such as *Skype* or *FaceTime*, by telephone, through email, or by mail. In general, you will want to use interviews to find information you can't find elsewhere. Below is some advice on planning and conducting an interview.

Before the interview

1. Once you identify someone you want to interview, email or phone to ask the person, stating your purpose for the interview and what you hope to learn.
2. Once you've set up an appointment, send a note or email confirming the time and place. If you wish to record the interview, be sure to ask for permission to do so. If you plan to conduct the interview by mail or email, state when you will send your questions.
3. Write out questions. Plan questions that invite extended response and supporting details: "What accounts for the recent spike in gasoline prices?" forces an explanation, whereas "Is the recent spike in gas prices a direct result of global politics?" is likely to elicit only a yes or a no.

At the interview

4. Record the full name of the person you interview, along with the date, time, and place of the interview; you'll need this information to cite and document the interview accurately.

5. Take notes, even if you are recording the interview.
6. Keep track of time: don't take more than you agreed to beforehand unless both of you agree to keep talking. End by thanking your subject and offering to provide a copy of your final product.

After the interview

7. Flesh out your notes with details as soon as possible after the interview, while you still remember them. What did you learn? What surprised you? Summarize both the interviewee's words and your impressions.
8. Make sure you've reproduced quotations from the interview accurately and fairly. Avoid editing quotations in ways that distort the speaker's intended meaning.
9. Be sure to send a thank-you note or email.

Observation. Some writing projects are based on information you get by observing something. For a sociology report, you may observe how students behave in large lectures. For an education course, you may observe one child's progress as a writer over a period of time. The following advice can help you conduct observations.

Before observing

1. Think about your research purpose: What are you looking for? What do you expect to find? How will your presence as an observer affect what you observe? What do you plan to do with what you find?
2. If necessary, set up an appointment. You may need to ask permission of the people you wish to observe and of your school as well. (Check with your instructor about your school's policy in this area.) Be honest and open about your goals and intentions; college students doing research assignments are often welcomed where others may not be.

While observing

3. If you're taking notes on paper, you may want to divide each page down the middle vertically and write only on the left side of the page, reserving the right side for information you will fill in later. If you're using a laptop, you can set up two columns or a split screen.

4. Note descriptive details about the setting. What do you see? What do you hear? Do you smell anything? Get down details about color, shape, size, sound, and so on. Consider photographing or making a sketch of what you see.
5. Who is there, and what are they doing? Describe what they look like, and make notes about what they say. Note any significant demographic details—about gender, race, occupation, age, dress, and so on.
6. What is happening? Who's doing what? What's being said? Make note of these kinds of narrative details.

After observing

7. As soon as possible after you complete your observations, use the right side of your notes to fill in gaps and include additional details.
8. Analyze your notes, looking for patterns. Did some things appear or happen more than once? Did anything stand out? surprise or puzzle you? What did you learn?

Questionnaires and surveys. Various kinds of questionnaires and surveys can provide information or opinions from a large number of people. For a political science course, you might conduct a survey to ask students who they plan to vote for. Or, for a marketing course, you might distribute a questionnaire asking what they think about an advertising campaign. The advice in this section will help you create useful questionnaires and surveys.

Define your goal. The goal of a questionnaire or survey should be limited and focused, so that every question will contribute to your research question. Also, people are more likely to respond to a brief, focused survey.

Define your sample. A survey gets responses from a representative sample of the whole group. The answers to these questions will help you define that sample:

1. Who should answer the questions? The people you contact should represent the whole population. For example, if you want to survey undergraduate students at your school, your sample should reflect your school's enrollment in terms of gender, year, major, age, ethnicity, and so forth as closely as possible.

2. How many people make up a representative sample? In general, the larger your sample, the more the answers will reflect those of the whole group. But if your population is small—200 students in a history course, for example—your sample must include a large percentage of that group.

Decide on a medium. Will you ask the questions face-to-face? over the phone? on a website such as *SurveyMonkey*? by mail? by email? Face-to-face questions work best for simple surveys or for gathering impersonal information. You're more likely to get responses to more personal questions with printed or online questionnaires, which should be neat and easy to read. Phone interviews may require well-thought-out scripts that anticipate possible answers and make it easy to record these answers.

Design good questions. The way you ask questions will determine the usefulness of the answers you get, so take care to write questions that are clear and unambiguous. Here are some typical question types:

- *Multiple-choice*

  What is your current age?

  ____ 15–20 ____ 21–25 ____ 26–30 ____ 31–35 ____ Other

- *Rating scale*

  How would you rate the service at the campus bookstore?

  ____ Excellent ____ Good ____ Fair ____ Poor

- *Agreement scale*

  How much do you agree with the following statements?

	Strongly Agree	Agree	Disagree	Strongly Disagree
The bookstore has sufficient numbers of textbooks available.	❒	❒	❒	❒

	Strongly Agree	Agree	Disagree	Strongly Disagree
Staff at the bookstore are knowledgeable.	❒	❒	❒	❒
Staff at the bookstore are courteous.	❒	❒	❒	❒

- *Open-ended*

  How often do you visit the campus bookstore?

  How can the campus bookstore improve its service?

Include all potential alternatives when phrasing questions to avoid biasing the answers. And make sure each question addresses only one issue—for example, "Bookstore staff are knowledgeable and courteous" could lead to the response "knowledgeable, agree; courteous, disagree."

When arranging questions, place easier ones at the beginning and harder ones near the end (but if the questions seem to fall into a different natural order, follow it). Make sure each question asks for information you will need—if a question isn't absolutely necessary, omit it.

Include an introduction. Start by stating your survey's purpose and how the results will be used. It's also a good idea to offer an estimate of the time needed to complete the questions. Remind participants of your deadline.

Test the survey or questionnaire. Make sure your questions elicit the kinds of answers you need by asking three or four people who are part of your target population to answer them. They can help you find unclear instructions, questions that aren't clear or that lack sufficient alternatives, or other problems that you should correct to make sure your results are useful. But if you change the questionnaire as a result of their responses, don't include their answers in your total.

265–72
280–82

IF YOU NEED MORE HELP

See EVALUATING SOURCES for help determining their usefulness. See also Chapter 24 for help TAKING NOTES on your sources.

Evaluating Sources 22

Searching the *Health Source* database for information on the incidence of meningitis among college students, you find seventeen articles. A *Google* search on the same topic produces over 600,000 hits. How do you decide which sources to read? This chapter presents advice on evaluating sources—first to determine whether a source might be useful for your purposes and is worth looking at more closely and then to read with a critical eye the ones you choose.

Considering Whether a Source Might Be Useful

Think about your purpose. Are you trying to persuade readers to believe or do something? to inform them about something? If the former, it will be especially important to find sources representing various positions; if the latter, you may need sources that are more factual or informative. Reconsider your audience. What kinds of sources will they find persuasive? If you're writing for readers in a particular field, what counts as evidence in that field? Following are some questions that can help you judge whether a possible source you've found deserves your time and attention:

- ***Is it reliable?*** Is it SCHOLARLY? peer-reviewed? published in a reputable journal or magazine, or by a reputable publisher? Did you find it in a library database? on the web? Evaluating web-based texts may require more work than using results from library databases. But whatever kind of search you do, skim the results quickly to evaluate their reliability. 243–46
- ***Is it relevant?*** How does the source relate to your purpose? What will it add to your work? Look at the title and at any introductory material—a preface, abstract, or introduction—to see what the source covers.

- *What are the author's credentials?* How is the author qualified to write on the subject? Are they associated with a particular position on the issue? See whether the source mentions other works this author has written. In any case, you might do a web search to see what else you can learn about the author.
- *What is the stance?* Consider whether a source covers various perspectives or advocates one particular point of view. Does its title suggest a certain slant? If it's online, you might check to see whether it includes links to other sites and, if so, what their perspectives are. You'll want to consult sources with a variety of viewpoints.
- *Who is the publisher or sponsor?* If it's a book, what kind of company published it; if an article, what kind of periodical did it appear in? Books published by university presses and articles in scholarly journals are reviewed by experts before they are published. Books and articles written for the general public typically do not undergo rigorous review—and they may lack the kind of in-depth discussion that is useful for research.

  If the source is online, is the site maintained by an organization? an interest group? a government agency? an individual? Look for clues in the URL: *.edu* is used mostly by colleges and universities, *.gov* by government agencies, *.org* by nonprofit organizations, *.mil* by the military, and *.com* by commercial organizations. Evaluate the publisher's or sponsor's motives: to present information even-handedly? to promote a certain point of view, belief, or position? to sell something?
- *What is the level?* Can you understand the material? Texts written for a general audience might be easier to understand but not authoritative enough for academic work. Texts written for scholars will be more authoritative but may be hard to comprehend.
- *When was it published?* See when books and articles were published. Check to see when online sources were created and last updated. (If the site lists no date, see if links to other sites still work.) Recent does not necessarily mean better—some topics may require very current information whereas others may call for older sources.

- ***Does it include other useful information?*** Is there a bibliography that might lead you to other sources? How current are the sources it cites?
- ***Is it available?*** Is it a source you can get hold of? If it's a book and your school's library doesn't have it, can you get it through interlibrary loan?

Once you've decided that a source should be examined more closely, use the following questions to give it critical scrutiny.

Reading Sources with a Critical Eye

- ***What arguments does the author make?*** Does the author present a number of different positions, or do they argue for a particular position? Do you need to analyze the argument?
- ***How persuasive do you find the argument?*** What reasons and evidence does the author provide in support of any position(s)? Are there citations or links—and if so, are they credible? Is any evidence presented without citations? Do you find any of the author's assumptions questionable? How thoroughly does the author consider opposing arguments?
- ***What is the author's stance?*** Does the author strive for objectivity, or does the content or language reveal a particular bias? Does the author consider opposing views and treat them fairly?
- ***Do you recognize ideas you've run across in other sources?*** Does the source leave out any information or perspective that other sources include—or include any that other sources leave out?
- ***Does this source support or challenge your own position—or does it do both?*** Does it support your thesis? offer a different argument altogether? Does it represent a position you may need to acknowledge or refute? Don't reject a source just because it challenges your views; your sources should reflect a variety of views on your topic, showing that you've considered the subject thoroughly.
- ***What can you tell about the intended audience and purpose?*** Is the author writing to a general audience, to a subset of that audience, to specialists in a particular field? Are you a member of that audience? If not, does

that affect the way you interpret what you read? Is the main purpose to inform readers about a topic or to argue a certain point?

Comparing Sources

You may find that two or more of your sources present similar information or arguments. How do you decide which one to use? Compare them, using these questions as a guide:

- *Which source is most current?* Generally, a more recent source is better than an older one, because the newer source includes information or data that is more up to date—and may include (or refute) the information in the earlier source. Be aware, though, that in some fields, such as literary criticism, decades-old sources may still be important.
- *Which argument is more persuasive?* Examine the claims, reasons, and evidence presented in each source. Which source's argument is most logical? Which one has the best supporting reasons and evidence? Which one best acknowledges, accommodates, or refutes opposing arguments?
- *Which author or authors are most authoritative?* An expert in the subject is more authoritative than, say, a journalist writing on the subject. An article published in a scholarly journal is more authoritative than one published in a general-circulation magazine or website. The journalist's article may be easier to read and more interesting, but you're best off looking for the best information—not the best read.
- *Which source has the most appropriate stance?* In general, look for sources that strive for objectivity, rather than a particular bias. Also, be aware that we all tend to favor information that agrees with our views—and that may lead us to choose sources we agree with rather than sources that present all sides of an issue.
- *Which source best fits your needs?* All other things being equal, the best source to choose is the one that will give you the information you need, support the argument you're making, and perhaps provide useful quotations to add to your writing. The best source will show that you've done appropriate research and will enhance your own credibility as a thinker, reader, researcher, and writer.

A Note of Caution: False News

As you read to find sources or simply to find out what's happening in the world, you need to be on guard against false or "fake" news. False news—propaganda, hoaxes, misinformation, and lies—includes satires and counterfeit news stories. Satires, which range from Jonathan Swift's "A Modest Proposal" to *Onion* stories like "NFL to Curb Excessive Celebrations by Removing Areas of Players' Brains Responsible for Emotions" and episodes of *The Daily Show*, offer humorous exaggerations to expose and criticize people and governments. Counterfeit news stories, though, are malicious fabrications created usually for political ends. World War II Nazi propaganda and recent fraudulent stories such as "Pope Francis Endorses Donald Trump," a story that went viral on Facebook, are intended to mislead readers. Further complicating things, some politicians and other public figures have taken to calling news reports with which they disagree and even entire newspapers and networks "fake news"—even though the stories reported are verifiably true and the news outlets are considered trustworthy.

Although false news has been around at least since the invention of the printing press, the internet and social media have led to a huge increase in false news stories, especially during the 2016 presidential election, seriously challenging and muddying "real" news. Each false story can rapidly multiply over sites such as *Facebook* and *Twitter* and through email. As a reader and researcher, you need to be able to see whether or not a story is false. As a writer, you risk harming your credibility if you cite a false news story as evidence.

All news outlets have a bias, but some are more trustworthy than others. Here is some advice on how to determine whether a potential news source is unfairly biased or can be safely used as a source in your own research.

Investigate the source. Some news media outlets' political bias is well known, but to determine the bias of other sources, you may have to do some research: Read the "About" pages of online sources to see how the source characterizes itself, who owns or runs it, and how the site may be contacted. A site without such information (or with only a link to a personal email account) is probably not a good source. If a site includes a disclaimer to the effect of, "We are not responsible for the reliability or accuracy of this information," assume that it's a site to avoid.

- See what websites that evaluate news sources say about the bias of the source. These sites rate the bias of sources using a combination of research into the content of a news source and votes on the site's judgment by the website's readers. While these sites acknowledge that such judgments are by nature subjective, they present a rough consensus on the direction and extent of bias.
- See whether the site appears in lists of websites that post fake or satirical stories. FactCheck.org and Wikipedia are two sites that publish such lists.
- Check the URL of online sources. Counterfeit websites mimic real news sources but either alter the URL (Breaking-CNN.com imitates CNN.com) or add a .co or .ma to a legitimate URL (usatoday.com.co or Bloomberg.com.ma). While reputable sites usually end in .org, .net, or .com, these endings don't necessarily mean the site is trustworthy—so exercise caution, especially with .com addresses.
- Check to see if other news media are reporting the same story. If the story appears in only one source, it's likely false.
- Check the date of the story and dates within the story. Sometimes old stories resurface as "news." They aren't any truer now than they were then.
- Do a search for the story's author. Does the author appear to be an expert on your topic? Does the author write for or belong to other organizations or sites that are biased or suspect? What other articles has the author written? If there's no author listed, the site is probably not trustworthy.

Use Your Own Judgment. Sometimes you need to judge the trustworthiness of your sources yourself. Begin by assessing the story's plausibility: how likely is it to be true, given what you already know about the world? For example, the likelihood of a U.S. senator's father being involved in the assassination of President John F. Kennedy or that vast, secret conspiracies are running the world is pretty slim—though such stories are common on the internet and believed by some people.

A story that seems designed to generate a strong emotional response in readers, especially anger or fear, rather than appealing to logic or sound evidence, may be false. For example, stories circulating on the internet asserting that childhood immunizations cause autism—and even that the president enacted a temporary ban on vaccinations—prey on parents' fears for their children's safety. But they are completely false.

You should also consider the source in light of the rhetorical situation:

Purpose	Consider the headline: Is it inflammatory or outrageous? Read beyond the headline. Does the story match the headline? Is the piece meant to inform? persuade? entertain? confirm readers' current beliefs? Is the story written to manipulate your emotions by making you angry? sad? Something else?
Audience	For whom is the piece written? Would this piece be considered reliable by the extreme political partisans on one side or another? To what extent does the piece confirm or challenge the expectations of its readers? Does the story appear only on social media, or is it also on other publication sites?
Genre	Is the genre of the piece appropriate for its purpose and audience? If it's an argument, does it offer multiple perspectives on the topic? What evidence is offered—and can it be confirmed through links, references, or other sources? Do links or references actually exist and support the claims in the story? Does the information in the piece appear in other, reputable publications?
Stance	What is the author's attitude toward the subject: objective? serious? angry? outraged? astonished? amused? snide? disrespectful? Is the author's tone appropriate for the content of the story?

Media/Design	Does the website appear to be well designed or the work of an amateur? Does the headline or the story use ALL CAPS? Are photographs, charts, or tables included in the story? Do they seem real—again, do they appear in other, reputable sources—or doctored? Could a photograph, for example, have been Photoshopped?

Consider, too, the effect of your own biases. Does the story confirm what you already believe? Confirmation bias (our tendency to believe things that match what we already believe) makes us more likely to accept stories that confirm our beliefs and to discount information that doesn't. Be wary of assuming a story or article is trustworthy just because you agree with the author—you need to step back and make sure your own beliefs aren't clouding your judgment.

As a final check, you can go to sites whose purpose is investigating news for its veracity. Some to visit:

- FactCheck.org
- Snopes.com
- PolitiFact.com
- *The Washington Post* Fact Checker
- AllSides.com
- mediabiasfactcheck.com

280–92
293–97

IF YOU NEED MORE HELP

See QUOTING, PARAPHRASING, AND SUMMARIZING for help in taking notes on your sources and deciding how to use them in your writing. See also ACKNOWLEDGING SOURCES, AVOIDING PLAGIARISM for advice on giving credit to the sources you use.

Synthesizing Ideas 23

To analyze the works of a poet, you show how she uses similar images in three different poems to explore a recurring concept. To solve a crime, a detective studies several eyewitness accounts to figure out who did it. To trace the history of photojournalism, a professor compares the uses of photography during the Civil War and during the Vietnam War. These are all cases where someone *synthesizes*—brings together material from two or more sources in order to generate new information or to support a new perspective. When you do research, you need to go beyond what your sources say; you need to use what they say to inspire and support *what you want to say*. This chapter focuses on how to synthesize ideas you find in other sources as the basis for your own ideas.

Reading for Patterns and Connections

Your task as a writer is to find as much information as you can on your topic—and then to sift through all that you have found to determine and support what you yourself will write. In other words, you'll need to synthesize ideas and information from the sources you've consulted to figure out first what arguments *you* want to make and then to provide support for those arguments.

When you synthesize, you group similar bits of information together, looking for patterns or themes or trends and trying to identify the key points. In the brief report on the following page, writer Jude Stewart synthesizes several pieces of research on boredom. Stewart's report originally appeared in *The Atlantic*, which uses an abbreviated documentation style.

Boredom has, paradoxically, become quite interesting to academics lately. The International Interdisciplinary Boredom Conference gathered humanities scholars in Warsaw for the fifth time in April. In early May, its less scholarly forerunner, London's Boring Conference, celebrated seven years of delighting in tedium. At this event, people flock to talks about toast, double yellow lines, sneezing, and vending-machine sounds, among other snooze-inducing topics.

This question allows Stewart to bring together four ways boredom can be measured.

What, exactly, is everybody studying? One widely accepted psychological definition of boredom is "the aversive experience of wanting, but being unable, to engage in satisfying activity." [1] But how can you quantify a person's boredom level and compare it with someone else's? In 1986, psychologists introduced the Boredom Proneness Scale, [2] designed to measure an individual's overall propensity to feel bored (what's known as "trait boredom"). By contrast, the Multidimensional State Boredom Scale, [3] developed in 2008, measures a person's feelings of boredom in a given situation ("state boredom"). A German-led team has since identified five types of state boredom: indifferent, calibrating, searching, reactant, and apathetic (indifferent boredom—characterized by low arousal—was the mellowest, least unpleasant kind; reactant—high arousal—was the most aggressive and unpleasant). [4] Boredom may be miserable, but let no one call it simple.

Stewart synthesizes seven different studies under one category, "behavior issues."

One study builds on a previous study.

Boredom has been linked to behavior issues, including bad driving, [5] mindless snacking, [6] binge-drinking, [7] risky sex, [8] and problem gambling. [9] In fact, many of us would take pain over boredom. One team of psychologists discovered that two-thirds of men and a quarter of women would rather self-administer electric shocks than sit alone with their thoughts for 15 minutes. [10] Probing this phenomenon, another team asked volunteers to watch boring, sad, or neutral films, during which they could self-administer electric shocks. The bored volunteers shocked themselves more and harder than the sad or neutral ones did. [11]

Again, Stewart creates a category that includes two different studies.

Stewart shows how one study relates to an earlier one's findings.

But boredom isn't all bad. By encouraging contemplation and daydreaming, it can spur creativity. An early, much-cited study gave participants abundant time to complete problem-solving and word-association exercises. Once all the obvious answers were exhausted, participants gave more and more inventive answers to fend off boredom. [12] A British study took these findings one step further, asking subjects to complete a creative challenge (coming up with a list of alternative uses for a household item). One group of subjects did a boring activity first, while the others went straight to the creative task. Those whose boredom pumps had been primed were more prolific. [13]

In our always-connected world, boredom may be an elusive state, 5
but it is a fertile one. Watch paint dry or water boil, or at least put away your smartphone for a while. You might unlock your next big idea.

Conclusion brings together all the research, creating a synthesis of the findings of all 13 sources.

The Studies

[1] Eastwood et al., "The Unengaged Mind" (*Perspectives on Psychological Science*, Sept. 2012)

[2] Farmer and Sundberg, "Boredom Proneness" (*Journal of Personality Assessment*, Spring 1986)

[3] Fahlman et al., "Development and Validation of the Multidimensional State Boredom Scale" (*Assessment*, Feb. 2013)

[4] Goetz et al., "Types of Boredom" (*Motivation and Emotion*, June 2014)

[5] Steinberger et al., "The Antecedents, Experience, and Coping Strategies of Driver Boredom in Young Adult Males" (*Journal of Safety Research*, Dec. 2016)

[6] Havermans et al., "Eating and Inflicting Pain Out of Boredom" (*Appetite*, Feb. 2015)

[7] Biolcati et al., " 'I Cannot Stand the Boredom' " (*Addictive Behaviors Reports*, June 2016)

[8] Miller et al., "Was Bob Seger Right?" (*Leisure Sciences*, Jan. 2014)

[9] Mercer and Eastwood, "Is Boredom Associated with Problem Gambling Behaviour?" (*International Gambling Studies*, April 2010)

[10] Wilson et al., "Just Think: The Challenges of the Disengaged Mind" (*Science*, July 2014)

[11] Nederkoorn et al., "Self-Inflicted Pain Out of Boredom" (*Psychiatry Research*, March 2016)

[12] Schubert, "Boredom as an Antagonist of Creativity" (*Journal of Creative Behavior*, Dec. 1977)

[13] Mann and Cadman, "Does Being Bored Make Us More Creative?" (*Creativity Research Journal*, May 2014)

—Jude Stewart, "Boredom Is Good for You: The Surprising Benefits of Stultification"

Here are some tips for reading to identify patterns and connections:

- Read all your sources with an open mind. Withhold judgment, even of sources that seem wrong-headed or implausible. Don't jump to conclusions.
- 288–89 Take notes and write a brief **SUMMARY** of each source to help you see relationships, patterns, and connections among your sources. Take notes on your own thoughts, too.
- Pay attention to your first reactions. You'll likely have many ideas to work with, but your first thoughts can often lead somewhere that you 213–16 will find interesting. Try **FREEWRITING**, **CLUSTERING**, or **LISTING** to see where they lead. How do these thoughts and ideas relate to your topic? 217–19 Where might they fit into your rough **OUTLINE**?
- Try to think creatively, and pay attention to thoughts that flicker at the edge of your consciousness, as they may well be productive.
- Be playful. Good ideas sometimes come when we let our guard down or take ideas to extremes just to see where they lead.

Ask yourself these questions about your sources:

- What sources make the strongest arguments? What makes them so strong?
- Do some arguments recur in several sources?
- Which arguments do you agree with? disagree with? Of those you disagree with, which ones seem strong enough that you need to acknowledge them in your text?
- Are there any disagreements among your sources?
- Are there any themes you see in more than one source?
- Are any data—facts, statistics, examples—or experts cited in more than one source?
- Do several of your sources use the same terms? Do they use the terms similarly, or do they use them in different ways?

- What have you learned about your topic? How have your sources affected your thinking on your topic? Do you need to adjust your thesis? If so, how?
- Have you discovered new questions you need to investigate?
- Keep in mind your rhetorical situation—have you found the information you need that will achieve your purpose, appeal to your audience, and suit your genre and medium?

What is likely to emerge from this questioning is a combination of big ideas, including new ways of understanding your topic and insights into recent scholarship about it, and smaller ones, such as how two sources agree with each other but not completely and how the information in one source supports or undercuts the argument of another. These ideas and insights will become the basis for your own ideas and for what *you* have to say about the topic.

Synthesizing Ideas Using Notes

You may find that identifying connections among your sources is easier if you examine them together rather than reading them one by one. For example, taking notes on note cards and then laying the cards out on a desk or table (or on the floor) lets you see passages that seem related. Doing the same with photocopies or printouts of your sources can help you identify similarities as well.

In doing research for an essay arguing that the sale of assault weapons should be banned, you might find several sources that address the scope of U.S. citizens' right to bear arms. On the next page are notes taken on three such sources: Joe Klein, a journalist writing in *Time.com*; Antonin Scalia, a former U.S. Supreme Court justice, quoted in an online news article; and Drew Westen, a professor of psychology writing in a blog sponsored by the *New York Times*. Though the writers hold very different views, juxtaposing these notes and highlighting certain passages show a common thread running through the sources. In this example, all three sources might be used to support the thesis that restrictions on the owning of weapons—but not an outright ban—are both constitutional and necessary.

Source 1

Limits of gun ownership

Although the U.S. Constitution includes the right to bear arms, that right is not absolute. "No American has the right to own a stealth bomber or a nuclear weapon. Armor-piercing bullets are forbidden. The question is where you draw a reasonable bright line."
—Klein, "How the Gun Won" — quote

Source 4

Limits of gun ownership

Supreme Court Justice Antonin M. Scalia has noted that when the Constitution was written and ratified, some weapons were barred. So limitations could be put on owning some weapons, as long as the limits are consistent with those in force in 1789.
—Scalia, quoted in Woods — paraphrase

Source 3

Limits of gun ownership

Westen's "message consulting" research has shown that Americans are ambivalent about guns but react very positively to a statement of principle that includes both the right to own guns and restrictions on their ownership, such as prohibiting large ammunition clips and requiring all gun purchasers to undergo background checks for criminal behavior or mental illness.
—Westen — paraphrase

Synthesizing Information to Support Your Own Ideas

If you're doing research to write a report, your own ideas will be communicated primarily through which information you decide to include from the sources you cite and how you organize that information. If you're writing a textual analysis, your synthesis may focus on the themes, techniques, or other patterns you find. If you're writing a research-based argument, on the other hand, your synthesis of sources must support the position you take in that argument. No matter what your genre, the challenge is to synthesize information from your research to develop ideas about your topic and then to support those ideas.

Entering the Conversation

As you read and think about your topic, you will come to an understanding of the concepts, interpretations, and controversies relating to your topic—and you'll become aware that there's a larger conversation going on. When you begin to find connections among your sources, you will begin to see your own place in that conversation, to discover your own ideas and your own stance on your topic. This is the exciting part of a research project, for when you write out your own ideas on the topic, you will find yourself entering that conversation. Remember that your stance as an author needs to be clear: simply stringing together the words and ideas of others isn't enough. You need to show readers *how* your source materials relate to one another and to your thesis.

IF YOU NEED MORE HELP

See Chapter 24, QUOTING, PARAPHRASING, AND SUMMARIZING, for help in integrating source materials into your own text. See also Chapter 25 on ACKNOWLEDGING SOURCES, AVOIDING PLAGIARISM for advice on giving credit to the sources you cite.

280–92
293–97

24 Quoting, Paraphrasing, and Summarizing

In an oral presentation about the rhetoric of Abraham Lincoln, you quote a memorable line from the Gettysburg Address. For an essay on the Tet Offensive in the Vietnam War, you paraphrase arguments made by several commentators and summarize some key debates about that war. When you work with the ideas and words of others, you need to clearly distinguish those ideas and words from your own and give credit to their authors. This chapter will help you with the specifics of quoting, paraphrasing, and summarizing source materials that you use in your writing.

Taking Notes

When you find material you think will be useful, take careful notes. How do you determine how much to record? You need to write down enough information so that when you refer to it later, you will be reminded of its main points and have a precise record of where it comes from.

- *Use a computer file, note cards, or a notebook,* labeling each entry with the information that will allow you to keep track of where it comes from—author, title, and the pages or the URL (or DOI [digital object identifier]). You needn't write down full bibliographic information (you can abbreviate the author's name and title) since you'll include that information in your **WORKING BIBLIOGRAPHY**. 239–41
- *Take notes in your own words, and use your own sentence patterns.* If you make a note that is a detailed **PARAPHRASE**, label it as such so that you'll know to provide appropriate **DOCUMENTATION** if you use it. 285–88 298–301

- ***If you find wording that you'd like to quote,*** be sure to enclose it in quotation marks to distinguish your source's words from your own. Double-check your notes to be sure any quoted material is accurately quoted—and that you haven't accidentally **PLAGIARIZED** your sources.

293–97

- ***Label each note with a number to identify the source and a subject heading*** to relate the note to a subject, supporting point, or other element in your essay. Doing this will help you to sort your notes easily and match them up with your rough outline. Restrict each note to a single subject.

Here are a few examples of one writer's notes on a source discussing synthetic dyes, bladder cancer, and the use of animals to determine what causes cancers. Each note includes a subject heading and brief source information and identifies whether the source is quoted or paraphrased.

Source 3

Synthetic dyes

The first synthetic dye was mauve, invented in 1854 and derived from coal. Like other coal-derived dyes, it contained aromatic amines.

Steingraber, "Pesticides," 976 — paraphrase

Source 3

Synthetic dyes & cancer

Bladder cancer was common among textile workers who used dyes. Steingraber: "By the beginning of the twentieth century, bladder cancer rates among this group of workers had skyrocketed."

Steingraber, "Pesticides," 976 — paraphrase and quote

Source 3

Synthetic dyes & cancer

In 1938, Wilhelm Hueper exposed dogs to aromatic amines and showed that the chemical caused bladder cancer.

Steingraber, "Pesticides," 976 — paraphrase

Deciding Whether to Quote, Paraphrase, or Summarize

222–24
282–85
285–88
288–89

When it comes time to **DRAFT**, you'll need to decide *how* to use any source you want to include—in other words, whether to quote, paraphrase, or summarize it. You might follow this rule of thumb: **QUOTE** texts when the wording is worth repeating or makes a point so well that no rewording will do it justice, when you want to cite the exact words of a known authority on your topic, when an authority's opinions challenge or disagree with those of others, or when the source is one you want to emphasize. **PARAPHRASE** sources that are not worth quoting but contain details you need to include. **SUMMARIZE** longer passages whose main points are important but whose details are not.

Quoting

289–92

Quoting a source is a way of weaving someone else's exact words into your text. You need to reproduce the source exactly, though you can modify it to omit unnecessary details (with ellipses) or to make it fit smoothly into your text (with brackets). You also need to distinguish quoted material from your own by enclosing short quotations in quotation marks, setting off longer quotes as a block, and using appropriate **SIGNAL PHRASES**.

Incorporate short quotations into your text, enclosed in quotation marks. If you are following MLA style, short quotations are defined as four typed lines or fewer; if using APA style, as below, short means fewer than forty words.

> Gerald Graff (2003) has argued that colleges make the intellectual life seem more opaque than it needs to be, leaving many students with "the misconception that the life of the mind is a secret society for which only an elite few qualify" (p. 1).

If you are quoting three lines or fewer of poetry, run them in with your text, enclosed in quotation marks. Separate lines with slashes, leaving one space on each side of the slashes.

> Emma Lazarus almost speaks for the Statue of Liberty with the words inscribed on its pedestal: "Give me your tired, your poor, / Your huddled masses yearning to breathe free, / The wretched refuse of your teeming shore" (58).

Set off long quotations block style. If you are using MLA style, set off quotations of five or more typed lines by indenting the quote one-half inch from the left margin. If you are using APA style, indent quotations of forty or more words one-half inch (or five to seven spaces) from the left margin. In either case, do not use quotation marks, and put any parenthetical documentation *after* any end punctuation.

> Nonprofit organizations such as Oxfam and Habitat for Humanity rely on visual representations of the poor. What better way to get our attention, asks rhetorician Diana George:
>
> > In a culture saturated by the image, how else do we convince Americans that—despite the prosperity they see all around them—there is real need out there? The solution for most nonprofits has been to show the despair. To do that they must represent poverty as something that can be seen and easily recognized: fallen down shacks and trashed out public housing, broken windows, dilapidated porches, barefoot kids with stringy hair, emaciated old women and men staring out at the camera with empty eyes. (210)

If you are quoting four or more lines of poetry, they need to be set off block style in the same way.

Indicate any omissions with ellipses. You may sometimes delete words from a quotation that are unnecessary for your point. Insert three ellipsis marks (leaving a space before the first and after the last one) to indicate the deletion. If you omit a sentence or more in the middle of a quotation, put a period before the three ellipsis dots. Be careful not to distort the source's meaning, however.

> Faigley points out that Gore's "Information Superhighway" metaphor "associated the economic prosperity of the 1950s and . . . 1960s facilitated by new highways with the potential for vast . . . commerce to be conducted over the Internet" (253).

> According to Welch, "Television is more acoustic than visual. . . . One can turn one's gaze away from the television, but one cannot turn one's ears from it without leaving the area where the monitor leaks its aural signals into every corner" (102).

Indicate additions or changes with brackets. Sometimes you'll need to change or add words in a quotation—to make the quotation fit grammatically within your sentence, for example, or to add a comment. In the following example, the writer changes the passage "one of our goals" to clarify the meaning of "our."

> Writing about the dwindling attention among some composition scholars to the actual teaching of writing, Susan Miller notes that "few discussions of writing pedagogy take it for granted that one of [writing teachers'] goals is to teach how to write" (480).

Here's an example of brackets used to add explanatory words to a quotation:

> Barbosa observes that Buarque's lyrics have long included "many a metaphor of *saudades* [yearning] so characteristic of *fado* music" (207).

Use punctuation correctly with quotations. When you incorporate a quotation into your text, you have to think about the end punctuation in the quoted material and also about any punctuation you need to add when you insert the quote into your own sentence.

Periods and commas. Put periods or commas *inside* closing quotation marks, except when you have parenthetical documentation at the end, in which case you put the period or comma after the parentheses.

> "Country music," Tichi says, "is a crucial and vital part of the American identity" (23).

After long quotations set off block style with no quotation marks, however, the period goes *before* the documentation, as in the example on page 283.

Question marks and exclamation points. These go *inside* closing quotation marks if they are part of the quoted material but *outside* when they are not. If there's parenthetical documentation at the end of the quotation, any punctuation that's part of your sentence comes after it.

> Speaking at a Fourth of July celebration in 1852, Frederick Douglass asked, "What have I, or those I represent, to do with your national independence?" (35).

> Who can argue with W. Charisse Goodman's observation that media images persuade women that "thinness equals happiness and fulfillment" (53)?

Colons and semicolons. These always go *outside* closing quotation marks.

> It's hard to argue with W. Charisse Goodman's observation that media images persuade women that "thinness equals happiness and fulfillment"; nevertheless, American women today are more overweight than ever (53).

Paraphrasing

When you paraphrase, you restate information from a source in your own words, using your own sentence structures. Paraphrase when the source material is important but the original wording is not. Because it includes all the main points of the source, a paraphrase is usually about the same length as the original.

Here is a paragraph about synthetic dyes and cancer, followed by two paraphrases of it that demonstrate some of the challenges of paraphrasing:

ORIGINAL SOURCE

In 1938, in a series of now-classic experiments, exposure to synthetic dyes derived from coal and belonging to a class of chemicals called aromatic amines was shown to cause bladder cancer in dogs. These results helped explain why bladder cancers had become so prevalent among dyestuffs workers. With the invention of mauve in 1854, synthetic dyes began replacing natural plant-based dyes in the coloring of cloth and leather. By the beginning of the twentieth century, bladder cancer rates among this group of workers had skyrocketed, and the dog experiments helped unravel this mystery. The International Labor Organization did not wait for the results of these animal tests, however, and in 1921 declared certain aromatic amines to be human carcinogens. Decades later, these dogs provided a lead in understanding why tire-industry workers, as well as machinists and metalworkers, also began falling victim to bladder cancer: aromatic amines had been added to rubbers and cutting oils to serve as accelerants and antirust agents.

—Sandra Steingraber, "Pesticides, Animals, and Humans"

The following paraphrase borrows too much of the language of the original or changes it only slightly, as the highlighted words and phrases show:

UNACCEPTABLE PARAPHRASE: WORDING TOO CLOSE

Now-classic experiments in 1938 showed that when dogs were exposed to aromatic amines, chemicals used in synthetic dyes derived from coal, they developed bladder cancer. Similar cancers were prevalent among dyestuffs workers, and these experiments helped to explain why. Mauve, a synthetic dye, was invented in 1854, after which cloth and leather manufacturers replaced most of the natural plant-based dyes with synthetic dyes. By the early twentieth century, this group of workers had skyrocketing rates of bladder cancer, a mystery the dog experiments helped to unravel. As early as 1921, though, before the test results proved the connection, the International Labor Organization had labeled certain aromatic amines carcinogenic. Even so, decades later many metalworkers, machinists, and tire-industry workers began developing bladder cancer. The animal tests helped researchers understand that rubbers and cutting oils contained aromatic amines as accelerants and antirust agents (Steingraber 976).

The next paraphrase uses original language but follows the sentence structure of Steingraber's text too closely:

UNACCEPTABLE PARAPHRASE: SENTENCE STRUCTURE TOO CLOSE

In 1938, several pathbreaking experiments showed that being exposed to synthetic dyes that are made from coal and belong to a type of chemicals called aromatic amines caused dogs to get bladder cancer. These results helped researchers identify why cancers of the bladder had become so common among textile workers who worked with dyes. With the development of mauve in 1854, synthetic dyes began to be used instead of dyes based on plants in the dyeing of leather and cloth. By the end of the nineteenth century, rates of bladder cancer among these workers had increased dramatically, and the experiments using dogs helped clear up this oddity. The International Labor Organization anticipated the results of these tests on animals, though, and in 1921 labeled some aromatic amines carcinogenic. Years later these experiments with dogs helped researchers explain why workers in the tire industry, as well as metalworkers and machinists, also started dying of bladder cancer: aromatic amines had been put into rubbers and cutting oils as rust inhibitors and accelerants (Steingraber 976).

Patchwriting, a third form of unacceptable paraphrase, combines the other two. Composition researcher Rebecca Moore Howard defines it as "copying from a source text and then deleting some words, altering grammatical structures, or plugging in one-for-one synonym-substitutes." Here is a patchwrite of the first two sentences of the original source: (The source's exact words are shaded in yellow; paraphrases are in blue.)

PATCHWRITE

Scientists have known for a long time that chemicals in the environment can cause cancer. For example, in 1938, in a series of important experiments, being exposed to synthetic dyes made out of coal and belonging to a kind of chemicals called aromatic amines was shown to cause dogs to develop bladder cancer. These experiments explain why this type of cancer had become so common among workers who handled dyes.

Here is an acceptable paraphrase of the entire passage:

ACCEPTABLE PARAPHRASE

Biologist Sandra Steingraber explains that pathbreaking experiments in 1938 demonstrated that dogs exposed to aromatic amines (chemicals used in coal-based synthetic dyes) developed cancers of the bladder that were similar to cancers common among dyers in the textile industry. After mauve, the first synthetic dye, was invented in 1854, leather and cloth manufacturers replaced most natural dyes made from plants with synthetic dyes, and by the early 1900s textile workers had very high rates of bladder cancer. The experiments with dogs proved the connection, but years before, in 1921, the International Labor Organization had labeled some aromatic amines carcinogenic. Even so, years later many metal-workers, machinists, and workers in the tire industry started to develop unusually high rates of bladder cancer. The experiments with dogs helped researchers understand that the cancers were caused by aromatic amines used in cutting oils to inhibit rust and in rubbers as accelerants (976).

Some guidelines for paraphrasing

- ***Use your own words and sentence structure.*** It is acceptable to use some words from the original, but as much as possible, the phrasing and sentence structures should be your own.
- 289–92 ***Introduce paraphrased text with*** **SIGNAL PHRASES**.
- ***Put in quotation marks any of the source's original phrasing that you use.***
- ***Indicate the source.*** Although the wording may be yours, the ideas and information come from another source; be sure to name the author and include documentation to avoid the possibility of **PLAGIARISM**. 293–97

Summarizing

A summary states the main ideas in a source concisely and in your own words. Unlike a paraphrase, a summary does *not* present all the details, and it is generally as brief as possible. Summaries may boil down an entire book or essay into a single sentence, or they may take a paragraph or more to present the main ideas. Here, for example, is a one-sentence summary of the Steingraber paragraph:

> Steingraber explains that experiments with dogs demonstrated that aromatic amines, chemicals used in synthetic dyes, cutting oils, and rubber, cause bladder cancer (976).

In the context of an essay, the summary might take this form:

> Medical researchers have long relied on experiments using animals to expand understanding of the causes of disease. For example, biologist and ecologist Sandra Steingraber notes that in the second half of the nineteenth century, the rate of bladder cancer soared among textile workers. According to Steingraber, experiments with dogs demonstrated that synthetic chemicals in dyes used to color the textiles caused the cancer (976).

Some guidelines for summarizing

- *Include only the main ideas; leave out the details.* A summary should include just enough information to give the reader the gist of the original. It is always much shorter than the original, sometimes even as brief as one sentence.
- *Use your own words.* If you quote phrasing from the original, enclose the phrase in quotation marks.
- *Indicate the source.* Although the wording may be yours, the ideas and information come from another source. Name the author, either in a signal phrase or parentheses, and include an appropriate in-text citation to avoid the possibility of **PLAGIARISM**. 296–97

Introducing Source Materials Using Signal Phrases

You need to introduce quotations, paraphrases, and summaries clearly, usually letting readers know who the author is—and, if need be, something about their credentials. Consider this sentence:

> Professor and textbook author Elaine Tyler May argues that many high school history books are too bland to interest young readers (531).

The beginning ("Professor and textbook author Elaine Tyler May argues") functions as a *signal phrase*, telling readers who is making the assertion and why she has the authority to speak on the topic—and making clear that everything between the signal phrase and the parenthetical citation comes from that source. Since the signal phrase names the author, the parenthetical citation includes only the page number; had the author not been identified in the signal phrase, she would have been named in the parentheses:

> Even some textbook authors believe that many high school history books are too bland to interest young readers (May 531).

MLA and APA have different conventions for constructing signal phrases. In MLA, the language you use in a signal phrase can be neutral—like X *says* or Y *thinks* or *according to* Z. Or it can suggest something about the stance—the source's or your own. The example above referring to the textbook author uses the verb *argues*, suggesting that what she says is open to dispute (or that the writer believes it is). How would it change your understanding if the signal verb were *observes* or *suggests*?

In addition to the names of sources' authors, signal phrases often give readers information about institutional affiliations and positions authors have, their academic or professional specialties, and any other information that lets readers judge the credibility of the sources. You should craft each signal phrase you use so as to highlight the credentials of the author. Here are some examples:

> A study done by Anthony M. Armocida, professor of psychology at Duke University, showed that . . .

The signal phrase identifies the source's author, his professional position, and his university affiliation, emphasizing his title.

> Science writer Isaac McDougal argues that . . .

This phrase acknowledges that the source's author may not have scholarly credentials but is a published writer; it's a useful construction if the source doesn't provide much information about the writer.

Writing in *Psychology Today*, Amanda Chao-Fitz notes that . . .

This is the sort of signal phrase you use if you have no information on the author; you establish credibility on the basis of the publication in which the source appears.

If you're writing using APA style, signal phrases are typically briefer, giving only the author's last name and the date of publication:

According to Benzinger (2010), . . .

Quartucci (2011) observed that . . .

SOME COMMON SIGNAL VERBS

acknowledges	claims	disagrees	observes
admits	comments	disputes	points out
advises	concludes	emphasizes	reasons
agrees	concurs	grants	rejects
argues	confirms	illustrates	reports
asserts	contends	implies	responds
believes	declares	insists	suggests
charges	denies	notes	thinks

Verb tenses. MLA and APA also have different conventions regarding the tenses of verbs in signal phrases. MLA requires present-tense verbs (*writes, asserts, notes*) in signal phrases to introduce a work you are quoting, paraphrasing, or summarizing.

In *Poor Richard's Almanack*, Benjamin Franklin notes, "He that cannot obey, cannot command" (739).

If, however, you are referring to the act of writing or saying something rather than simply quoting someone's words, you might not use the present tense. The writer of the following sentence focuses on the year in which the source was written—therefore, the verb is necessarily in the past tense:

> Back in 1941, Kenneth Burke wrote that "the ethical values of work are in its application of the competitive equipment to cooperative ends" (316).

If you are following APA style, use the past tense or present-perfect tense to introduce sources composed in the past.

> Dowdall, Crawford, and Wechsler (1998) observed that women attending women's colleges are less likely to engage in binge drinking than are women who attend coeducational colleges (p. 713).

APA requires the present tense, however, to discuss the results of an experiment or to explain conclusions that are generally agreed on.

> The findings of this study suggest that excessive drinking has serious consequences for college students and their institutions.
>
> The authors of numerous studies agree that smoking and drinking among adolescents are associated with lower academic achievement.

IF YOU NEED MORE HELP

293–97

See Chapter 25 for help ACKNOWLEDGING SOURCES and giving credit to the sources you use.

Acknowledging Sources, Avoiding Plagiarism 25

Whenever you do research-based writing, you find yourself entering a conversation—reading what many others have had to say about your topic, figuring out what you yourself think, and then putting what you think in writing—"putting in your oar," as the rhetorician Kenneth Burke once wrote. As a writer, you need to *acknowledge* any words and ideas that come from others—to give credit where credit is due, to recognize the various authorities and many perspectives you have considered, to show readers where they can find your sources, and to situate your own arguments in the ongoing conversation. Using other people's words and ideas without acknowledgment is *plagiarism,* a serious academic and ethical offense. This chapter will show you how to acknowledge the materials you use and avoid plagiarism.

Acknowledging Sources

When you insert in your text information that you've obtained from others, your reader needs to know where your source's words or ideas begin and end. Therefore, you should usually introduce a source by naming the author in a **SIGNAL PHRASE** and then provide brief documentation of the specific material from the source in a parenthetical reference following the material. (Sometimes you can put the author's name in the parenthetical reference as well.) You need only brief documentation of the source here, since your readers will find full bibliographic information about it in your list of works cited or references.

289–92

Sources that need acknowledgment. You almost always need to acknowledge any information that you get from a specific source. Material you should acknowledge includes the following:

- ***Direct quotations.*** Unless they are well known (see p. 296 for some examples), any quotations from another source must be enclosed in quotation marks, cited with brief bibliographic information in parentheses, and usually introduced with a signal phrase that tells who wrote or said it and provides necessary contextual information, as in the following sentence:

  In a dissenting opinion on the issue of racial preferences in college admissions, Supreme Court justice Ruth Bader Ginsburg argues, "The stain of generations of racial oppression is still visible in our society, and the determination to hasten its removal remains vital" (*Gratz v. Bollinger*).

- ***Arguable statements and information that may not be common knowledge.*** If you state something about which there is disagreement or for which arguments can be made, cite the source of your statement. If in doubt about whether you need to give the source of an assertion, provide it. As part of an essay on "fake news" programs, for example, you might make the following assertion:

  The satire of *The Daily Show* complements the conservative bias of FOX News, since both have abandoned the stance of objectivity maintained by mainstream news sources, contends Michael Hoyt, executive editor of the *Columbia Journalism Review* (43).

  Others might argue with the contention that the FOX News Channel offers biased reports of the news, so the source of this assertion needs to be acknowledged. In the same essay, you might present information that should be cited because it's not widely known, as in this example:

  According to a report by the Pew Research Center, 12 percent of Americans under thirty got information about the 2012 presidential campaign primarily from "fake news" and comedy shows like *The Daily Show* and *Saturday Night Live* (2).

- ***The opinions and assertions of others.*** When you present the ideas, opinions, and assertions of others, cite the source. You may have rewritten the concept in your own words, but the ideas were generated by someone else and must be acknowledged, as they are here:

  > David Boonin, writing in the *Journal of Social Philosophy,* asserts that, logically, laws banning marriage between people of different races are not discriminatory since everyone of each race is affected equally by them. Laws banning same-sex unions are discriminatory, however, since they apply only to people with a certain sexual orientation (256).

- ***Any information that you didn't generate yourself.*** If you did not do the research or compile the data yourself, cite your source. This goes for interviews, statistics, graphs, charts, visuals, photographs—anything you use that you did not create. If you create a chart using data from another source, you need to cite that source.
- ***Collaboration with and help from others.*** In many of your courses and in work situations, you'll be called on to work with others. You may get help with your writing at your school's writing center or from fellow students in your writing courses. Acknowledging such collaboration or assistance, in a brief informational note, is a way of giving credit—and saying thank you. See guidelines for writing notes in the MLA and APA sections of this book.

Sources that don't need acknowledgment. Widely available information and common knowledge do not require acknowledgment. What constitutes common knowledge may not be clear, however. When in doubt, provide a citation, or ask your instructor whether the information needs to be cited. You generally do not need to cite the following:

- ***Information that most readers are likely to know.*** You don't need to acknowledge information that is widely known or commonly accepted as fact. For example, in a literary analysis, you wouldn't cite a source saying that Harriet Beecher Stowe wrote *Uncle Tom's Cabin*; you can assume your readers already know that. On the other hand, you should cite the source from which you got the information that the book was first published in installments in a magazine and then, with revisions, in book form, because that information isn't common knowledge. As you do research in areas you're not familiar with, be aware that what constitutes common knowledge isn't always clear; the history of the novel's publication would be known to Stowe scholars and would likely need no acknowledgment in an essay written for them. In this case, too, if you aren't sure whether to acknowledge information, do so.

- *Information and documents that are widely available.* If a piece of information appears in several sources or reference works or if a document has been published widely, you needn't cite a source for it. For example, the date when astronauts Neil Armstrong and Buzz Aldrin landed a spacecraft on the moon can be found in any number of reference works. Similarly, the Declaration of Independence and the Gettysburg Address are reprinted in thousands of sources, so the ones where you found them need no citation.
- *Well-known quotations.* These include such famous quotations as Lady Macbeth's "Out, damned spot!" and John F. Kennedy's "Ask not what your country can do for you; ask what you can do for your country." Be sure, however, that the quotation is correct. Winston Churchill is said to have told a class of schoolchildren, "Never, ever, ever, ever, ever, ever, ever give up. Never give up. Never give up. Never give up." His actual words, however, are much different and begin "Never give in."
- *Material that you created or gathered yourself.* You need not cite photographs that you took, graphs that you composed based on your own findings, or data from an experiment or survey that you conducted—though you should make sure readers know that the work is yours.

A good rule of thumb: *when in doubt, cite your source.* You're unlikely to be criticized for citing too much—but you may invite charges of plagiarism by citing too little.

Avoiding Plagiarism

When you use the words or ideas of others, you need to acknowledge who and where the material came from; if you don't credit those sources, you are guilty of plagiarism. Plagiarism is often committed unintentionally—as when a writer paraphrases someone else's ideas in language that is too close to the original. It is essential, therefore, to know what constitutes plagiarism: (1) using another writer's words or ideas without acknowledging the source, (2) using another writer's exact words without quotation marks, and (3) paraphrasing or summarizing someone else's ideas using language or sentence structures that are too close to theirs.

To avoid plagiarizing, take careful **NOTES** as you do your research, clearly labeling as quotations any words you quote directly and being careful to use your own phrasing and sentence structures in paraphrases and summaries. Be sure you know what source material you must **DOCUMENT**, and give credit to your sources, both in the text and in a list of references or works cited.

280–82

298–301

Be aware that it's easy to plagiarize inadvertently when you're working with online sources, such as full-text articles, that you've downloaded or cut and pasted into your notes. Keep careful track of these materials, since saving copies of your sources is so easy. Later, be sure to check your draft against the original sources to make sure your quotations are accurately worded—and take care, too, to include quotation marks and document the source correctly. Copying online material right into a document you are writing and forgetting to put quotation marks around it or to document it (or both) is all too easy to do. You must acknowledge information you find on the web just as you must acknowledge all other source materials.

And you must recognize that plagiarism has consequences. Scholars' work will be discredited if it too closely resembles another's. Journalists found to have plagiarized lose their jobs, and students routinely fail courses or are dismissed from their school when they are caught cheating—all too often by submitting as their own essays that they have purchased from online "research" sites. If you're having trouble completing an assignment, seek assistance. Talk with your instructor, or if your school has a writing center, go there for advice on all aspects of your writing, including acknowledging sources and avoiding plagiarism.

26 Documentation

In everyday life, we are generally aware of our sources: "I read it on Megan McArdle's blog." "Amber told me it's your birthday." "If you don't believe me, ask Mom." Saying how we know what we know and where we got our information is part of establishing our credibility and persuading others to take what we say seriously.

The goal of a research project is to study a topic, combining what we learn from sources with our own thinking and then composing a written text. When we write up the results of a research project, we cite the sources we use, usually by quoting, paraphrasing, or summarizing, and we acknowledge those sources, telling readers where the ideas came from. The information we give about sources is called documentation, and we provide it not only to establish our credibility as researchers and writers but also so that our readers, if they wish to, can find the sources themselves.

Understanding Documentation Styles

The Norton Field Guide covers the documentation styles of the Modern Language Association (MLA) and the American Psychological Association (APA). MLA style is used chiefly in the humanities; APA is used in the social sciences, sciences, education, and nursing. Both are two-part systems, consisting of (1) brief in-text parenthetical documentation for quotations, paraphrases, or summaries and (2) more-detailed documentation in a list of sources at the end of the text. MLA and APA require that the end-of-text documentation provide the following basic information about each source you cite:

- author, editor, or creator of the source
- title of source (and of publication or site where it appears)
- place of publication (for print sources; APA only)
- name of publisher
- date of publication
- retrieval information (for online sources)

MLA and APA are by no means the only documentation styles. Many other publishers and organizations have their own style, among them the University of Chicago Press and the Council of Science Editors. We focus on MLA and APA here because those are styles that college students are often required to use. On the following page are examples of how the two parts—the brief parenthetical documentation in your text and the more detailed information at the end—correspond in each of these systems.

The examples here and throughout this book are color-coded to help you see the crucial parts of each citation: tan for author and editor, yellow for title, and gray for publication information: place of publication, name of publisher, date of publication, page number(s), and so on.

As the examples of in-text documentation show, in either MLA or APA style you should name the author either in a signal phrase or in parentheses following the source information. But there are several differences between the two styles in the details of the documentation. In MLA, the author's full name is used in a signal phrase; in APA, only the last name is used. In APA, the abbreviation *p.* is used with the page number, which is provided only for a direct quotation; in MLA, a page number (if there is one) is always given, but with no abbreviation before it. Finally, in APA the date of publication always appears just after the author's name.

Comparing the MLA and APA styles of listing works cited or references also reveals some differences: MLA includes an author's first name while APA gives only initials; MLA puts the date near the end while APA places it right after the author's name; APA requires the place of publication while MLA usually does not; MLA capitalizes most of the words in a book's title and subtitle while APA capitalizes only the first words and proper nouns and proper adjectives in each.

MLA Style

IN-TEXT DOCUMENTATION

As Lester Faigley puts it, "The world has become a bazaar from which to shop for an individual 'lifestyle'" (12).

As one observer suggests, "The world has become a bazaar from which to shop for an individual 'lifestyle'" (Faigley 12).

WORKS-CITED DOCUMENTATION

Faigley, Lester. *Fragments of Rationality: Postmodernity and the Subject of Composition.* U of Pittsburgh P, 1992.

APA Style

IN-TEXT DOCUMENTATION

As Faigley (1992) suggested, "The world has become a bazaar from which to shop for an individual 'lifestyle'" (p. 12).

As one observer has noted, "The world has become a bazaar from which to shop for an individual 'lifestyle'" (Faigley, 1992, p. 12).

REFERENCE-LIST DOCUMENTATION

Faigley, L. (1992). *Fragments of rationality: Postmodernity and the subject of composition.* Pittsburgh, PA: University of Pittsburgh Press.

author title publication

Some of these differences are related to the nature of the academic fields in which the two styles are used. In humanities disciplines, the authorship of a text is emphasized, so both first and last names are included in MLA documentation. Scholarship in those fields may be several years old but still current, so the publication date doesn't appear in the in-text citation. In APA style, as in many documentation styles used in the sciences, education, and engineering, emphasis is placed on the date of publication because in these fields, more recent research is usually preferred over older studies. However, although the elements are arranged differently, both MLA and APA—and other documentation styles as well—require similar information about author, title, and publication.

part 7

Genres

When we make a shopping list, we automatically write each item we need in a single column. When we email a friend, we begin with a salutation: "Hi, Jordan." Whether we are writing a letter, a résumé, or a proposal, we know generally what it should contain and what it should look like because we are familiar with each of those genres. Genres are kinds of writing, and texts in any given genre share goals and features—a proposal, for instance, generally starts out by identifying a problem and then suggests a certain solution.

Genres

Abstracts 27

Abstracts are summaries written to give readers the gist of a report or presentation. Sometimes they are published in conference proceedings or databases. In courses in the *sciences*, *social sciences*, and *engineering*, you may be asked to create abstracts of your proposed projects and completed reports and essays. Abstracts are brief, typically 100–200 words, sometimes even shorter. Two common kinds are *informative abstracts* and *proposal abstracts*.

INFORMATIVE ABSTRACTS

Informative abstracts state in one paragraph the essence of a whole paper about a study or a research project. That one paragraph must mention all the main points or parts of the paper: a description of the study or project, its methods, the results, and the conclusions. Here is an example of the abstract accompanying a seven-page article that appeared in the *Journal of Clinical Psychology*:

> The relationship between boredom proneness and health-symptom reporting was examined. Undergraduate students ($N = 200$) completed the Boredom Proneness Scale and the Hopkins Symptom Checklist. A multiple analysis of covariance indicated that individuals with high boredom-proneness total scores reported significantly higher ratings on all five subscales of the Hopkins Symptom Checklist (Obsessive–Compulsive, Somatization, Anxiety, Interpersonal Sensitivity, and Depression). The results suggest that boredom proneness may be an

> important element to consider when assessing symptom reporting. Implications for determining the effects of boredom proneness on psychological- and physical-health symptoms, as well as the application in clinical settings, are discussed.
>
> —Jennifer Sommers and Stephen J. Vodanovich, "Boredom Proneness"

The first sentence states the nature of the study being reported. The next summarizes the method used to investigate the problem, and the following one gives the results: students who, according to specific tests, are more likely to be bored are also more likely to have certain medical or psychological symptoms. The last two sentences indicate that the paper discusses those results and examines the conclusion and its implications.

PROPOSAL ABSTRACTS

Proposal abstracts contain the same basic information as informative abstracts, but their purpose is very different. You prepare proposal abstracts to persuade someone to let you write on a topic, pursue a project, conduct an experiment, or present a paper at a scholarly conference. This kind of abstract is not written to introduce a longer piece but rather to stand alone, and often the abstract is written before the paper itself. Titles and other aspects of the proposal deliberately reflect the theme of the proposed work, and you may use the future tense, rather than the past, to describe work not yet completed. Here is a possible proposal for doing research on boredom:

> Undergraduate students will complete the Boredom Proneness Scale and the Hopkins Symptom Checklist. A multiple analysis of covariance will be performed to determine the relationship between boredom-proneness total scores and ratings on the five subscales of the Hopkins Symptom Checklist (Obsessive–Compulsive, Somatization, Anxiety, Interpersonal Sensitivity, and Depression).

Key Features / Abstracts

A summary of basic information. An informative abstract includes enough information to substitute for the report itself, and a proposal abstract gives an overview of the planned work.

Objective description. Abstracts present information on the contents of a report or a proposed study; they do not present arguments about or personal perspectives on those contents. The informative abstract on boredom proneness, for example, offers only a tentative conclusion: "The results *suggest* that boredom proneness *may* be an important element to consider."

Brevity. Although the length of abstracts may vary, journals and organizations often restrict them to 120–200 words—meaning you must carefully select and edit your words.

A BRIEF GUIDE TO WRITING ABSTRACTS

Considering the Rhetorical Situation

Purpose	Are you giving a brief but thorough overview of a completed study? only enough information to create interest? a proposal for a planned study or presentation?
Audience	For whom are you writing this abstract? What information about your project will your readers need?
Stance	Whatever your stance in the longer work, your abstract must be objective.
Media/Design	How will you set off your abstract from the rest of the text? If you are publishing it online, should it be on a separate page? What format do your readers expect?

Generating Ideas and Text

Write the paper first, the abstract last. You can then use the finished work as the guide for the abstract, which should follow the same basic structure. *Exception:* You may need to write a proposal abstract months before the work it describes will be complete.

Copy and paste key statements. If you've already written the work, highlight your thesis, objective, or purpose; basic information on your methods; your results; and your conclusion. Copy and paste those sentences into a new document to create a rough version of your abstract.

288–89

Pare down the rough abstract. SUMMARIZE the key ideas in the document, editing out any nonessential words and details. In your first sentence, introduce the overall scope of your study. Also include any other information that seems crucial to understanding your paper. Avoid phrases that add unnecessary words, such as "It is concluded that." In general, you probably won't want to use "I"; an abstract should cover ideas, not say what you think or will do.

Conform to any requirements. In general, an informative abstract should be at most 10 percent of the length of the entire work and no longer than the maximum length allowed. Proposal abstracts should conform to the requirements of the organization calling for the proposal.

Ways of Organizing an Abstract

Organizing abstracts is straightforward: in a single paragraph, briefly state the nature of the report or presentation, followed by an overview of the paper or the proposal.

[An informative abstract]

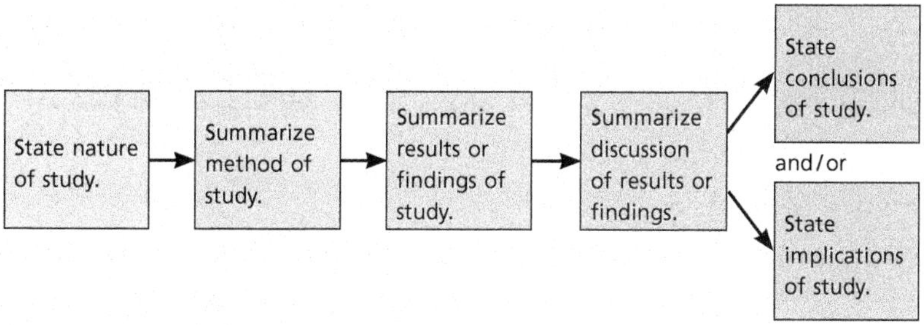

[A proposal abstract]

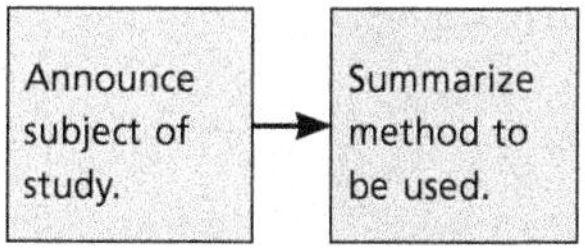

Taking Stock of Your Work

Take stock of what you've written by writing out answers to these questions:

- How did you decide on the type of abstract—informative or proposal—to write?
- How did you identify key statements in your finished work?
- What did you do well in this piece? What could still be improved? What would you do differently next time?

IF YOU NEED MORE HELP

See Chapter 18 for guidelines on DRAFTING, and Chapter 19 on EDITING AND PROOFREADING.

222–24
225–29

28 Annotated Bibliographies and Reviews of Scholarly Literature

When we do research, we may consult annotated bibliographies to evaluate potential sources and literature reviews when we need an overview of the important research ("literature") on a topic. In some courses, you may be asked to create annotated bibliographies or literature reviews to demonstrate that you have researched your topic thoroughly. This chapter offers advice on writing both.

ANNOTATED BIBLIOGRAPHIES

Annotated bibliographies describe, give publication information for, and sometimes evaluate each work on a list of sources. There are two kinds of annotations, *descriptive* and *evaluative*; both may be brief, consisting only of phrases, or more formal, consisting of sentences and paragraphs. Sometimes an annotated bibliography is introduced by a short statement explaining its scope.

Descriptive annotations simply summarize the contents of each work, without comment or evaluation. They may be very short, just long enough to capture the flavor of the work, like the examples in the following excerpt from a bibliography of books and articles on teen films, published in the *Journal of Popular Film and Television.*

MICHAEL BENTON, MARK DOLAN, AND REBECCA ZISCH

Teen Film$

In the introduction to his book *The Road to Romance and Ruin,* Jon Lewis points out that over half of the world's population is currently under the age of twenty. This rather startling fact should be enough to make most Hollywood producers drool when they think of the potential profits from a target movie audience. Attracting the largest demographic group is, after all, the quickest way to box-office success. In fact, almost from its beginning, the film industry has recognized the importance of the teenaged audience, with characters such as Andy Hardy and locales such as Ridgemont High and the 'hood.

Beyond the assumption that teen films are geared exclusively toward teenagers, however, film researchers should keep in mind that people of all ages have attended and still attend teen films. Popular films about adolescents are also expressions of larger cultural currents. Studying the films is important for understanding an era's common beliefs about its teenaged population within a broader pattern of general cultural preoccupations.

This selected bibliography is intended both to serve and to stimulate interest in the teen film genre. It provides a research tool for those who are studying teen films and their cultural implications. Unfortunately, however, in the process of compiling this list we quickly realized that it was impossible to be genuinely comprehensive or to satisfy every interest.

Doherty, Thomas. *Teenagers and Teenpics: The Juvenilization of American Movies in the 1950s*. Unwin Hyman, 1988. Historical discussion of the identification of teenagers as a targeted film market.

Foster, Harold M. "Film in the Classroom: Coping with 'Teenpics.'" *English Journal*, vol. 76, no. 3, Mar. 1987, pp. 86–88. Evaluation of the potential of using teen films such as *Sixteen Candles*, *The Karate Kid*, *Risky Business*, *The Flamingo Kid*, and *The Breakfast Club* to instruct adolescents on the difference between film as communication and film as exploitation.

Washington, Michael, and Marvin J. Berlowitz. "Blaxploitation Films and High School Youth: Swat Superfly." *Jump Cut*, vol. 9, Oct.–Dec. 1975, pp. 23–24. Marxist reaction to the trend of youth-oriented black action films. Article seeks to illuminate the negative influences the films have on high school students by pointing out the false ideas about education, morality, and the black family espoused by the heroes in the films.

These annotations are purely descriptive; the authors express none of their own opinions. They describe works as "historical" or "Marxist" but do not indicate whether they're "good." The bibliography entries are documented in MLA style.

Evaluative annotations offer opinions on a source as well as describe it. They are often helpful in assessing how useful a source will be for your own writing. The following evaluative annotations are from a bibliography by Kelly Green, a student at Arizona State University. Following her instructor's directions, she labeled each required part of her annotation—summary, degree of advocacy, credibility, and reliability.

KELLY GREEN

Researching Hunger and Poverty

Abramsky, Sasha. "The Other America, 2012: Confronting the Poverty Epidemic." *The Nation,* vol. 294, no. 20, 25 Apr. 2012, https://www.thenation.com/article/other-america-2012-confronting-poverty-epidemic/. Accessed 10 Oct. 2017.

The author presents the image of American poverty in 2012 with examples from various families living in poverty. The author explores the conditions that make up the new recession and suggests that people in America notice the scale of the issue and take action to solve it [Summary]. The author advocates poverty reform and shows bias toward the interests of low-income families. He acknowledges other perspectives on the issue respectfully [Degree of Advocacy]. Abramsky is a freelance journalist with experience in several magazines and newspapers. He has written several books on the topic of poverty [Credibility]. *The Nation* is one of the oldest-running magazines in the United States and contains opinions on politics and culture [Reliability].

Ambler, Marjane. "Sustaining Our Home, Determining Our Destiny." *Tribal College Journal,* vol. 13, no. 3, Spring 2002, http://www.tribalcollegejournal.org/sustaining-home-determining-destiny/. Accessed 14 Oct. 2017.

The author examines the causes of poverty on Native American reservations, the factors that lead to solutions to Native American poverty, and the ways in which tribal colleges have helped improve life on reservations [Summary]. The author is strongly biased toward Native American interests and advocates that effective solutions to poverty originate within the reservations, especially in tribal colleges and universities [Degree of Advocacy]. Marjane Ambler was an editor for the *Tribal College Journal* for 9 years and worked in national park service for nearly a decade [Credibility]. This article was published in 2002 in the *Tribal College Journal*, a national magazine published by the American Indian Higher Education Consortium [Reliability].

These annotations not only summarize the sources in detail but also evaluate their bias, or "degree of advocacy"; credibility; and reliability.

Key Features / Annotated Bibliographies

A statement of scope. Sometimes you need or are asked to provide a brief introductory statement to explain what you're covering. The authors of the bibliography on teen films introduce their bibliography with three paragraphs establishing a context for the bibliography and announcing their purpose for compiling it.

Complete bibliographic information. Provide all the information about each source using one documentation system (MLA, APA, or another one) so that you, your readers, or other researchers will be able to find the source easily. It's a good idea to include sources' URLs or PERMALINKS to make accessing online sources easier. 241

A concise description of the work. A good annotation describes each item as carefully and objectively as possible, giving accurate information and showing that you understand the source. These qualities will help to build authority—for you as a writer and for your annotations.

Relevant commentary. If you write an evaluative bibliography, your comments should be relevant to your purpose and audience. The best way to achieve relevance is to consider what questions a potential reader might have about each source: What are the main points of the source? What is its argument? How even-handed or biased is it? How current and reliable is it? Will the source be helpful for your project?

Consistent presentation. All annotations should follow a consistent pattern: if one is written in complete sentences, they should all be. Each annotation in the teen films bibliography, for example, begins with a phrase (not a complete sentence) characterizing the work.

A BRIEF GUIDE TO WRITING ANNOTATED BIBLIOGRAPHIES

Considering the Rhetorical Situation

Purpose	Will your bibliography need to demonstrate the depth or breadth of your research? Will your readers actually track down and use your sources? Do you need or want to convince readers that your sources are good?
Audience	For whom are you compiling this bibliography? What does your audience need to know about each source?
Stance	Are you presenting yourself as an objective describer or evaluator? Or are you expressing a particular point of view toward the sources you evaluate?
Media / Design	If you are publishing the bibliography electronically, will you provide links from each annotation to the source itself? Online or offline, should you distinguish the bibliographic information from the annotation by using a different font?

Generating Ideas and Text

Decide what sources to include. You may be tempted to include in a bibliography every source you find or look at. A better strategy is to include only those sources that you or your readers may find potentially useful in researching your topic. For an academic bibliography, you need to consider the qualities in the list below. Some of these qualities should not rule a source in or out; they simply raise issues you need to think about.

- *Appropriateness.* Is this source relevant to your topic? Is it a primary source or a secondary source? Is it aimed at an appropriate audience? General or specialized? Elementary, advanced, or somewhere in between?
- *Credibility.* Is the author reputable? Is the publication, publishing company, or sponsor of the site reputable? Do the ideas more or less agree with those in other sources you've read?
- *Balance.* Does the source present enough evidence for its assertions? Does it show any particular bias? Does it present countering arguments fairly?
- *Timeliness.* Is the source recent enough? Does it reflect current thinking or research about the subject?

If you need help FINDING SOURCES, see Chapter 21. 243–64

Compile a list of works to annotate. Give the sources themselves in whatever documentation style is required.

Determine what kind of bibliography you need to write. Will your bibliography be descriptive or evaluative? Will your annotations be in the form of phrases? complete sentences? paragraphs? The form will shape your reading and note taking. If you're writing a descriptive bibliography, your reading goal will be just to understand and capture the writer's message as clearly as possible. If you're writing an evaluative bibliography, you will also need to assess the source as you read in order to include your own opinions of it.

322–31

Read carefully. To write an annotation, you must understand the source's argument, but when you are writing an annotated bibliography as part of a **PROPOSAL**, you may have neither the time nor the need to read the whole text. Here's a way of quickly determining whether a source is likely to serve your needs:

- Check the publisher or sponsor (university press? scholarly journal? popular magazine? website sponsored by a reputable organization?).
- Read the preface (of a book), abstract (of a scholarly article), introduction (of an article in a nonscholarly magazine or a website).
- Skim the table of contents or the headings.
- Read the parts that relate specifically to your topic.

Research the writer, if necessary. If you are required to indicate the writer's credentials, you may need to do additional research. You may find information by typing the writer's name into a search engine or looking up the writer in *Contemporary Authors*. In any case, information about the writer should take up no more than one sentence in your annotation.

Summarize the work in a sentence or two. Describe it as objectively as possible: even if you are writing an evaluative annotation, you can evaluate the central point of a work better by stating it clearly first. *If you're writing a descriptive annotation, you're done.*

265–72

Establish criteria for evaluating sources. If you're **EVALUATING** sources for a project, you'll need to evaluate them in terms of their usefulness for your project, their stance, and their overall credibility.

Write a brief evaluation of the source. If you can generalize about the worth of the entire work, fine. You may find, however, that some parts are useful while others are not, and what you write should reflect that mix.

Be consistent—in content, sentence structure, and format.

- *Content.* Try to provide about the same amount of information for each entry. If you're evaluating, don't evaluate some sources and just describe others.

- *Sentence structure.* Use the same style throughout—complete sentences, brief phrases, or a mix.
- *Format.* Use one documentation style throughout; use a consistent **FONT** for each element in each entry—for example, italicize or underline all book titles. 368–69

Ways of Organizing an Annotated Bibliography

Depending on their purpose, annotated bibliographies may or may not include an introduction. Most annotated bibliographies cover a single topic and so are organized alphabetically by author's or editor's last name. When a work lacks a named author, alphabetize it by the first important word in its title. Consult the documentation system you're using for additional details about alphabetizing works appropriately.

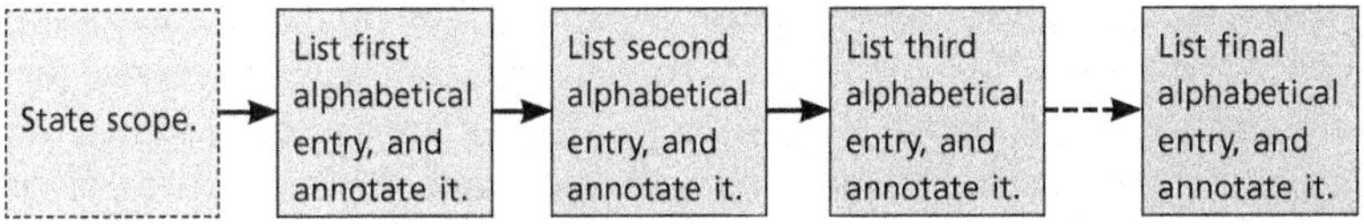

Sometimes an annotated bibliography needs to be organized into several subject areas (or genres, periods, or some other category); if so, the entries are listed alphabetically within each category. For example, a bibliography about terrorism breaks down into subjects such as "Global Terrorism" and "Weapons of Mass Destruction."

[Multicategory bibliography]

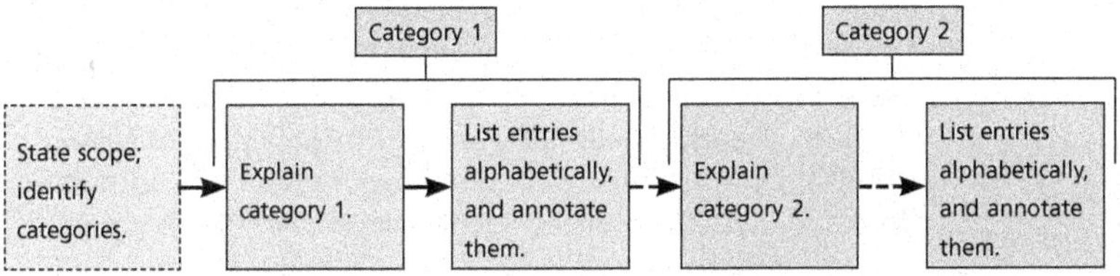

Taking Stock of Your Work

Take stock of what you've written by writing out answers to these questions:

- How did you go about researching the entries in this bibliography?
- How did you decide which sources to include and which to leave out?
- How did you go about drafting your bibliography?
- Did you cite your sources accurately?
- What did you do well? What could still be improved? What would you do differently next time?

REVIEWS OF SCHOLARLY LITERATURE

Reviews of scholarly literature describe and evaluate important research ("literature") available on a topic. In writing a literature review, your goal is to give an overview of the literature on a topic. You do that by discussing the literature that is most relevant to your topic and your purposes, providing clear and accurate summaries of appropriate source material, and describing relationships among facts and concepts. Here is a brief excerpt from a literature review that describes scholarship in zombie movies by a student at the University of Mary Washington.

CAMERON CARROLL

Zombie Film Scholarship: A Review of the Literature

Zombies are the shambling undead creatures that attack in hordes and strike terror into the hearts of moviegoers with their mindless aggression. Monsters on the big screen fascinate American audiences and scholars alike as representations of cultural fears and reflections of public perceptions, and they have done so since they first shuffled into theaters. The walking dead first haunted cinemas in 1932 with the release of *White Zombie* and have gone through cycles of popularity both at the box office and in scholarly debate. Without a doubt, the height of zombie scholarship began in the mid-2000s with only shallow mentions made in horror analyses before then. Only the English discipline gave the zombie credit as a subject worthy of study. As author and English professor Kyle Bishop wrote in 2010, "The zombie phenomenon has yet to be plumbed to its depths by the academic and literary markets."[1] Although significant zombie research has only surfaced in the 2000s, a valiant effort is currently being made to explore zombie symbolism and its historical and cultural context across non-traditional scholarly fields, such as anthropology, psychology, sociology, and philosophy.

. . .

Zombies, as creatures that waver between living and dead, necessarily bring forth questions on the nature of being and thus also fall into the realm of philosophy as seen in *Zombies, Vampires, and Philosophy: New Life for the Undead* published in 2010 and edited by Richard Greene and K. Silem Mohammed, professors of philosophy and English, respectively. Philosophers in the study of zombies seek to answer such questions as, is it better to be undead or dead? Richard Greene argues that since death is a state of non-existence and Undeath is at least a primal existence, the question comes down to the classic "to be, or not to be?" For him, Undeath is the only option for a state of being, since death is non-existence. Existence in any form is inherently better than utterly ceasing to be.[16] Greene's philosophy colleague, William Larkin, counters that zombies are driven to actions seen as evil and mindless, both states that humans do not usually choose. He cites how zombie films repeatedly depict survivors who ask their friends and family to kill them should it appear that they will turn into zombies, so desperate are they to avoid Undeath.[17] Simon Clark, a writer with a master's degree in Fine Arts, discusses morality in relation to zombies: if zombies are non-moral and whether or not they are the freest creatures because of their lack of morality. Clark writes that they become ultimately free in their modern incarnations from turn of the millennium cinema.[18] Zombies break through barriers that survivors put up to keep them confined and are so primal that they cannot be held accountable for their actions, making them truly liberated. A fictional creature encourages real discussions in philosophical debate, demonstrating yet another area that inspires scholars to reexamine their own field because of zombies.

. . .

The message to take away from zombie scholarship is that what it represents is evolutionary and infinitely debatable, but the victory for zombie studies is that zombies are being studied at all. After decades of being underrepresented in horror scholarship, zombies are finally getting their due as a cultural icon, complete with varying opinions and interpretations. Scholarly debate proves that the zombie is a valid resource for understanding American culture and worthy of the enthusiastic pursuit of interdepartmental scholarship. As shown within the scholarly works above, the debate over the meaning of the living dead is quite lively, indeed.

Notes

1. Kyle William Bishop, *American Zombie Gothic: The Rise and Fall (and Rise) of the Walking Dead in Popular Culture* (Jefferson, NC: McFarland, 2010), 7.

. . .

16. Richard Greene and K. Silem Mohammed, eds., *Zombies, Vampires, and Philosophy: New Life for the Undead* (Chicago: Open Court, 2010), 13.
17. Greene and Mohammed, *Zombies, Vampires, and Philosophy*, 20.
18. Greene and Mohammed, *Zombies, Vampires, and Philosophy*, 208.

Carroll begins by establishing a context for her discussion and then focuses on her topic, the scholarship of zombies in film. In her review, she discusses the history of zombie scholarship in general and then in psychology, social trends, fiction, and, in this excerpt, philosophy. A history major, she follows Chicago *style; in addition to the notes, she included a bibliography listing all her sources, including the two noted here.*

Key Features / Reviews of Scholarly Literature

Careful, thorough research. A review of scholarly literature demands that you research all the major literature on the topic—or at least the major literature available to you, given the time you have.

Accurate, objective summaries of the relevant literature. Readers expect a literature review to objectively summarize the main ideas or conclusions of the texts reviewed.

Critical evaluation for the literature. A literature review offers considered selection of the most important, relevant, and useful sources of information on its topic, so you must evaluate each source to decide whether it should be included and then to determine how it advances understanding of the topic.

SYNTHESIS of the scholarship. A literature review differs from an annotated bibliography in that the review identifies key concepts, similarities, and differences within the body of literature, showing how the sources relate to one another by method, study findings, themes, main ideas, or something else. 273–79

A clear focus. Because a literature review provides an overview of your topic's main issues and explains the main concepts underlying your research, it must be carefully organized and clearly focused on your specific topic.

Taking Stock of Your Work

Take stock of what you've written by writing out answers to these questions:

- How did you go about researching the sources you used?
- How did you decide which sources to include and which to leave out?
- What led you to group related sources together as you did?
- How did you go about synthesizing similar sources?
- What did you do well? What could still be improved? What would you do differently next time?

IF YOU NEED MORE HELP

See Chapter 18 for guidelines on DRAFTING, and Chapter 19 on EDITING AND PROOFREADING. See Chapter 36 if you are required to submit your bibliography in a writing PORTFOLIO.

222–24
225–30
397–408

29 Proposals

Proposals are part of our personal lives: lovers propose marriage, friends propose sharing dinner and a movie, you offer to pay half the cost of a car and insurance if your parents will pay the other half. They are also part of our academic and professional lives: student leaders lobby for lights on bike paths. Musicians, artists, writers, and educators apply for grants. Researchers in all fields of the humanities, social sciences, sciences, and technology seek funding for their projects. In business, contractors bid on building projects, and companies and freelancers solicit work from potential clients. These are all examples of proposals, ideas put forward for consideration that say, "Here is a solution to a problem" or "This is what ought to be done." For example, here is a proposal for reducing the costs of college textbooks, written by an accounting professor at the University of Texas who is chairman of the university's Co-op Bookstore and himself a textbook author.

MICHAEL GRANOF

Course Requirement: Extortion

By now, entering college students and their parents have been warned: textbooks are outrageously expensive. Few textbooks for semester-long courses retail for less than $120, and those for science and math courses typically approach $180. Contrast this with the $20 to $30 cost of most hardcover best sellers and other trade books.

Perhaps these students and their parents can take comfort in knowing that the federal government empathizes with them, and in an attempt to ease their pain Congress asked its Advisory Committee on Student Financial Assistance to suggest a cure for the problem.

Unfortunately, though, the committee has proposed a remedy that would only worsen the problem.

The committee's report, released in May, mainly proposes strengthening the market for used textbooks—by encouraging college bookstores to guarantee that they will buy back textbooks, establishing online book swaps among students, and urging faculty to avoid switching textbooks from one semester to the next. The fatal flaw in that proposal (and similar ones made by many state legislatures) is that used books are the cause of, not the cure for, high textbook prices.

Yet there is a way to lighten the load for students in their budgets, if not their backpacks. With small modifications to the institutional arrangements between universities, publishers, and students, textbook costs could be reduced—and these changes could be made without government intervention.

Today the used-book market is exceedingly well organized and 5
efficient. Campus bookstores buy back not only the books that will be used at their university the next semester but also those that will not. Those that are no longer on their lists of required books they resell to national wholesalers, which in turn sell them to college bookstores on campuses where they will be required. This means that even if a text is being adopted for the first time at a particular college, there is almost certain to be an ample supply of used copies.

As a result, publishers have the chance to sell a book to only one of the multiple students who eventually use it. Hence, publishers must cover their costs and make their profit in the first semester their books are sold—before used copies swamp the market. That's why the prices are so high.

As might be expected, publishers do what they can to undermine the used-book market, principally by coming out with new editions every three or four years. To be sure, in rapidly changing fields like biology and physics, the new editions may be academically defensible. But in areas like algebra and calculus, they are nothing more than a transparent attempt to ensure premature textbook obsolescence. Publishers also try to discourage students from buying used books by bundling the text with extra materials like workbooks and CDs that are not reusable and therefore cannot be passed from one student to another.

The system could be much improved if, first of all, colleges and publishers would acknowledge that textbooks are more akin to computer software than to trade books. A textbook's value, like that of a software program, is not in its physical form, but rather in its intellectual content. Therefore, just as software companies typically "site license" to colleges, so should textbook publishers.

Here's how it would work: A teacher would pick a textbook, and the college would pay a negotiated fee to the publisher based on the number of students enrolled in the class. If there were 50 students in the class, for example, the fee might be \$15 per student, or \$750 for the semester. If the text were used for ten semesters, the publisher would ultimately receive a total of \$150 (\$15 × 10) for each student enrolled in the course, or as much as \$7,500.

In other words, the publisher would have a stream of revenue for 10
as long as the text was in use. Presumably, the university would pass on this fee to the students, just as it does the cost of laboratory supplies and computer software. But the students would pay much less than the \$900 a semester they now typically pay for textbooks.

Once the university had paid the license fee, each student would have the option of using the text in electronic format or paying more to purchase a hard copy through the usual channels. The publisher could set the price of hard copies low enough to cover only its production and distribution costs plus a small profit, because it would be covering most of its costs and making most of its profit by way of the license fees. The hard copies could then be resold to other students or back to the bookstore, but that would be of little concern to the publisher.

A further benefit of this approach is that it would not affect the way courses are taught. The same cannot be said for other recommendations from the Congressional committee and from state legislatures, like placing teaching materials on electronic reserve, urging faculty to adopt cheaper "no frills" textbooks, and assigning mainly electronic textbooks. While each of these suggestions may have merit, they force faculty to weigh students' academic interests against their fiscal concerns and encourage them to rely less on new textbooks.

Neither colleges nor publishers are known for their cutting-edge innovations. But if they could slightly change the way they do business, they would make a substantial dent in the cost of higher education and provide a real benefit to students and their parents.

This proposal clearly defines the problem—some textbooks cost a lot—and explains why. It proposes a solution to the problem of high textbook prices and offers reasons why this solution will work better than others. Its tone is reasonable and measured, yet decisive.

Key Features / Proposals

A well-defined problem. Some problems are self-evident and relatively simple, and you would not need much persuasive power to make people act—as with the problem "This university discards too much paper." While some people might see nothing wrong with throwing paper away, most are likely to agree that recycling is a good thing. Other issues are controversial: some people see them as problems while others do not, such as this one: "Motorcycle riders who do not wear helmets risk serious injury and raise health-care costs for everyone." Some motorcyclists believe that wearing or not wearing a helmet should be a personal choice; you would have to present arguments to convince your readers that not wearing a helmet is indeed a problem needing a solution. Any written proposal must establish at the outset that there is a problem—and that it's serious enough to require a solution. For some topics, visual or audio evidence of the problem may be helpful.

A recommended solution. Once you have defined the problem, you need to describe the solution you are suggesting and to explain it in enough detail for readers to understand what you are proposing. Again, photographs, diagrams, or other visuals may help. Sometimes you might suggest several solutions, weigh their merits, and choose the best one.

A convincing argument for your proposed solution. You need to convince readers that your solution is feasible—and that it is the best way to solve the problem. Sometimes you'll want to explain in detail how your proposed solution would work. See, for example, how the textbook proposal details the way a licensing system would operate. Visuals may strengthen this part of your argument as well.

Granof's proposal for reducing textbook prices via licensing fees might benefit from a photograph like this one, which provides a comparison of other approaches to the problem, such as buying used books or renting them.

A response to anticipated questions. You may need to consider any questions readers may have about your proposal—and to show how its advantages outweigh any disadvantages. Had the textbook proposal been written for college budget officers, it would have needed to anticipate and answer questions about the costs of implementing the proposed solution.

A call to action. The goal of a proposal is to persuade readers to accept your proposed solution. This solution may include asking readers to take action.

An appropriate tone. Since you're trying to persuade readers to act, your tone is important—readers will always react better to a reasonable, respectful presentation than to anger or self-righteousness.

A BRIEF GUIDE TO WRITING PROPOSALS

Deciding on a Topic

Choose a problem that can be solved. Complex, large problems, such as poverty, hunger, or terrorism, usually require complex, large solutions. Most of the time, focusing on a smaller problem or a limited aspect of a large problem will yield a more manageable proposal. Rather than tackling the problem of world poverty, for example, think about the problem faced by people in your community who have lost jobs and need help until they find employment.

Considering the Rhetorical Situation

Purpose	Do you have a stake in a particular solution, or do you simply want to eliminate the problem by whatever solution might be adopted?
Audience	Do your readers share your view of the problem as a serious one needing a solution? Are they likely to be open to possible solutions or resistant? Do they have the authority to carry out a proposed solution?
Stance	How can you show your audience that your proposal is reasonable and should be taken seriously? How can you demonstrate your own authority and credibility?
Media/Design	How will you deliver your proposal? In print? Electronically? As a speech? Would visuals, or video or audio clips help support your proposal?

Generating Ideas and Text

Explore potential solutions to the problem. Many problems can be solved in more than one way, and you need to show your readers that you've examined several potential solutions. You may develop solutions

231

on your own; more often, though, you'll need to do **RESEARCH** to see how others have solved—or tried to solve—similar problems. Don't settle on a single solution too quickly—you'll need to compare the advantages and disadvantages of several solutions in order to argue convincingly for one.

Decide on the most desirable solution(s). One solution may be head and shoulders above others—but be open to rejecting all the possible solutions on your list and starting over if you need to, or to combining two or more potential solutions in order to come up with an acceptable fix.

Think about why your solution is the best one. Why did you choose your solution? Why will it work better than others? What has to be done to enact it? What will it cost? What makes you think it can be done? Writing out answers to these questions will help you argue for your solution: to show that you have carefully and objectively outlined a problem, analyzed the potential solutions, weighed their merits, and determined the reasons the solution you propose is the best.

Ways of Organizing a Proposal

You can organize a proposal in various ways, but always you will begin by establishing that there is a problem. You may then identify several possible solutions before recommending one of them or a combination of several. Sometimes, however, you might discuss only a single solution.

[Several possible solutions]

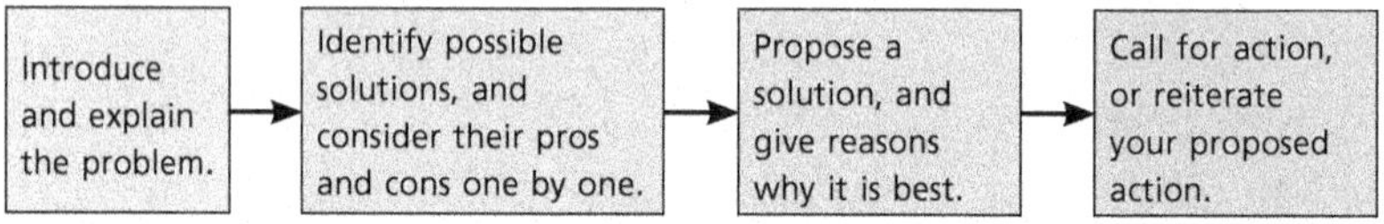

[A single solution]

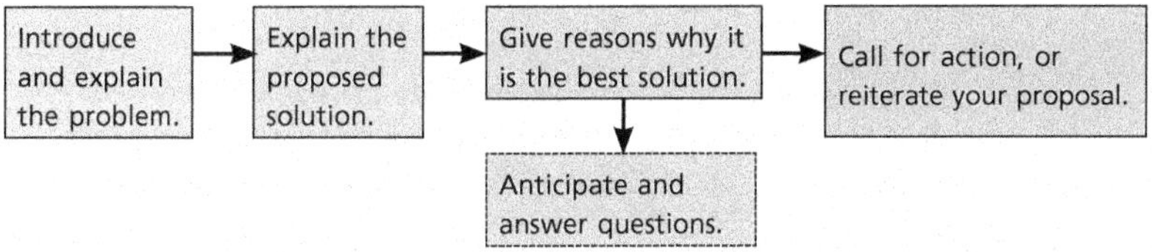

Taking Stock of Your Work

Take stock of what you've written by writing out answers to these questions:

- How did you decide on and limit your topic?
- How did you go about researching your topic?
- How did you determine the best solution to the problem you defined?
- Did you use visual elements (tables, graphs, diagrams, photographs), audio elements, or links effectively? If not, would they have helped?
- What did you do well in this piece? What could still be improved? What would you do differently next time?
- What have you learned about the processes of writing from writing this piece? What do you need to work on in the future?

TOPIC PROPOSALS

Instructors often ask students to write topic proposals to ensure that their topics are appropriate or manageable. Some instructors may also ask for an ANNOTATED BIBLIOGRAPHY showing that appropriate sources of information are available—more evidence that the project can be carried out. Here a student proposes a topic for an assignment in a writing course in which she has been asked to take a position on a global issue. 310–18

CATHERINE THOMS

Social Media and Data Privacy

The relationship between social media and data privacy is an issue that has recently risen to the forefront of many social media users' concerns. While we have been posting and sharing online, major companies like Facebook, Twitter, and Google have been silently collecting information about our personal lives and leaving that data vulnerable to potentially harmful exposure. As someone who has had their private information compromised multiple times by large-scale data breaches, I feel compelled to share my research on the dangers of such security breaches and how they can happen.

In this paper, I will argue that it is crucial for consumers to be aware of the ways in which social media platforms can gain access to consumers' private data and what those platforms can do with that data. In March 2018, it was revealed that 87 million Facebook profiles were exposed to manipulation by the political consulting firm Cambridge Analytica during the 2016 presidential election. I will use this scandal as an example of how the unlawful exposure of personal data can have far-reaching effects on external world events, and I plan to analyze how this scandal has functioned as a global catalyst for further scrutiny into the privacy mechanisms of social media.

I will concentrate on the specific ways personal data may be misused. Although sharing thoughts and pictures on social media may not seem like anything to think twice about, many people don't realize just how much is at stake should enough of that personal data fall into the wrong hands. Much of my research will be done on specific social media applications such as Facebook and Google Analytics, as that is where the heart of the issue resides and where consumers can learn the most about their personal data exposure and protection.

Thoms defines and narrows her topic (from data breaches to the specific ways consumers' data may be misused), discusses her interest, outlines her argument, and discusses her research strategy. Her goal is to convince her instructor that she has a realistic writing project and a clear plan.

Key Features / Topic Proposals

You'll need to explain what you want to write about, why you want to explore it, and what you'll do with your topic. Unless your instructor has additional requirements, here are the features to include:

A concise discussion of the subject. Topic proposals generally open with a brief discussion of the subject, outlining any important areas of controversy or debate associated with it and clarifying the extent of the writer's current knowledge of it. In its first two paragraphs, Thoms's proposal includes a concise statement of the topic she wishes to address.

A clear statement of your intended focus. State what aspect of the topic you intend to write on as clearly as you can, narrowing your focus appropriately. Thoms does so by stating her intended topic—data breaches—and then showing how she will focus on the specific ways consumers' data may be misused.

A rationale for choosing the topic. Tell your instructor why this topic interests you and why you want to write about it. Thoms both states what made her interested in her topic and hints at a practical reason for choosing it: plenty of information is available.

Mention of resources. To show your instructor that you can achieve your goal, you need to identify the available research materials.

IF YOU NEED MORE HELP

See Chapter 18 for guidelines on DRAFTING, and Chapter 19 on EDITING AND PROOFREADING. See Chapter 36 if you are required to submit your proposal in a writing PORTFOLIO.

222–24
225–30
397–408

30 Reflections

Sometimes we write essays just to think about something—to speculate, ponder, probe; to play with an idea, develop a thought; or simply to share something. Reflective essays are our attempt to think something through by writing about it and to share our thinking with others. If such essays make an argument, it is about things we care or think about more than about what we believe to be "true." In college, you might be asked in courses across the curriculum to write formal or informal reflections in the form of essays, journals, design reports, or learning logs. Have a look at one example of a reflection by Edan Lepucki, a novelist and nonfiction writer. This essay originally appeared on the Op-Ed page of the *New York Times*.

EDAN LEPUCKI

Our Mothers as We Never Saw Them

In one of my favorite photographs of my mother, she's about 18 and very tan, with long, blond hair. It's the 1970s and she's wearing a white midriff and cutoffs. My dad is there, too, hugging her from behind, and from the looks of it, they're somewhere rural—maybe some pastoral patch of small-town New Jersey where they met.

I haven't seen this photo for years, I have no idea where it is now, but I still think of it—and, specifically, my mom in it. She looks really sexy; wars have been waged over less impressive waist-to-hip ratios. And she is so young and innocent. She hasn't yet dropped out of college, or gotten married. The young woman in this photo has no idea that life will bring her five children and five grandchildren, a conversion to Judaism, one divorce, two marriages, a move across the country.

For me, as for many daughters, the time before my mother became a mother is a string of stories, told and retold: the time she got hit by a car and had amnesia; the time she sold her childhood Barbie to buy a ticket to Woodstock; the time she worked as a waitress at Howard Johnson's, struggling to pay her way through her first year at Rutgers. The old photos of her are even more compelling than the stories because they're a historical record, carrying the weight of fact, even if the truth there is slippery: the trick of an image, and so much left outside the frame. These photos serve as a visual accompaniment to the myths. Because any story about your mother is part myth, isn't it?

After finishing my most recent novel, in part about mother-daughter relationships, I put out a call on social media for photos from women of their mothers before they were mothers. A character in the book, a young artist, does something similar, so I'd thought a lot about what the process might be like. I wasn't prepared, however, for how powerful the images I received would be.

The young women in these pictures are beautiful, fierce, sassy, 5
goofy, cool, sweet—sometimes all at once. I asked contributors to tell me about their moms or the photo submitted, and they often wrote that something specific and special about their present-day mother—her smile, say, or her posture—was present in this earlier version. What solace to know that time, aging and motherhood cannot take away a woman's essential identity. For daughters who closely resemble their moms, it must be an even bigger comfort; these mothers and daughters are twins, separated by a generation, and an old photo serves as a kind of mirror: How do I look? Even if there isn't a resemblance, we can't help but compare ourselves to our young mothers before they were mothers.

Adalena can see her own expression in this image of her mother, Hua Sou, which she contributed to the author's project.

"I locate something of myself in the slope of her shoulders," said one contributor, Molly. "This makes me feel adjacent to her coolness."

Sometimes, too, a photo deepens the mystery of a mother. Emma, whose mom died when she was 8, says that she "cobbles together" an image of her mother from other people's memories. "Those points only give an outline," she writes, "let alone a shadow or full likeness of a person." She's heard plenty of stories about her mother's childhood, and about her early years as a mother, but very little about the years after her mother graduated college and before she got married. Emma calls this period her mother's "lost years." She notes that she, at age 29, is in that same phase of life now.

Many of us find a breezy toughness in the bygone versions of our mothers, and we envy it. Before a kid or two tied her down, Mom was hitchhiking, or she was playing softball with guys, or like Julia's mom, she was "transcribing tapes from her time as a war reporter like it's the most casual thing in the world." Paria, whose mother fled Iran during the Revolution, notes her mother's resilience; then, as now, her mom maintains a "joie de vivre."

Julia's mother, Anne, during her time as a war reporter.

The photos women sent me offer a key to how we, as daughters, want to perceive young womanhood. Pluck, sex appeal, power, kindness, persistence: We admire and celebrate these characteristics, and we long for the past versions of our moms to embody them. But if these characteristics are a prerequisite for a properly executed womanhood, does becoming a mother divest a woman of such qualities? In studying these photos, and each daughter's interpretation of them, I've come to wonder what traits we allow our mothers to have, and which ones we view as temporary, expiring with age and the beginning of motherhood. Can a woman be both sexual and maternal, daring and responsible, innocent and wise? Mothers are either held up as paragons of selflessness, or they're discounted and parodied. We often don't see them in all their complexity.

For daughters, these old photos of our mothers feel like both a 10
chasm and a bridge. The woman in the picture is someone other than the woman we know. She is also exactly the person in the photo—still, right now. Finally, we see that the woman we've come

Zan submitted this photo of her mother, Darcy, to the project.

to think of as Mom—whether she's nurturing, or disapproving, or thoughtful, or delusional, or pestering, or supportive, or sentimental—is also a mysterious, fun, brave babe.

She's been here all this time.

Photographs of people's mothers when they were young sparks Lepucki's reflection on the lenses through which we see our mothers. She considers the stories our mothers tell and the way photos complement the stories, then examines several photos contributed by others, noting how we compare ourselves to our parents. Finally, her reflections lead her to explore how "we, as daughters, want to perceive young womanhood"—and how the women in the photos combine distance, familiarity, and youthful allure.

Key Features / Reflections

A topic that intrigues you. A reflective essay has a dual purpose: to ponder something you find interesting or puzzling and to share your thoughts with an audience. Your topic may be anything that interests you. You might write about someone you have never met and are curious about, an object or occurrence that makes you think, a place where you feel comfortable or safe. Your goal is to explore the meaning that the person, object, event, or place has for you in a way that will interest others. One way to do that is by making connections between your personal experience and more general ones that readers may share. Lepucki writes about her own and other women's photos of their mothers, and in doing so she raises questions and offers insights about the way people relate to their mothers.

Some kind of structure. A reflective essay can be structured in many ways, but it needs to *be* structured. It may seem to wander, but all its paths and ideas should relate, one way or another. The challenge is to keep your readers' interest as you explore your topic and to leave readers satisfied that the journey was pleasurable, interesting, and profitable. Lepucki begins by describing a remembered photo of her mother and relating it to her mother's stories. She then explores the significance of several photos of other women's mothers and examines the ways daughters interpret photos of their mothers as young women—and how those interpretations may change when those young women become mothers.

Specific details. You'll need to provide specific details to help readers understand and connect with your subject, especially if it's an abstract or unfamiliar one. Lepucki offers a wealth of details about a favorite photo: "She's about 18 and very tan, with long, blond hair. It's the 1970s and she's wearing a white midriff and cutoffs. My dad is there, too, hugging her from behind." Anecdotes can bring your subject to life. Writing of that photo, Lepucki continues: "And she is so young and innocent. She hasn't yet dropped out of college, or gotten married. The young woman in this photo has no idea that life will bring her five children and five grandchildren, a conversion to Judaism, one divorce, two marriages, a move across the country." Reflections may be about causes, such as how our parents affect our self-images; comparisons, such as when Lepucki compares the photos sent to her; and examples, as the photos included in Lepucki's essay exemplify the "beautiful, fierce, sassy, goofy, cool, sweet" young women she sees in all the photos sent to her.

A questioning, speculative tone. In a reflective essay, you are working toward answers, not providing them neatly organized and ready for consumption. So your tone is usually tentative and open, demonstrating a willingness to entertain, accept, and reject various ideas as your essay progresses from beginning to end. Lepucki achieves this tone by questioning her own insights: "Any story about your mother is part myth, isn't it?"; and by admitting that she doesn't have all the answers: "In studying these photos, and each daughter's interpretation of them,

I've come to wonder what traits we allow our mothers to have, and which ones we view as temporary, expiring with age and the beginning of motherhood."

A BRIEF GUIDE TO WRITING REFLECTIONS

Deciding on a Topic

Choose a subject you want to explore. Write a list of things that you think about, wonder about, find puzzling or annoying. They may be big things—life, relationships—or little things—quirks of certain people's behavior, curious objects, everyday events. Try **CLUSTERING** one or more of those things, or begin by **FREEWRITING** to see what comes to mind as you write.

215–16
213–14

Considering the Rhetorical Situation

Purpose	What's your goal in writing this essay? To introduce a topic that interests you? Entertain? Provoke readers to think about something? What aspects of your subject do you want to ponder and reflect on?
Audience	Who is the audience? How familiar are they with your subject? How will you introduce it in a way that will interest them?
Stance	What is your attitude toward the topic you plan to explore? Questioning? Playful? Critical? Curious? Something else?
Media/Design	Will your essay be a print document? an oral presentation? Will it be posted on a website or blog? Would it help to include any visuals or video or audio files?

Generating Ideas and Text

Explore your subject in detail. Reflections often include descriptive details. Lepucki, for example, describes the aspects of the women in the photos that help her see how daughters want to see young women: as having "pluck, sex appeal, power, kindness, persistence." She also provides details in the form of several photographs. You may also make your point by defining, comparing, even classifying. Virtually any organizing pattern will help you explore your subject.

214–15
217–19
222–24

Back away. Ask yourself why your subject matters: why is it important or intriguing or significant? You may try **LISTING** or **OUTLINING** possibilities, or you may want to start **DRAFTING** to see where the writing takes your thinking. Your goal is to think on screen (or paper) about your subject, to play with its possibilities.

Think about how to keep readers with you. Reflections may seem loose or unstructured, but they must be carefully crafted so that readers can follow your train of thought. It's a good idea to sketch out a rough thesis to help focus your thoughts. You may not include the thesis in the essay itself, but every part of the essay should in some way relate to it.

Ways of Organizing a Reflective Essay

Reflective essays may be organized in many ways because they mimic the way we think, associating one idea with another in ways that make sense but do not necessarily form a "logical" progression. In general, you might consider organizing a reflection using this overall strategy:

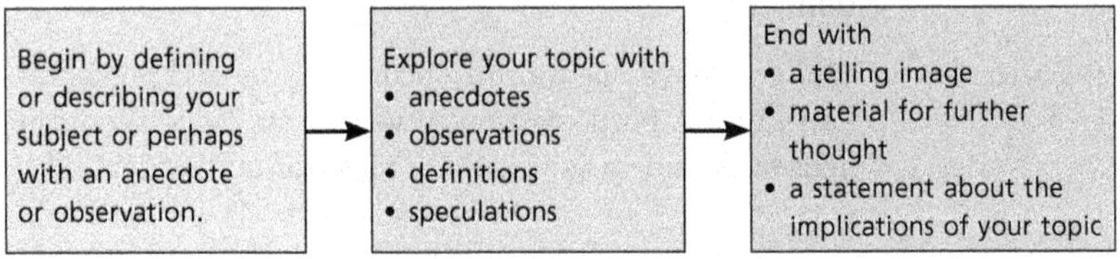

Another way to organize this type of essay is as a series of brief reflections that together create an overall impression:

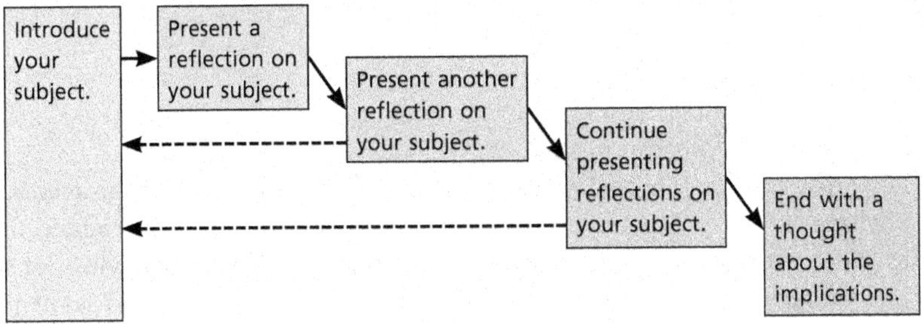

Taking Stock of Your Work

Take stock of what you've written by writing out answers to these questions:

- How did you decide on your topic?
- Why did you organize it as you did?
- Did you use visual elements (photographs, diagrams, drawings), audio elements, or links? If so, what did they add? If not, what might you have used?
- What did you do well in this piece? What could still be improved? What would you do differently next time?
- What have you learned about your writing ability from writing this piece? What do you need to work on in the future?

IF YOU NEED MORE HELP

See Chapter 18 for guidelines on DRAFTING, and Chapter 19 on EDITING AND PROOFREADING. See Chapter 36 if you are required to submit your reflection in a writing PORTFOLIO.

222–24
225–30
397–408

31

Résumés and Job Letters

Résumés summarize our education, work experience, and other accomplishments for prospective employers. Application letters introduce us to those employers. When you send a letter and résumé applying for a job, you are making an argument for why that employer should want to meet you and perhaps hire you. In a way, the two texts together serve as an advertisement selling your talents and abilities to someone who likely has to sift through many applications to decide whom to invite for an interview. That's why résumés and application letters require a level of care that few other documents do. In the same way, sending a thank-you letter following an interview completes your presentation of yourself to potential employers. Résumés, application letters, and thank-you letters are obviously very different genres—yet they share one common purpose: to help you find a job. Thus, they are presented together in this chapter.

Understanding Your Audiences

When you apply for a job, you will likely post your application materials online. They may then be read by a recruiter or a hiring manager. Before that happens, though, your résumé may be searched by an ATS, or applicant tracking system. These systems are designed to ease recruiters' and managers' workloads by ranking applicants, usually on the basis of keywords that appear in their résumés. These keywords usually match the words used in the job posting, so to increase your chances of success, you should describe your skills and experience using the same keywords. One way to do this is to paste the job posting into an online word cloud generator, such as *Wordle, WordItOut,* or *Jobscan.* For example, here is a posting for an internship and a word cloud; the larger the word, the more often it is used in the posting:

> Interns will receive full-on training in their respective departments and be responsible for generating sales, conducting presentations, scheduling promotions, and working within our team.
>
> You will assist Account Executives in their events or retail demonstration and sales and marketing campaigns.
>
> Our company generates over $1 million in revenue through direct marketing campaigns. Interns must be prepared to interact with clients and customers and deliver sales presentations.
>
> This is a hands-on opportunity and interns will gain experience and skills in promotional sales, direct marketing, and working in a team atmosphere and with clients.
>
> **Requirements**: student mentality; goal-oriented; confidence; self-motivation; punctuality; reliability; strong work ethic; desire to make a difference; passionate about helping people

The word cloud suggests that these words should appear in an applicant's résumé: *Sales*, *marketing*, *clients*, *business*, *interns*, *team*, and *customers*. (While it's tempting to use "soft skill" terms as listed under the requirements, you're better off describing actions that demonstrate those skills.

For example, "self-motivation" and "passionate about helping people" might be shown by volunteer work at a homeless shelter.)

Social Media and Job Hunting

Social media have become important aspects of finding a job, for both good and ill. In fact, over half of all employers always search for job applicants' online profiles—and in many cases, those profiles reduce the applicants' chances of being hired. So it's important to create or revise your profiles on *Facebook, LinkedIn,* and *Twitter,* the three most-searched social media sites, as well as other sites. Emphasize any volunteer or charity work you do, and highlight potential qualifications for and interest in the kind of work you want. Make sure your profiles contain no profanity or references to your sexual activity, or use of alcohol, guns, or illegal drugs—and proofread your posts for grammar and spelling. Your photos of yourself should project a professional image, too. Also, Google yourself to see what a search reveals about you.

You can also use social media to improve your job search. Read the descriptions of positions you would like to have, looking for keywords that describe what employers want in such employees; then use those keywords in your profiles. Also, join *LinkedIn* groups related to your desired job or industry to stay current with the conversations in those fields; then follow the companies where you'd like to work, as new job opportunities are sometimes posted there before they appear in other places.

RÉSUMÉS

A résumé is one of a job seeker's most important tools. If done well, a résumé not only tells potential employers about your education and work history, it says a lot about your attention to detail, writing skills, and professionalism. Taking the time to craft an excellent résumé, then, is time well spent. Here's an example, a résumé written by a college student applying for an internship before her senior year.

Emily W. Williams
28 Murphy Lane
Springfield, Ohio 45399
Phone: 937-555-2640
Email: ewilliams22@gmail.com
LinkedIn: www.linkedin.com/EmilyWWilliams

Name in boldface.

SKILLS

- Communicating in writing and verbally, face-to-face and in various media
- Organizing and analyzing data
- Collaborating with other people on a team to achieve goals within deadlines
- Fluent in French
- Software: Microsoft Word, Microsoft Excel, SPSS, ATLAS.ti, Avid Pro Tools

EDUCATION

Wittenberg University, Springfield, Ohio
- BA in Marketing expected in May 2020
- Minor in Psychology
- Current GPA: 3.67
- Recipient, Community Service Scholarship

Clark State Community College, Springfield, Ohio
- AA in Business Administration, 2018
- GPA: 3.88
- Honors: Alpha Lambda Delta National Honor Society

EXPERIENCE

Work experience in reverse chronological order.

Aug. 2018–Present: Department of Psychology, Wittenberg University, Springfield, Ohio
Research Assistant
- Collect and analyze data
- Interview research study participants

Summer 2018: Landis and Landis Public Relations, Springfield, OH
Events Coordinator
- Organized local charity campaigns
- Coordinated database of potential donors
- Produced two radio spots for event promotion

Summers 2016–17: Springfield Aquatic Club, Springfield, OH
Assistant Swim Coach
- Instructed children ages 5–18 in competitive swimming

Format to fill entire page.

Emily Williams's résumé is arranged to highlight her social media presence and skills; her education and experience are arranged chronologically. Because she is in college, readers can assume that she graduated from high school, so that information isn't needed here. She describes her skills and work responsibilities using action verbs to highlight what she actually did—"communicating," "collaborating," "produced," "instructed"—and so on.

Key Features / Résumés

A structure that suits your goals and experience. There are conventional ways of organizing a résumé but no one right way. You can organize a résumé chronologically or functionally, and it can be targeted (customized for a particular job application) or not. A *chronological résumé* is the most general, listing pretty much all your academic and work experience from the most recent to the earliest. A *targeted résumé* will generally announce the specific goal up top, just beneath your name, and will offer information selectively, showing only the experience and skills relevant to your goal. A *functional résumé* is organized around various kinds of experience and is not chronological. You might write a functional résumé if you wish to demonstrate a lot of experience in more than one area and perhaps if you wish to downplay dates. *Combination résumés*, like Emily Williams's, allow you to combine features from various types of résumés to present yourself in the best light; Emily's initial emphasis on skills is functional, while her education and experience are listed chronologically.

Succinct. A résumé should almost always be short—one page if at all possible. Entries should be parallel but do not need to be written in complete sentences—"Produced two radio spots," for instance, rather than "I produced two radio spots." Use action verbs ("instructed," "produced") to emphasize what you accomplished.

A design that highlights key information. It's important for a résumé to look good and to be easy to skim; typography, white space, and alignment matter. Your name should be bold at the top, and the information you want your readers to see first should be near the top of the page. Major sections should be labeled with headings, all of which should be in one slightly larger or bolder font. And you need to surround each section and the text as a whole with adequate white space to make the parts easy to read—and to make the entire document look professional.

A BRIEF GUIDE TO WRITING RÉSUMÉS

Considering the Rhetorical Situation

Purpose	Are you seeking a job? an internship? some other position? How will the position for which you're applying affect what you include on your résumé?
Audience	What sort of employee is the company or organization seeking? What experience and qualities will the person doing the hiring be looking for?
Stance	What personal and professional qualities do you want to convey? Think about how you want to come across—as eager? polite? serious? ambitious?—and choose your words accordingly.
Media/Design	Are you planning to send your résumé and letter as PDFs? on paper? as an email attachment? Whatever your medium, be sure both documents are formatted appropriately and proofread carefully.

Generating Ideas and Text for a Résumé

Define your objective. Are you looking for a particular job for which you should create a targeted résumé? Are you preparing a generic chronological résumé to use in a search for work of any kind? Defining your objective as specifically as possible helps you decide on the form the résumé will take and the information it will include.

Consider how you want to present yourself. Begin by gathering the information you will need to include. As you work through the steps of putting your résumé together, think about the method of organization that works best for your purpose—chronological, targeted, functional, or combination.

- ***Contact information.*** At the top of your résumé, list your full name, a permanent address (rather than your school address), and a permanent telephone number with area code.
- ***Your email address.*** Your email address should sound professional; addresses like hotbabe334@gmail.com do not make a good first impression on potential employers. If possible, get an address that uses your name and a common provider, such as Gmail, iCloud mail, or Outlook.
- ***Your social media presence.*** Many employers routinely check applicants' social media presence to evaluate their personality and character, so yours should reflect your professional self and highlight your skills. Anything from an inappropriate photo or reference to drinking to poor writing can hurt your chances, while evidence of communication skills and a professional image can help them, so you should shape your social media presence to highlight or demonstrate your qualifications and skills. Don't scrub your sites and post nothing, though—use your online presence to enhance your employability. That includes checking for jobs on company *Facebook* pages and *Twitter* feeds and in *LinkedIn* groups.
- ***Your skills.*** What have you learned to do, both in school and in jobs or volunteer work that you've done? Make a list, and phrase each one in terms of what you can *do*, as Williams does. Avoid such phrases as "hard worker," "detail-oriented," and "self-starter." As you revise your résumé to fit different job postings, choose skills from your list that match the job's requirements. As you list your education, experience, and other activities, think in terms of the skills you acquired and add them to your list.

- ***Your education.*** Start with the most recent: degree, major, college attended, and minor (if any). You may want to list your GPA (if it's over 3.0) and any academic honors you've received. If you don't have much work experience, list education first.
- ***Your work experience.*** As with education, list your most recent job first and work backward. Include job title, organization name, city and state, start and end dates, and responsibilities. Describe them in terms of your duties and accomplishments. If you have extensive work experience in the area in which you're applying, list that first.
- ***Community service, volunteer, and charitable activities.*** Many high school students are required to perform community service, and many students participate in various volunteer activities that benefit others. List the skills and aptitudes that participation helped you develop or demonstrate.
- ***Other activities, interests, and abilities.*** What do you do for fun? What skills do your leisure activities require? (For example, if you play a sport, you probably have a good grasp of the value of teamwork and the drive to practice something until you've mastered it. You should describe your skills in a way that an employer might find attractive.)

Choose references. It's assumed that if you get to the interview stage, employers will ask you to provide references, so you don't need to list them on your résumé or say "References on request." Before you start applying for jobs, ask people to serve as references, so they will be ready. It's a good idea to provide each reference with a one-page summary of relevant information about you (for example, give professors a list of courses you took with them, including the grades you earned and the titles of papers you wrote).

Choose your words carefully. Remember, your résumé is a sales document—you're trying to present yourself as someone worth a second look. Focus on your achievements, using action verbs that say what you've done. Be honest—employers expect truthfulness, and embellishing the truth can cause you to lose a job later.

Consider key design elements. Make sure your résumé is centered on the page and that it looks clean and clear. It's usually best to use a single, simple **FONT** (Times New Roman, Calibri, Arial, and Cambria are good ones) throughout and to print on white paper. Use bold type and bullets to make the résumé easy to read, and limit it to no more—and no less—than one full page.

368–69

Edit and proofread carefully. Your résumé must be perfect. Show it to others, and proofread again. You don't want even one typo or other error.

Send the résumé as a PDF. PDFs look the same on all devices, whereas *Word* or other formats may not. Make sure potential employers see your résumé as you intended.

Ways of Organizing a Résumé

If you don't have much work experience or if you've just gone back to school to train for a new career, put education before work experience; if you have extensive work experience in the area in which you're applying, list work before education.

[Chronological]

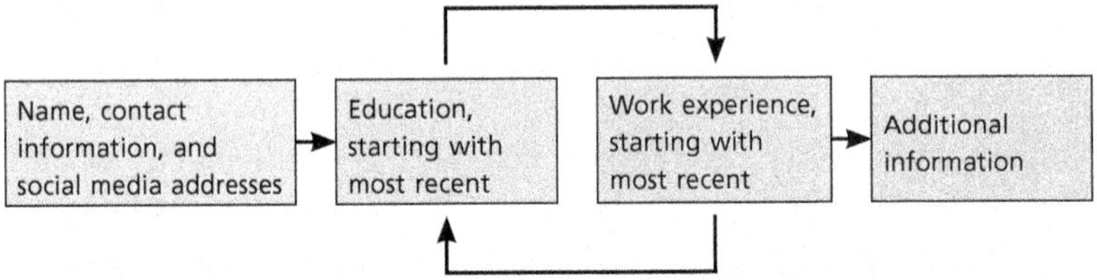

If you have limited work experience, gaps in your employment or education, or wish to focus on your skills, rather than your work history, use a functional résumé.

[Functional]

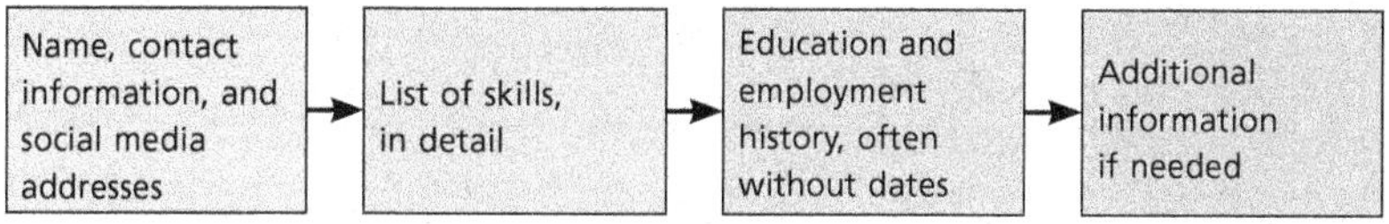

A combination résumé is flexible: it lets you focus on both your skills and your experience by listing skills and also your education and employment history, and it can be tailored to specific job prospects.

[Combination]

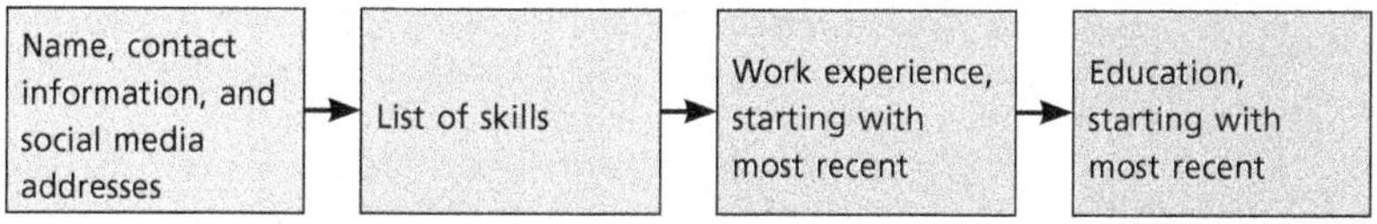

APPLICATION AND THANK-YOU LETTERS

The application letter argues that the writer should be taken seriously as a candidate for a job or some other opportunity. Generally, it is sent together with a résumé, so it doesn't need to give that much information. It does, however, have to make a favorable impression: the way it's written and presented can get you in for an interview—or not. On the following page is an application letter that Emily Williams wrote seeking a position at the end of her junior year. Williams tailored her letter to one specific reader at a specific organization. The letter cites details, showing that it is not a generic application letter being sent to many possible employers. Rather, it identifies a particular position—the public relations internship—and

Application Letter

Equal space at top and bottom of page, all text aligning at left margin.

Street address, city, state, ZIP, date.

28 Murphy Lane
Springfield, OH 45399
May 19, 2019

Line space.

Recipient's name and title, organization, address.

Barbara Jeremiah, President
Jeremiah Enterprises
44322 Commerce Way
Worthington, OH 45322

Line space.

Re: Public Relations Internship Opening (Ref. ID: 27C)

Subject line with position information.

Line space.

Salutation, with a colon.

Dear Ms. Jeremiah:

Position identified.

I am writing to apply for the public relations internship advertised in the Sunday, May 15, *Columbus Dispatch*. The success of your company makes me eager to work with you and learn from you.

Line space between paragraphs.

Match between experience and job description.

My grasp of public relations goes beyond the theories I have learned in the classroom. I applied those theories last summer at Landis and Landis, the Springfield public relations firm, where I was responsible for organizing two charity events that drew over two hundred potential donors each. I also learned to use sound productions software to produce promotional radio spots. Since Jeremiah Enterprises focuses on nonprofit public relations, my experience, training, and initiative will allow me to contribute to your company's public relations team..

Show knowledge of company.

Availability.

I will be available to begin any time after May 23, when the spring term at Wittenberg ends. I have attached my résumé, which provides detailed information about my background. I will phone this week to see if I might arrange an interview.

Line space.

Closing.

Sincerely,

4 lines space for signature if mailed. Electronic letters need only typed name.

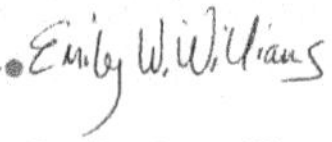

Emily W. Williams

Sender's name, typed.

stresses the fit between Williams's credentials and the position. Williams also states her availability. Send a thank-you email to each person who interviewed you within twenty-four hours of the interview; follow up by mailing a printed note that follows the same format as the application letter. Doing so is a way of showing appreciation for the interview and restating your interest in the position. It also shows that you have good manners and understand proper business etiquette. Below is an email that Emily Williams sent to the person who interviewed her. Williams thanks the interviewer for her time and the opportunity to meet, and she reiterates her interest in the position and her qualifications for it.

Thank-You Email

Dear Ms. Jeremiah: — *Salutation, with a colon.*

Line space.

Thank you for the opportunity to meet with you yesterday. I enjoyed talking with you and meeting the people who work with you, and I continue to be very interested in becoming an intern with Jeremiah Enterprises. — *Thanks and confirmation of interest.*

Line space between paragraphs.

As we discussed, I worked with a public relations firm last summer, and since then I have completed three courses in marketing and public relations that relate directly to the work I would be doing as an intern. — *Brief review of qualifications.*

I have attached a list of references, as you requested. — *Attachments.* If you need any more information, please do not hesitate to contact me by email at ewilliams22@gmail.com or by phone at 937-555-2640. — *Invitation for further contact.* Thanks again; I hope to hear from you soon. — *Repeat thanks.*

Line space.

Sincerely, — *Closing.*

Emily W. Williams

Key Features / Application and Thank-You Letters

A succinct indication of your qualifications. In an application letter, you need to make clear why you're interested in the position or the organization—and at the same time give some sense of why the person you're writing to should at least want to meet you. In a thank-you letter, you should remind the interviewer of your qualifications.

A reasonable and pleasing tone. When writing application and thank-you letters, you need to go beyond simply stating your accomplishments or saying thank you. Through your words, you need to demonstrate that you will be the kind of employee the organization wants. Presentation is also important—your letter should be neat and error-free.

A conventional, businesslike format. Application and thank-you letters typically follow a prescribed format. The most common is the block format shown in the examples. It includes the writer's address, the date, the recipient's name and address, a salutation, the message, a closing, and a signature.

A BRIEF GUIDE TO WRITING JOB LETTERS

Generating Ideas and Text for Application and Thank-You Letters

Focus. Application and thank-you letters are not personal and should not be chatty. Keep them focused: when you're applying for a position, include only information relevant to the position. Don't make your audience wade through irrelevant side issues. Stay on topic.

State the reason for the letter. Unlike essays, which develop a thesis over several paragraphs, or emails, which announce their topic in a subject line, letters need to explicitly introduce their reason for being written, usually in the first paragraph. When you're applying for something or thanking someone, say so in the first sentence: "I am writing to apply for the Margaret Branscomb Peabody Scholarship for students majoring in veterinary science." "Thank you for meeting with me."

Think of your letter as an argument. When you're asking for a job, you're making an argument. You're making a claim—that you're qualified for a certain position—and you need to support your claim with reasons and evidence. Therefore, it's important to read the position's requirements carefully and tailor the letter to show that you meet them. In her letter, for example, Williams shows how her combined education and work experience make her successful in her summer job, and she connects that experience to the specific internship she's applying for.

Choose an appropriate salutation. If you know the person's name and title, use it: "Dear Professor Turnigan." If you don't know the person's title, one good solution is to address them by first and last name: "Dear Julia Turnigan." If, as sometimes happens, you must write to an unknown reader, your options include "To Whom It May Concern" and the more old-fashioned "Dear Sir or Madam." Another option in such situations might be to omit the salutation completely and instead use a subject line, for example: "Subject: Public Relations Internship Application." Whenever possible, though, write to a specific person; research or contact the organization and find out whom to write to. Once you've had an interview, write to your interviewer.

Consider the medium. If you're applying for a job with a printed letter and résumé, follow standard business-letter format, as Williams does. If you're applying via email, paste your entire letter into the body of the email, but move your contact information below your signature. Also, list the job for which you are applying in your subject line—and if the employer asks for specific information in the subject line, be sure to include it exactly.

Proofread. Few writing situations demand greater perfection than professional letters—especially job letters. Employers receive dozens, sometimes hundreds, of applications, and often can't look at them all. Typos, grammar errors, and other forms of sloppiness prejudice readers against applicants: an employer is likely to think that if this applicant can't take the time and care to **PROOFREAD**, how badly do they want this position? To compete, strive for perfection.

228–29

Ways of Organizing an Application or Thank-You Letter

Application and thank-you letters should both follow a conventional organization, though you might vary the details somewhat. Here are two standard organizations:

[Application letter]

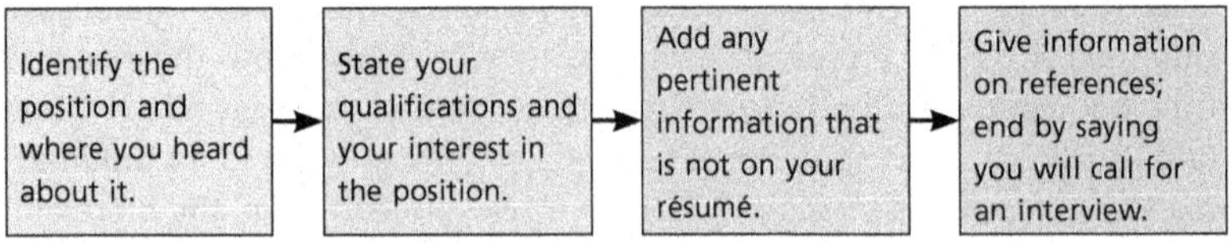

[Thank-you letter]

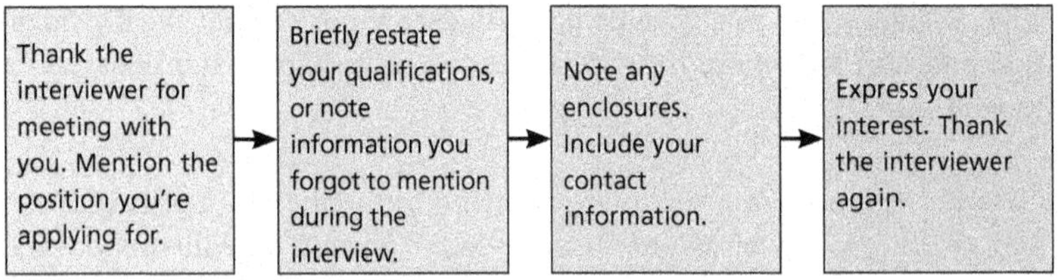

Taking Stock of Your Work

Take stock of what you've written by writing out answers to these questions:

- How did you go about identifying your strengths and qualifications?
- Why did you choose the résumé structure you did?

- Did you maintain an appropriate tone throughout your job letters?
- What did you do well in your résumé and letters? What could still be improved?
- What have you learned about your writing ability and your job qualifications from writing these pieces? What do you need to work on in the future?

IF YOU NEED MORE HELP

See Chapter 18 for guidelines on DRAFTING, and Chapter 19 on EDITING AND PROOFREADING.

222–24
225–30

part 8

Media / Design

Consciously or not, we design all the texts we write, choosing typefaces, setting up text as lists or charts, deciding whether to add headings—and then whether to center them or align them on the left. Sometimes our genre calls for certain design elements—essays begin with titles, letters begin with salutations ("Dear Auntie Em"). Other times we design texts to meet the demands of particular audiences, formatting documentation in MLA or APA or some other style, setting type larger for young children, and so on. And our designs always depend upon our medium. A memoir might take the form of an essay in a book, be turned into a bulleted list for a slide presentation, or include links to images or other pages if presented on a website. The chapters in this part offer advice for CHOOSING MEDIA; working with DESIGN, IMAGES, and SOUND; and GIVING PRESENTATIONS.

Media / Design

Choosing Media 32

USA Today reports on contract negotiations between automakers and autoworkers with an article that includes a large photo and a colorful graph; the article on the same story on the *New York Times* website includes a video of striking workers. In your economics class, you give a presentation about the issue that includes *Prezi* slides.

These examples show how information about the same events can be delivered using three different media: print (*USA Today*), digital (*nytimes.com*), and spoken (the main medium for your class presentation). They also show how different media offer writers different modes of expressing meaning, ranging from words to images to sounds and hyperlinks. A print text can include written words and still visuals; online, the same text can also incorporate links to moving images and sound as well as to other written materials. A presentation with slides can include both spoken and written words, can incorporate video and audio elements—and can also include print handouts.

In college writing, the choice of medium often isn't up to you: your instructor may require a printed essay or a classroom talk, a website, or some combination of media. Sometimes, though, you'll be the one deciding. Because your medium will play a big part in the way your audience receives and reacts to your message, you'll need to think hard about what media best suit your audience, purpose, and message. This chapter will help you choose media when the choice is yours.

Print

When you have a choice of medium, print has certain advantages over spoken and digital text in that it's more permanent and doesn't depend on audience access to technology. Depending on your own access to technology, you can usually insert photos or other visuals and can present data and other information as graphs or charts. Obviously, though, print documents are more work than digital ones to update or change, and they don't allow for sound, moving images, or links to other materials.

Digital

Online writing is everywhere: on course learning management systems and class websites; in virtual discussion groups and wikis; in emails, text messages, tweets, and other social media. And when you're taking an online course, you are, by definition, always using a digital medium. Remember that this medium has advantages as well as limitations and potential pitfalls. You can add audio, video, and links—but your audience may not have the same access to technology that you do. These are just some of the things you'll need to keep in mind when deciding, say, whether to include or link to videos or a site that has restricted access. Also, digital texts that circulate online, through blogs, websites, email, or social media, can take on a life of their own; others may forward, like, retweet, or repost your text to much larger audiences than you originally considered.

Spoken

If you deliver your text orally, as a speech or presentation, you have the opportunity to use your tone of voice, gestures, and physical bearing to establish credibility. But you must write your text so that it's easy to understand when it is heard rather than read. Speaking from memory or from notecards, rather than reading a script or essay, often makes it easier for the audience to follow your talk. The spoken medium can be used alone with a live, face-to-face audience, but it's often combined with print, in the form of handouts, or with digital media, in the form of presentation software like *PowerPoint* or *Prezi*, or designed for remote audiences in formats like webcasts, webinars, podcasts, or video-calling services such as *Skype*.

Multimedia

It's increasingly likely that you'll be assigned to create a multimedia text, one that includes some combination of print, oral, and digital elements. It's also possible that you'll have occasion to write a multimodal text, one that uses more than one mode of expression: words, images, audio, video, links, and so on. The words *multimedia* and *multimodal* are often used interchangeably, but *multimodal* is the term that's used most often in composition classes, whereas *multimedia* is the one used in other disciplines and in industry. In composition classes, the word generally refers to writing that includes more than just words.

For example, let's say that in a U.S. history class you're assigned to do a project about the effects of the Vietnam War on American society. You might write an essay using words alone to discuss such effects as increased hostility toward the military and government, generational conflict within families and society at large, and increased use of recreational drugs. But you could also weave such a text together with many other materials to create a multimodal composition.

If you're using print, for example, you could include photographs from the Vietnam era, such as of antiwar protests or military funerals. Another possibility might be a timeline that puts developments in the war in the context of events going on simultaneously elsewhere in American life, such as in fashion and entertainment or in the feminist and civil rights movements. If you're posting your project online, you might also incorporate video clips of TV news coverage of the war and clips from films focusing on it or its social effects, such as *Apocalypse Now* or *Easy Rider*. Audio elements could include recorded interviews with veterans who fought in the war, people who protested against it, or government officials who were involved in planning or overseeing it. Many of these elements could be inserted into your document as links.

If your assignment specifies that you give an oral presentation, you could play some of the music of the Vietnam era, show videos of government officials defending the war and demonstrators protesting it, maybe hang some psychedelic posters from the era.

397–408

You might do something similar with your own work by creating an electronic, or e-portfolio. Tips for compiling an **E-PORTFOLIO** may be found in Chapter 36.

Considering the Rhetorical Situation

Purpose — What's your purpose, and what media will best suit that purpose? A text or email may be appropriate for inviting a friend to lunch, but neither would be ideal for demonstrating to a professor that you understand a complex historical event; for that, you'd likely write a report, either in print or online—and you might include photos or maps or other such texts to provide visual context.

Audience — What media are your audience likely to expect—and be able to access? A blog may be a good way to reach people who share your interest in basketball or cupcakes, but to reach your grandparents, you may want to put a handwritten note in the mail. Some employers and graduate school admissions officers require applicants to submit résumés and applications online, while others prefer to receive them in print form.

Genre — Does your genre require a particular medium? If you're giving an oral presentation, you'll often be expected to include slides. Academic essays are usually formatted to be printed out, even if they are submitted electronically. An online essay based on field research might include audio files of those you've interviewed, but if your essay were in print, you'd need to quote (or paraphrase or summarize) what they said.

Stance — If you have a choice of media, think about whether a particular medium will help you convey your stance. A print document in MLA format, for instance, will make you seem scholarly and serious. Tweeting or blogging, however, might work better for a more informal stance. Presenting data in charts will sometimes help you establish your credibility as a knowledgeable researcher.

Once you decide on the media and modes of expression you're using, you'll need to design your text to take advantage of their possibilities and to deal with their limitations. The next chapters will help you do that.

33 Designing Text

You're trying to figure out why a magazine ad you're looking at is so funny, and you realize that the text's font is deliberately intended to make you laugh. An assignment for a research paper in psychology specifies that you are to follow APA format. Your classmates complain that the *PowerPoint* slides you use for a presentation are hard to read because there's not enough contrast between the words and the background. Another says you include too many words on each slide. Whether you're putting together your résumé, creating a website for your intramural soccer league, or writing an essay for a class, you need to think about how you design what you write.

Sometimes you can rely on established conventions: in MLA and APA styles, for example, there are specific guidelines for margins, headings, and the use of single-, double-, or triple-spaced lines of text. But often you'll have to make design decisions on your own—and not just about words and spacing. If what you're writing includes photos, charts, tables, graphs, or other visuals, you'll need to integrate these with your written text in the most attractive and effective way; online, you may also need to decide where and how to include video clips and links. You might even use scissors, glue, and staples to attach objects to a poster or create pop-ups in a brochure.

No matter what your text includes, its design will influence how your audience responds to it and therefore how well it achieves your purpose. This chapter offers general advice on designing print and online texts.

Considering the Rhetorical Situation

As with all writing tasks, your rhetorical situation should affect the way you design a text. Here are some points to consider:

Purpose	How can you design your text to help achieve your purpose? If you're reporting information, for instance, you may want to present statistical data in a chart or table rather than in the main text to help readers grasp it more quickly. If you're trying to get readers to care about an issue, a photo or pull quote—a brief selection of text "pulled out" and reprinted in a larger font—might help you do so.
Audience	How can you make your design appeal to your intended audience? By using a certain font style or size to make your text look stylish, serious, or easy to read? What kind of headings—big and bold, simple and restrained?—would your readers expect or find helpful? What colors would appeal to them?
Genre	Are you writing in a genre that has design conventions, such as an annotated bibliography, a lab report, or a résumé? Do you need to follow a format such as those prescribed in MLA or APA style?
Stance	How can your design reflect your attitude toward your audience and subject? Do you need a businesslike font or a playful one? Would tables and graphs help you establish your credibility? How can illustrations help you convey a certain tone?

Some Basic Principles of Design

Be consistent. To keep readers oriented while reading documents or browsing multiple webpages, any design elements should be used consistently. In a print academic essay, that task may be as simple as using the same font throughout for your main text and using boldface or italics for headings. If you're writing for the web, navigation buttons and other major elements should be in the same place on every page. In a presentation, each slide should use the same background and the same font unless there's a good reason to introduce differences.

Keep it simple. One of your main design goals should be to help readers see quickly—even intuitively—what's in your text and how to find specific information. Adding headings to help readers see the parts, using consistent colors and fonts to help them recognize key elements, setting off steps in lists, using white space to set off blocks of text or to call attention to certain elements, and (especially) resisting the temptation to fill pages with fancy graphics or unnecessary animations—these are all ways of making your text simple to read.

Look, for example, at a furniture store's simple, easy-to-understand webpage design on the next page. This webpage contains considerable information: a row of links across the top, directing readers to various products; a search option; a column down the right side that provides details about the chair shown in the wide left-hand column; thumbnail photos below the chair and ordering information; and more details across the bottom. Despite the wealth of content, the site's design is both easy to figure out and, with the generous amount of white space, easy on the eyes.

Aim for balance. On the webpage on the following page, the photo takes up about a quarter of the screen and is balanced by a narrower column of text, and the product information tabs and text across the page bottom balance the company logo and search box across the top. For a page without images, balance can be created through the use of margins, headings, and spacing. For example, you can use white space around an article title and an author's name, as well as set them in larger type or capital letters, to help to balance them vertically against a large block of text below them. A large initial letter at the start of the text can also help to balance a mass of smaller type that follows. MLA and APA styles have specific design guidelines for academic research papers that cover these elements. A magazine page might create a sense of balance by using pull quotes and illustrations to break up dense vertical columns of text.

Use color and contrast carefully. Academic readers usually expect black text on a white background, with perhaps one other color for headings. Presentation slides and webpages are most readable with a plain, light-colored background and dark text that provides contrast. Remember that not everyone can see all colors and that an online text that includes sev-

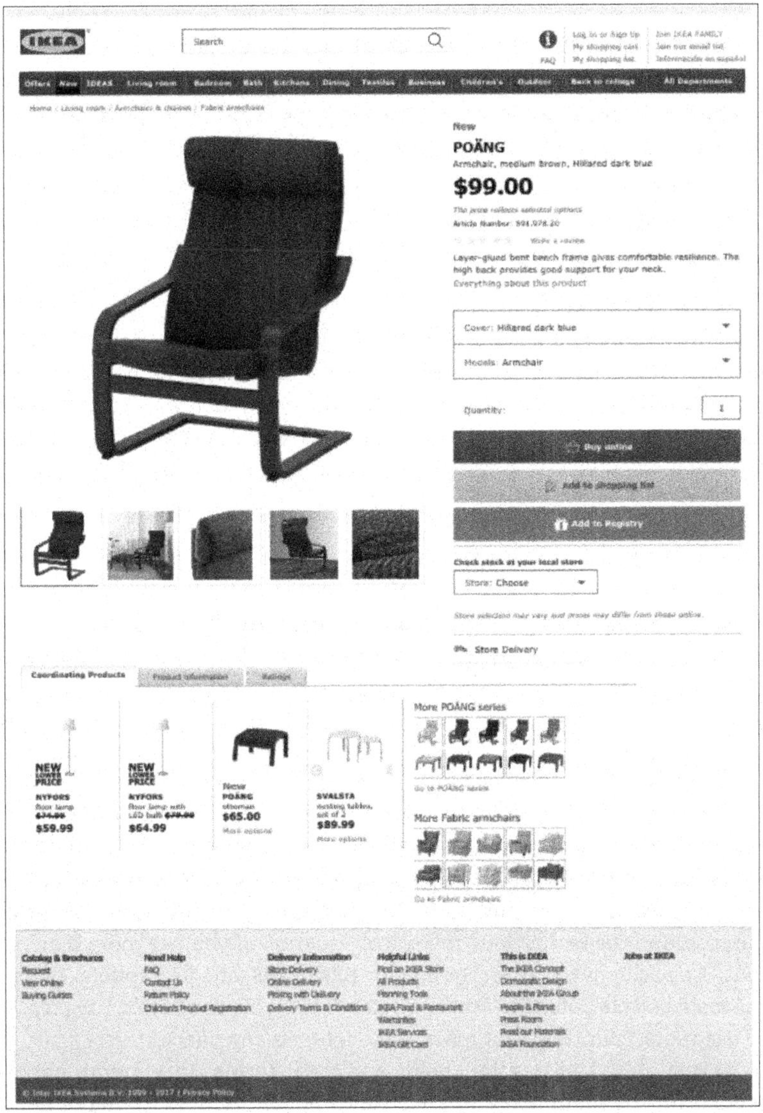
IKEA
Search
FAQ
New
POÄNG
Armchair, medium brown, Hillared dark blue
$99.00
Layer-glued bent beech frame gives comfortable resilience. The high back provides good support for your neck.
Everything about this product
Cover: Hillared dark blue
Models: Armchair
Quantity:
1
Add to Registry
Check stock at your local store
Store: Choose
Store Delivery
Coordinating Products
NEW LOWER PRICE
NYFORS
$59.99
NEW LOWER PRICE
NYFORS
$64.99
New
POÄNG
$65.00
SVALSTA
$89.99
More POÄNG series
More Fabric armchairs

eral colors might be printed out and read in black and white; make sure your audience will be able to distinguish any color variations well enough to grasp your meaning. Colored lines on a graph, for example, should be distinguishable even if readers cannot see the colors. Red-green contrasts are especially hard to see and should be avoided.

Use available templates. Good design takes time, and most of us do not have training as designers. If you're pressed for time or don't feel up to the challenge of designing your own text, take advantage of the many templates available. In *Microsoft Word*, for example, you can customize "styles" to specify the font, including its size and color; single- or double-spacing; paragraph indentations; and several other features that will then automatically apply to your document. Websites that host personal webpages and blogs offer dozens of templates that you can use or modify to suit your needs. And presentation software offers many templates that can simplify creating slides.

Some Elements of Design

Fonts. You can usually choose from among many fonts, and the one you choose will affect how well the audience can read your text and how they will perceive your tone. Times Roman will make a text look businesslike or academic; Comic Sans will make it look playful. For most academic writing, you'll want to use a font size between 10 and 12 points and a serif font (such as Times Roman or Bookman) rather than a sans serif font (such as Arial, Verdana, or Calibri) because serif fonts are generally easier to read. Reserve sans serif for headings and parts of the text that you want to highlight. Decorative fonts (such as Magneto, Amaze, Chiller, and Jokerman) should be used sparingly and only when they're appropriate for your audience, purpose, and the rest of your rhetorical situation. If you use more than one font, use each one consistently: one for **HEADINGS**, one for captions, one for the main body of your text. Don't go overboard—you won't often have reason to use more than two or, at most, three fonts in any one text.

370–72

Every font has regular, **bold**, and *italic* forms. In general, choose regular for the main text and lower-level headings, bold for major headings, and italic within the main text to indicate titles of books and other long works and, occasionally, to emphasize words or brief phrases. Avoid italicizing or boldfacing entire sentences or paragraphs, especially in academic writing. If you are following MLA, APA, or some other style format, be sure your use of fonts conforms to its requirements.

Finally, consider the line spacing of your text. Generally, academic writing is double-spaced, whereas **JOB LETTERS** and **RÉSUMÉS** are usually single-spaced. Some kinds of reports may call for single-spacing; check with your instructor if you're not sure. You'll often need to add extra space to set off parts of a text—items in a list, for instance, or headings. 340–56

Layout. Layout is the way text is arranged on a page. An academic essay, for example, will usually have a title centered at the top, one-inch margins all around, and double-spacing. A text can be presented in paragraphs—or in the form of **LISTS**, **TABLES**, **CHARTS**, **GRAPHS**, and so on. Sometimes you'll need to include other elements as well: headings, images and other graphics, captions, lists of works cited. 369–70 376

Paragraphs. Dividing text into paragraphs focuses information for readers and helps them process it by dividing it into manageable chunks. If you're writing a story for a print newspaper with narrow columns, for example, you'll divide your text into shorter paragraphs than you would if you were writing an academic essay. In general, indent paragraphs five to seven spaces (one-half inch) when your text is double-spaced; either indent or skip a line between single-spaced paragraphs.

Lists. Put into list form information that you want to set off and make easily accessible. Number the items in a list when the sequence matters (in instructions, for example); use bullets when the order is not important. Set off lists with an extra line of space above and below, and add extra space between the items if necessary for legibility. Here's an example:

> Darwin's theory of how species change through time derives from three postulates, each of which builds on the previous one:
>
> 1. The ability of a population to expand is infinite, but the ability of any environment to support populations is always finite.
> 2. Organisms within populations vary, and this variation affects the

ability of individuals to survive and reproduce.

3. The variations are transmitted from parents to offspring.

—Robert Boyd and Joan B. Silk, *How Humans Evolved*

Do not set off text as a list unless there's a good reason to do so, however. Some lists are more appropriately presented in paragraph form, especially when they give information that is not meant to be referred to more than once. In the following example, there is no reason to highlight the information by setting it off in a list—and bad news is softened by putting it in paragraph form:

> I regret to inform you that the Scholarship Review Committee did not approve your application for a Board of Rectors scholarship for the following reasons: your grade-point average did not meet the minimum requirements; your major is not among those eligible for consideration; and the required letter of recommendation was not received before the deadline.

Presented as a list, that information would be needlessly emphatic.

305–9

Headings. Headings make the structure of a text easier to follow and help readers find specific information. Some genres require standard headings—announcing an **ABSTRACT**, for example, or a list of works cited. Other times you will want to use headings to provide an overview of a section of text. You may not need any headings in brief texts, but when you do, you'll probably want to use one level at most, just to announce major topics. Longer texts, information-rich genres such as brochures or detailed reports, and websites may require several levels of headings. If you decide to include headings, you will need to decide how to phrase them, what fonts to use, and where to position them.

Phrase headings concisely. Make your headings succinct and parallel in structure. You might make all the headings nouns (**Mushrooms**), noun phrases (**Kinds of Mushrooms**), gerund phrases (**Recognizing Kinds of Mushrooms**), or questions (**How Do I Identify Mushrooms?**). Whatever form you decide on, use it consistently for each heading. Sometimes your phrasing will depend on your purpose. If you're simply helping readers find information, use brief phrases:

HEAD	**Forms of Social Groups among Primates**
SUBHEAD	*Solitary Social Groups*
SUBHEAD	*Monogamous Social Groups*

If you want to address your readers directly with the information in your text, consider writing your headings as questions:

How can you identify edible mushrooms?
Where can you find edible mushrooms?
How can you cook edible mushrooms?

Make headings visible. Headings need to be visible, so if you aren't following an academic style like MLA or APA, consider making them larger than the regular text, putting them in **bold** or *italics*, or using underlining—or a different font. For example, you could use a serif font like Times Roman for your main text and a sans serif font like Arial for your headings. On the web, consider making headings a different color from the body text. When you have several levels of headings, use capitalization, bold, and italics to distinguish among the various levels:

First-Level Head
Second-Level Head
Third-level head

APA format requires that each level of heading appear in a specific style: centered bold uppercase and lowercase for the first level, flush-left bold uppercase and lowercase for the second level, and so on.

Position headings appropriately. If you're following APA format, center first-level headings. If you are not following a prescribed format, you get to decide where to position your headings: centered, flush with the left margin, or even alongside the text in a wide left-hand margin. Position each level of head consistently throughout your text. Generally, online headings are positioned flush left.

White space. Use white space to separate the various parts of a text. In general, use one-inch margins for the text of an essay or report. Unless you're following MLA or APA format, include space above headings, above and below lists, and around photos, graphs, and other visuals. Review sample research papers to see examples of the formats required by MLA and APA styles.

Evaluating a Design

Does the design suit your purpose? Does the overall look of the design help convey the text's message, support its argument, or present information?

How well does the design meet the needs of your audience? Will the overall appearance of the text appeal to the intended readers? Is the font large enough for them to read? Are there headings to help them find their way through the text? Does the design help readers find the information they need?

How well does the text meet any genre requirements? Can you tell by looking at the text that it is an academic essay, a lab report, a résumé, a blog? Do its fonts, margins, headings, and page layout meet the requirements of MLA, APA, or whatever style is being followed?

How well does the design reflect your stance? Do the page layout and fonts convey the appropriate tone—serious, playful, adventuresome, conservative, or whatever other tone you intended?

Using Visuals, Incorporating Sound 34

For an art history class, you write an essay comparing two paintings by Willem de Kooning. For a business class, you create a proposal to improve department communication in a small local firm and incorporate diagrams to illustrate the new procedure. For a visual rhetoric class, you take an autobiographical photograph and include a two-page analysis of how the picture distills something essential about you. For an engineering class project, you design a model of a bridge and give an in-class presentation explaining the structures and forces involved, which you illustrate with slides. For a psychology assignment, you interview several people who've suffered foreclosures on their homes in recent years about how the experience affected them—and then create an online text weaving together a slideshow of photos of the people outside their former homes, a graph of foreclosure rates, video and audio clips from the interviews, and your own insights.

All of these writing tasks require you to incorporate and sometimes to create visuals and sound. Many kinds of visuals can be included in print documents: photos, drawings, diagrams, graphs, charts, and more. And with writing that's delivered online or as a spoken presentation, your choices expand to include audio and video, voice-over narration, and links to other materials.

Visuals and sound aren't always appropriate, however, or even possible—so think carefully before you set out to include them. But they can help you make a point in ways that words alone cannot. Election polling results are easier to see in a bar graph than in a paragraph; photos of an event may convey its impact more powerfully than words alone; an audio clip can make a written analysis of an opera easier to understand. This chapter provides some tips for using visuals and incorporating sound in your writing.

Considering the Rhetorical Situation

Use visuals and sounds that are appropriate for your audience, purpose, and the rest of your rhetorical situation. If you're trying to persuade voters in your town to back a proposal on an issue they don't know much about, for example, you might use dramatic pictures just to get their attention. But when it's important to come across as thoughtful and objective, maybe you need a more subdued look—or to make your points with written words alone. A newspaper article on housing prices might include a bar or line graph and also some photos. A report on that topic for an economics class would probably have graphs with no photos; a spoken presentation for a business class might use a dynamic graph that shows prices changing over time and an audio voice over for pictures of a neighborhood; a community website might have graphs, links to related sites, and a video interview with a home owner.

In your academic writing, especially, be careful that any visuals you use support your main point—and don't just serve to decorate the text. (Therefore, avoid clip art, which is primarily intended as decoration and comes off as unsophisticated and childish.) Images should validate or exemplify what you say elsewhere with written words and add information that words alone can't provide as clearly or easily.

Using Visuals

Photos, drawings, diagrams, videos, tables, pie charts, bar graphs—these are many kinds of visuals you could use. Visuals can offer support, illustration, evidence, and comparison and contrast in your document.

Photographs. Photos can support an argument, illustrate narratives and processes, present other points of view, and help readers "place" your information in time and space. You may use photos you take yourself, or you can download photos and other images from the internet—within limits. Most downloadable photos are copyrighted, meaning that you can use them without obtaining permission from the copyright owner only if

An essay discussing the theme of mother and child might compare this painting from the Italian Renaissance (left) with a modern photograph such as Dorothea Lange's Migrant Mother *(right).*

you are doing so for academic purposes, to fulfill an assignment. If you are going to publish your text, either in print or on the web, you must have permission. You can usually gain permission by emailing the copyright holder, but that often entails a fee, so think carefully about whether you need the image. Consider, too, the file size of digital images; large files can clog readers' email in-boxes, take a long time to display on their screens, or be hard for you to upload in the first place, so you may have to compress an image in a zip file or reduce its resolution (which can diminish its sharpness).

Videos. If you're writing online, you can include video clips for readers to play. If you're using a video already available online, such as on *YouTube*, you can show the opening image with an arrow for readers to click on to start the video, or you can simply copy the video's URL and paste it into your text as a **LINK**. In either case, you need to introduce the video in your text with a **SIGNAL PHRASE**. As with any other source, you need to provide an in-text citation and full documentation.

381–82
289–92

If you want to include a video you made yourself, you can edit it using such programs as *iMovie* or *Shotcut*. Once you're ready to insert it into your online document, the easiest way is to first upload it to *YouTube*, choosing the Private setting so only those you authorize may view it, and then create a link in your document.

Graphs, charts, and tables. Statistical and other numerical information is often best presented in graphs, charts, and tables. If you can't find the right one for your purpose, you can create your own, as long as it's based on sound data from reliable sources. To do so, you can use various spreadsheet programs such as *Excel* or online chart and graph generators such as *Plot.ly* or *Venngage*.

365 In any case, remember to follow basic design principles: be **CONSISTENT**,
366 label all parts clearly, and **KEEP THE DESIGN SIMPLE**, so readers can focus on the information and not be a distracted by a needlessly complex design. In particular, use color and contrast wisely to emphasize what's
366–98 most significant. Choose **COLORS** that are easy to distinguish from one another—and that remain so if the graph or chart is printed out in black and white. (Using distinct gradations of color from light to dark will show well in black and white.) Some common kinds of graphs, charts, and tables are shown on the facing page.

Diagrams, maps, flowcharts, and timelines. Information about place and time is often presented in diagrams, maps, flowcharts, and timelines. If you're using one of these infographics from the web or elsewhere,
298–301 be sure to **DOCUMENT** it. Otherwise you can create one of these yourself. Make diagrams and maps as simple as possible for the point you're making. Unnecessarily complex maps can be more of a distraction than a help. To draw a flowchart, you can use the Shape tab on the Insert section of *Microsoft Word*. For timelines, make sure the scale accurately depicts the passage of time about which you are writing and avoids gaps and bunches.

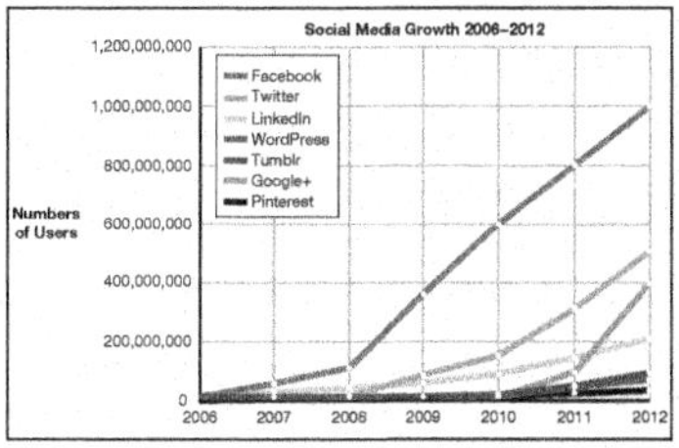

Line graphs are a good way of showing changes in data over time. Each line here represents a different social media platform. Plotting the lines together allows readers to compare the data at different points in time. Be sure to label the *x* and *y* axes and limit the number of lines to avoid confusion.

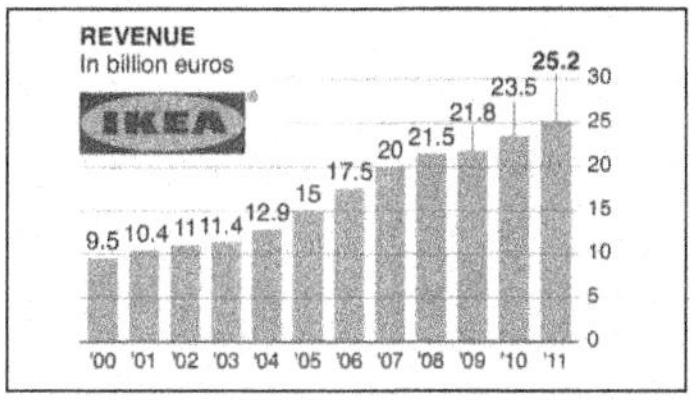

Bar graphs are useful for comparing quantitative data, measurements of how much or how many. The bars can be horizontal or vertical. This graph shows IKEA's earnings between 2000 and 2011. Some software offers 3-D and other special effects, but simple graphs are often easier to read.

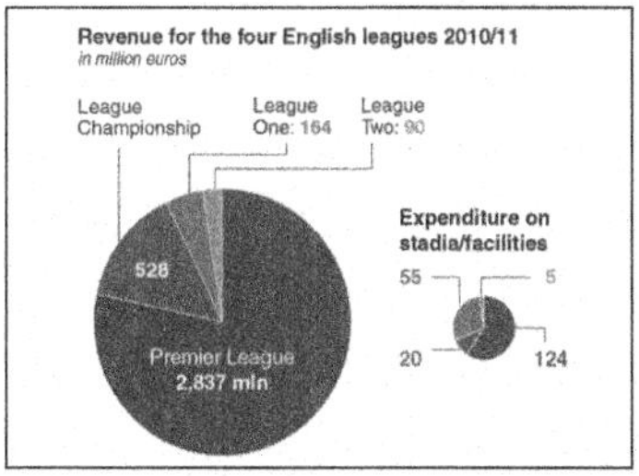

Pie charts can be used to show how a whole is divided into parts or how parts of a whole relate to one another. These two pie charts show and compare the revenue of four 2010–11 English soccer leagues and their expenditures. The segments in a pie should always add up to 100 percent, and each segment should be clearly labeled.

ECONOMY WATCH

A snapshot of key figures for the world's largest economies.

COUNTRY	GDP in billions in 2010	GDP GROWTH Y/year (%)	CURRENT ACC'T/GDP in 2010 (%)	INFLATION Year over year (%)	JOBLESS (%)
U.S.	$14,658	2.0†	-3.2	3.5	8.6
Euro zone	12,474*	1.4	-0.2*	3.0	10.3
China	5,878	9.1	5.2	5.5	4.1‡
Japan	5,459	5.6†	3.6	-0.1	4.5
Germany	3,316	2.5	5.3	2.8†	6.9
France	2,583	1.7	-2.1	2.5†	9.7
Britain	2,247	0.5	-2.5	5.0	8.3
Italy	2,055	0.8	-2.1*	3.7†	8.5
Brazil	1,601*	2.1	-1.5*	6.6	5.8
Canada	1,574	3.5†	-3.1	2.9	7.4
India	1,538	6.9	-3.2	9.7	n.a.
Russia	1,222*	4.8	4.1*	6.8	6.4
Mexico	1,039	4.5	-0.7*	3.5	5.0
South Korea	833*	3.5	3.9*	4.2	3.1

* Actual figures of 2009 ** Harmonized figures † Quarter on quarter annualized ‡ Urban and September

Tables are useful for displaying numerical information concisely, especially when several items are being compared. The table here presents economic information for fourteen countries: 2010 GDP, GDP growth, current account GDP, inflation, and joblessness. Presenting information in columns and rows permits readers to find data and identify relationships among them.

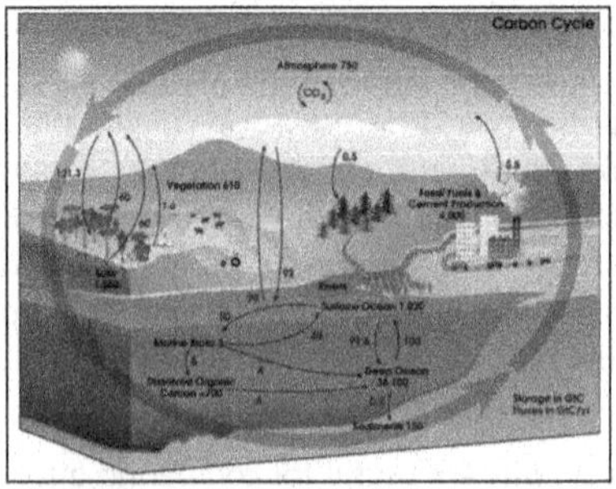

Diagrams and flowcharts are ways of showing relationships and processes. This diagram shows how carbon moves between the Earth and its atmosphere. Flowcharts can be made using widely available templates; diagrams, on the other hand, can range from simple drawings to works of art. Some simple flowcharts may be found in the genres chapters.

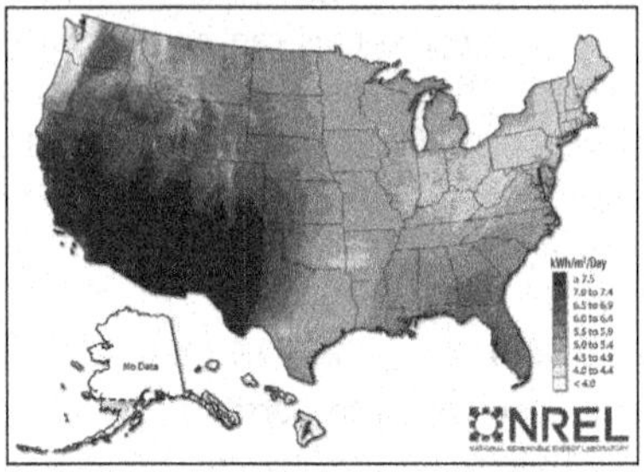

Maps show physical locations. This map shows the annual average direct solar resources for each of the U.S. states. Maps can be drawn to scale or purposefully out of scale to emphasize a point.

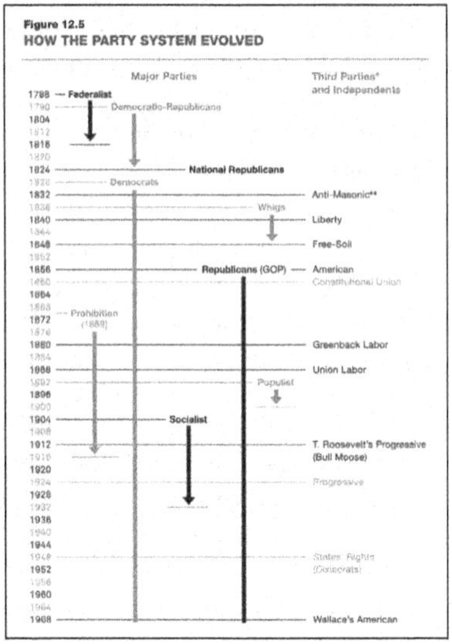

Timelines show change over time. These are useful to demonstrate cause and effect relationships or evolution. This timeline depicts how the American party system has evolved from 1788 to 2016. Timelines can be drawn horizontally or vertically.

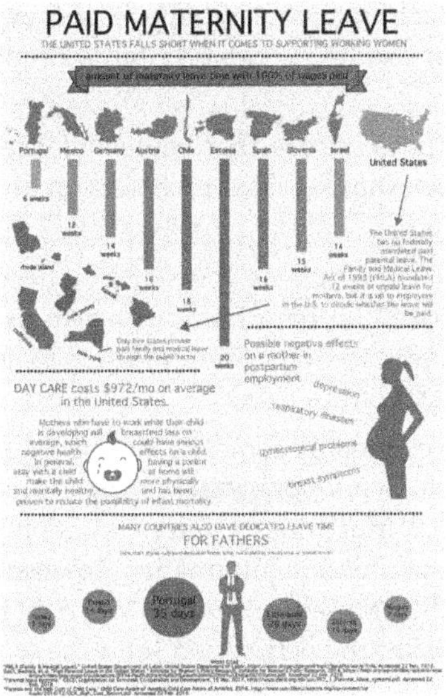

Infographics are eye-catching visual representations of information that help simplify a complicated subject. Infographics typically include an engaging title; a design that reflects the content being displayed; and a balance of charts, graphs, and other elements; readable fonts; and the sources of your information. Several websites offer templates to help you design and execute infographics, including *Piktochart*, *Infogram*, and several others.

SOME TIPS FOR USING VISUALS

- Position images as close as possible to the discussion to which they relate. In *Microsoft Word*, simply position your cursor where you want to insert an image; click the appropriate type of visual from the menu on the Insert tab; choose the appropriate image from your files; and click Insert. You may then need to adjust the way the text flows or wraps around the image: in the Page Layout tab, choose the appropriate option in Wrap Text.
- In academic writing, number all images, using separate sequences of numbers for figures (photos, graphs, diagrams, video clips, and drawings) and tables: Fig. 1, Fig. 2; Table 1, Table 2. Follow style guidelines (e.g., MLA or APA) for where to place the figure or table number and caption.
- Explain in your written text whatever information you present in an image—don't expect it to speak for itself. Refer to the image before it appears, identifying it and summarizing its point. For example: "As Table 1 shows, Italy's economic growth rate has been declining for thirty years."

- Provide a title or caption for each image to identify it and explain its significance for your text. For example: "Table 1: Italy's Economic Growth Rate, 1985–2015."
- Label the parts of visuals clearly to ensure that your audience will understand what they show. For example, label each section of a pie chart to show what it represents.
- Cite the source of any images you don't create yourself. You need not document visuals you create, based on data from your own experimental or field research, but if you use data from a source to create a graph or chart, **CITE THE SOURCE** of the data. 293–96
- In general, you may use visuals created by someone else in your academic writing as long as you include full **DOCUMENTATION**. 298–301 If you post your writing online, however, you must first obtain permission from the copyright owner and include permission information. For example: Photo courtesy of Victoria and Albert Museum, London. Copyright holders will often tell you how they want the permission sentence to read.

Incorporating Sound

Audio clips, podcasts, and other sound files can serve various useful purposes in online writing and spoken presentation. Music, for example, can create a mood for your text, giving your audience hints about how to interpret the meaning of your words and images or what emotional response you're evoking. Other types of sound effects—such as background conversations, passing traffic, birdsongs, crowd noise at sports events—can provide a sense of immediacy, of being part of the scene or event you're describing. Spoken words can serve as the primary way you present an online text or as an enhancement of or even a counterpoint to a written text. (And if your audience includes visually impaired people, an audio track can allow or help them to follow the text.)

You can download or link to various spoken texts online, or you can record voice and music as podcasts using programs such as *GarageBand* and *Audacity*. Remember to provide an in-text citation and full **DOCUMENTATION** 298–301 of any sound material you obtain from another source.

Adding Links

If you're writing an online text in which you want to include images, video, or sound material available on the web, it's often easier and more effective to create links to them within the text than to embed them by copying and pasting. Rather than provide the URL for the link, use relevant words to make it easier for a reader to decide to click on the link. (See the example below where the links are marked by blue color and words such as "Francis Davis Millet and Millet family papers.") Such links allow readers to see the materials' original context and to explore it if they wish. Be selective in the number of links you include: too many links can dilute a text.

The example below shows a blog post from the Archives of American Art with links to additional detail and documentation.

John Singer Sargent

This lively caricature from the Francis Davis Millet and Millet family papers features an artist fervently painting his subject, just in the background. Most likely it is John Singer Sargent at work on his painting *Carnation, Lily, Lily, Rose*. His posture and the expression on his face suggest an exuberance that matches the action of the paint dripping and splashing as it prepares to meet the canvas with energetic strokes.

Caricature of an artist painting vigorously, ca. 1885-1886. Francis Davis Millet and Millet family papers, Archives of American Art, Smithsonian Institution.

SOME TIPS FOR CREATING LINKS

289–92

- Indicate links with underlining and color (most often blue), and introduce them with a **SIGNAL PHRASE**.
- Don't include your own punctuation in a link. In the example on page 381, the period is not part of the link.
- Try to avoid having a link open in a new browser window. Readers expect links to open in the same window.

Editing Carefully—and Ethically

You may want to edit a photograph, cropping to show only part of it or using *Photoshop* or similar programs to enhance the colors or otherwise alter it. Similarly, you may want to edit a video, podcast, or other audio file to shorten it or remove irrelevant parts. If you are considering making a change of this kind, however, be sure not to do so in a way that misrepresents the content. If you alter a photo, be sure the image still represents the subject accurately; if you alter a recording of a speech or interview, be sure the edited version maintains the speaker's intent. Whenever you alter an image, a video, or a sound recording, tell your readers how you have changed it.

The same goes of editing charts and graphs. Changing the scale on a bar graph, for example, can change the effect of the comparison, making the quantities being compared seem very similar or very different, as shown in the two bar graphs of identical data in Figures 1 and 2.

Both charts show the increase in average housing costs in the United States between 2000 and 2015. However, by making the baseline in Figure 1 $200,000 instead of zero, the increase appears to be far greater than it was in reality. Just as you shouldn't edit a quotation or a photograph in a way that might misrepresent its meaning, you should not present statistical data in a way that could mislead readers.

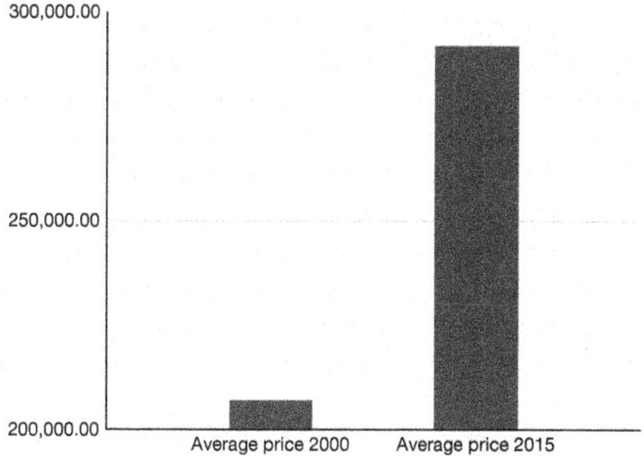

Fig. 1. Average housing prices in the United States, 2000–2015 (exaggerated).

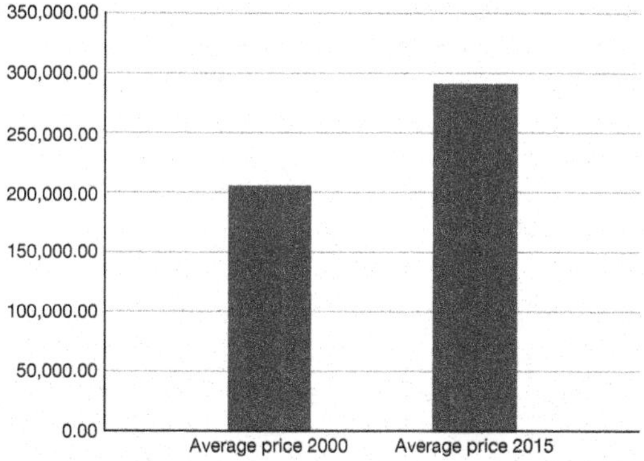

Fig. 2. Average housing prices in the United States, 2000–2015 (presented accurately).

35 Giving Presentations

In a marketing class, you give a formal presentation that includes slides and handouts as part of a research project on developing brand loyalty to clothing labels among college students. As a candidate for student government, you deliver several speeches to various campus groups that are simultaneously broadcast over the web. At a good friend's wedding, after you make a toast to the married couple, another friend who couldn't attend in person toasts them remotely using *Skype*; a third guest records both toasts on his cell phone and uploads them to *Facebook*. Whether or not you include digital and print media, whenever you are called on to give a spoken presentation, you need to make your points clear and memorable. This chapter offers guidelines to help you prepare and deliver effective presentations. We'll start with two good examples.

ABRAHAM LINCOLN

Gettysburg Address

Given by the sixteenth president of the United States, at the dedication of the Gettysburg battlefield as a memorial to those who died in the Civil War, this is one of the most famous speeches ever delivered in the United States.

Four score and seven years ago our fathers brought forth on this continent, a new nation, conceived in Liberty, and dedicated to the proposition that all men are created equal.

Now we are engaged in a great civil war, testing whether that nation, or any nation so conceived and so dedicated, can long endure.

We are met on a great battle-field of that war. We have come to dedicate a portion of that field, as a final resting place for those who here gave their lives that that nation might live. It is altogether fitting and proper that we should do this.

But, in a larger sense, we can not dedicate—we can not consecrate—we can not hallow—this ground. The brave men, living and dead, who struggled here, have consecrated it, far above our poor power to add or detract. The world will little note, nor long remember what we say here, but it can never forget what they did here. It is for us the living, rather, to be dedicated here to the unfinished work which they who fought here have thus far so nobly advanced. It is rather for us to be here dedicated to the great task remaining before us—that from these honored dead we take increased devotion to that cause for which they gave the last full measure of devotion—that we here highly resolve that these dead shall not have died in vain—that this nation, under God, shall have a new birth of freedom—and that government of the people, by the people, for the people, shall not perish from the earth.

You won't likely be called on to deliver such an address, but the techniques Lincoln used—brevity, rhythm, recurring themes—are ones you can use in your own spoken texts. The next example represents the type of spoken text we are sometimes called on to deliver at important occasions in the lives of our families.

JUDY DAVIS

Ours Was a Dad . . .

This short eulogy was given at the funeral of the writer's father, Walter Boock. Judy Davis lives in Davis, California, where she was for many years the principal of North Davis Elementary School.

Elsa, Peggy, David, and I were lucky to have such a dad. Ours was a dad who created the childhood for us that he did not have for himself.

The dad who sent us airborne on the soles of his feet, squealing with delight. The dad who built a platform in the peach tree so we could eat ourselves comfortably into peachy oblivion. The dad who assigned us chores and then did them with us. The dad who felt our pain when we skinned our knees.

Ours was the dad who took us camping, all over the U.S. and Canada, but most of all in our beloved Yosemite. The one who awed us with his ability to swing around a full pail of water without spilling a drop and let us hold sticks in the fire and draw designs in the night air with hot orange coals.

Our dad wanted us to feel safe and secure. On Elsa's eighth birthday, we acquired a small camping trailer. One very blustery night in Minnesota, Mom and Dad asleep in the main bed, David suspended in the hammock over them, Peggy and Elsa snuggled in the little dinette bed, and me on an air mattress on the floor, I remember the most incredible sense of well-being: our family all together, so snug, in that little trailer as the storm rocked us back and forth. It was only in the morning that I learned about the tornado warnings. Mom and Dad weren't sleeping: they were praying that when morning came we wouldn't find ourselves in the next state.

Ours was the dad who helped us with homework at the round oak table. He listened to our oral reports, taught us to add by looking for combinations of 10, quizzed us on spelling words, and when our written reports sounded a little too much like the *World Book* encyclopedia, he told us so.

Ours was a dad who believed our round oak table that seated 5
twelve when fully extended should be full at Thanksgiving. Dad called the chaplain at the airbase, asked about homesick boys, and invited them to join our family. Or he'd call International House in Berkeley to see if someone from another country would like to experience an American Thanksgiving. We're still friends with the Swedish couple who came for turkey forty-five years ago. Many people became a part of our extended family around that table. And if twelve around the table was good, then certainly fourteen would be better. Just last fall, Dad commissioned our neighbor Randy to make yet another leaf for the table. There were fourteen around the table for Dad's last Thanksgiving.

Ours was a dad who had a lifelong desire to serve. He delivered Meals on Wheels until he was eighty-three. He delighted in picking up

> the day-old doughnuts from Mr. Rollen's shop to give those on his route an extra treat. We teased him that he should be receiving those meals himself! Even after walking became difficult for him, he continued to drive and took along an able friend to carry the meals to the door.
>
> Our family, like most, had its ups and downs. But ours was a dad who forgave us our human failings as we forgave him his. He died in peace, surrounded by love. Elsa, Peggy, David, and I were so lucky to have such a dad.

This eulogy, in honor of the writer's father, provides concrete and memorable details that give the audience a clear image of the kind of man he was. The repetition of the phrase "ours was a dad" provides a rhythm and unity that moves the text forward, and the use of short, conventional sentences makes the text easy to understand—and deliver.

Key Features / Spoken Presentations

A clear structure. Spoken texts need to be clearly organized so that your audience can follow what you're saying. The beginning needs to engage their interest, make clear what you will be talking about, and perhaps forecast the central parts of your talk. The main part of the text should focus on a few main points—only as many as your listeners can be expected to absorb and retain. (Remember, they can't go back to reread!) The ending is especially important: it should leave your audience with something, to remember, think about, or do. Davis ends as she begins, saying that she and her sisters and brother "were so lucky to have such a dad." Lincoln ends with a dramatic resolution: "that government of the people, by the people, for the people, shall not perish from the earth."

Signpost language to keep your audience on track. You may need to provide cues to help your listeners follow your text, especially transitions that lead them from one point to the next. Sometimes you'll also want to stop and **SUMMARIZE** a complex point to help your audience keep track of your ideas and follow your development of them. 288–89

A tone to suit the occasion. Lincoln spoke at a serious, formal event, the dedication of a national cemetery, and his address is formal and even solemn. Davis's eulogy is more informal in tone, as befits a speech given for friends and loved ones. In a presentation to a panel of professors, you probably would want to take an academic tone, avoiding too much slang and speaking in complete sentences. If you had occasion to speak on the very same topic to a neighborhood group, however, you would likely want to speak more casually.

Repetition and parallel structure. Even if you're never called on to deliver a Gettysburg Address, you will find that repetition and parallel structure can lend power to a presentation, making it easier to follow—and more likely to be remembered. "We can not dedicate—we can not consecrate—we can not hallow": the repetition of "we can not" and the parallel forms of the three verbs are one reason these words stay with us more than 150 years after they were written and delivered. These are structures any writer can use. See how the repetition of "ours was a dad" in Davis's eulogy creates a rhythm that engages listeners and at the same time unifies the text.

Slides and other media. Depending on the way you deliver your presentation, you will often want or need to use other media—*PowerPoint, Prezi*, or other presentation slides, video and audio clips, handouts, flip charts, whiteboards, and so on—to present certain information and to highlight key points.

Considering the Rhetorical Situation

As with any writing, you need to consider your rhetorical situation when preparing a presentation:

Purpose	Consider what your primary purpose is. To inform? persuade? entertain? evoke another kind of emotional response?

Audience — Think about whom you'll be addressing and how well you know them. Will they be interested, or will you need to get them interested? Are they likely to be friendly? How can you get and maintain their attention, and how can you establish common ground with them? How much will they know about your subject—will you need to provide background or define any terms?

Genre — The genre of your text will affect the way you structure and present it. If you're making an argument, for instance, you'll need to consider counterarguments—and, depending on the way you're giving the presentation, perhaps to allow for questions and comments from members of the audience who hold other opinions. If you're giving a report, you may have reasons to prepare handouts with detailed information you don't have time to cover in your spoken text, or links to online documents or websites.

Stance — Consider the attitude you want to express. Is it serious? thoughtful? passionate? well informed? humorous? something else? Choose your words and any other elements of your presentation accordingly. Whatever your attitude, your presentation will be received better by your listeners if they perceive you as comfortable and sincere.

A Brief Guide to Writing Presentations

Whether you're giving a poster presentation at a conference or an oral report in class, what you say will differ in important ways from what you might write for others to read. Here are some tips for composing an effective presentation.

Budget your time. A five-minute presentation calls for about two and a half double-spaced pages of writing, and ten minutes means only four or five pages. Your introduction and conclusion should each take about one-tenth of the total time available; time for questions (if the format allows for them) should take about one-fifth; and the body of the talk, the rest. In a ten-minute presentation, then, allot one minute for your introduction, one minute for your conclusion, and two minutes for questions, leaving six minutes for the body of your talk.

Organize and draft your presentation. Readers can go back and reread if they don't understand or remember something the first time through a text. Listeners can't. Therefore, it's important that you structure your presentation so that your audience can follow your text—and remember what you say.

- *Craft an introduction* that engages your audience's interest and tells them what to expect. Depending on your rhetorical situation, you may want to begin with humor, with an anecdote, or with something that reminds them of the occasion for your talk or helps them see the reason for it. In any case, you always need to summarize your main points, provide any needed background information, and outline how you'll proceed.

- *In the body of your presentation,* present your main points in more detail and support them with reasons and evidence. As you draft, you may well find that you have more material than you can present in the time available, so you'll need to choose the most important points to focus on and leave out the rest.

- *Let your readers know you're concluding* (but try to avoid saying "in conclusion"), and then use your remaining time to restate your main points and to explain why they're important. End by saying "thank you" and offering to answer questions or take comments if the format allows for them.

Consider whether to use visuals. You may want or need to include some visuals to help listeners follow what you're saying. Especially when you're presenting complex information, it helps to let them see it as well as hear it. Remember, though, that visuals should be a means of conveying information, not mere decoration.

DECIDING ON THE APPROPRIATE VISUALS

- *Slides* are useful for listing main points and for projecting illustrations, tables, and graphs.
- *Videos, animations, and sounds* can add additional information to your presentations.
- *Flip charts, whiteboards, or chalkboards* allow you to create visuals as you speak or to keep track of comments from your audience.
- *Posters* sometimes serve as the main part of a presentation, providing a summary of your points. You then offer only a brief introduction and answer any questions. You should be prepared to answer questions from any portion of your poster.
- *Handouts* can provide additional information, lists of works cited, or copies of any slides you show.

What visual tools (if any) you decide to use is partly determined by how your presentation will be delivered. Will you be speaking to a crowd or a class, delivering your presentation through a podcast, or creating an interactive presentation for a web conference? Make sure that any necessary equipment and programs are available—and that they work. If at all possible, check out any equipment in the place where you'll deliver your presentation before you go live. If you bring your own equipment for a live presentation, make sure you can connect to the internet if you need to and that electrical outlets are in reach of your power cords. Also, make sure that your visuals can be seen. You may have to rearrange the furniture or the screen to make sure everyone can see.

And finally, have a backup plan. Computers fail; projector bulbs burn out; marking pens run dry. Whatever your plan is, have an alternative in case any problems occur.

Presentation software. *PowerPoint*, *Keynote*, and other presentation software can include images, video, and sound in addition to displaying written text. They are most useful for linear presentations that move audiences along one slide at a time. Cloud-based programs like *Prezi* also allow you to arrange words or slides in various designs, group related content together, and zoom in and out. Here are some tips for writing and designing slides:

369–70

- ***Use* LISTS *or images, not paragraphs.*** Use slides to emphasize your main points, not to reproduce your talk onscreen: keep your audience's attention focused on what you're saying. A list of brief points, presented one by one, reinforces your words. An image can provide additional information that your audience can take in quickly.

368–69

- ***Make your text easy for your audience to read.*** **FONTS** should be at least 18 points, and larger than that for headings. Projected slides are easier to read in sans serif fonts like Arial, Helvetica, and Tahoma than in serif fonts like Times New Roman. And avoid using all capital letters, which can be hard to read.
- ***Choose colors carefully.*** Your text and any illustrations must contrast with the background. Dark content on a light background is easier to read than the reverse. And remember that not everyone sees all colors; be sure your audience doesn't need to be able to see particular colors or contrasts in order to get your meaning. Red-green and blue-yellow contrasts are especially hard for some people to see and should be avoided.
- ***Use bells and whistles sparingly, if at all.*** Presentation software offers lots of decorative backgrounds, letters that fade in and out or dance across the screen, and sound effects. These features can be more distracting than helpful; use them only if they help to make your point.
- ***Mark your text.*** In your notes or prepared text, mark each place where you need to click a mouse to call up the next slide.

This Prezi presentation rotates, includes audio and video, and zooms in and out to let viewers take a closer look.

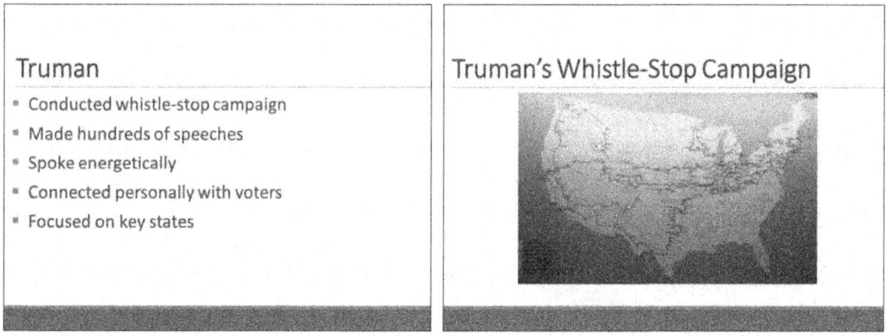

Two PowerPoint slides on the U.S. presidential election of 1948. The slide on the left outlines the main points; the one on the right shows a map of Truman's whistle-stop campaign, providing a graphic illustration of the miles he traveled as he campaigned to be president.

Handouts. When you want to give your audience information they can refer to later—reproductions of your visuals, bibliographic information about your sources, printouts of your slides—do so in the form of handouts. Refer to the handouts in your presentation, but unless they include material your audience needs to consult before or as you talk, wait until you are finished to distribute them so as not to distract listeners. Clearly label everything you give out, including your name and the date and title of the presentation.

Delivering a Presentation

The success of a presentation often hinges on how you deliver it. As you work on your spoken texts, bear in mind the following points:

Practice. Practice, practice, and then practice some more. The better you know your talk, the more confident you will be, and your audience will respond positively to that confidence. If you're reading a prepared text, try to write it as if you were talking. Then practice by recording it as you read it; listen for spots that sound as if you're reading, and work on your delivery to sound more relaxed. As you practice, pay attention to keeping within your time limit. If possible, rehearse your talk with a small group of friends to test their response and to get used to speaking in front of an audience.

Speak clearly. When you're giving a spoken presentation, your first goal is to be understood by your audience. If listeners miss important words or phrases because you don't pronounce them distinctly, your talk will not succeed. Make sure, too, that your pace matches your audience's needs. Often you'll need to make yourself speak more slowly than usual to explain complex material (or to compensate for nerves); sometimes you may need to speed up to keep your audience's attention. In general, though, strive for a consistent pace throughout, one that ensures you don't have to rush at the end.

Pause for emphasis. In writing, you have white space and punctuation to show readers where an idea or discussion ends. When speaking, you need to pause to signal the end of a thought, to give listeners a moment to consider something you've said, or to get them ready for a surprising or amusing statement.

Stand up (or sit up) straight and look at your audience. If you're in the same physical space as your audience, try to maintain some eye contact with them. If that's uncomfortable, fake it: pick a spot on the wall just above the head of a person in the back of the room, and focus on it. You'll appear as if you're looking at your audience even if you're not looking them in the eye. And if you stand or sit up straight, you'll project the sense that you have confidence in what you're saying. If you appear to believe in your words, others will, too. If you're speaking via an online forum like *Skype*, look at the computer's camera—not at the screen. Also, make sure the camera is positioned at your eye level, so you aren't looking down at it (and showing your viewers the ceiling behind you!).

Use gestures for emphasis. If you're not used to speaking in front of a group, you may let your nervousness show by holding yourself stiffly, elbows tucked in. To overcome some of that nervousness, take some deep breaths, try to relax, and move your arms and the rest of your body as you would if you were talking to a friend. Use your hands for emphasis: most public speakers use one hand to emphasize specific points and both hands to make larger gestures. Watch politicians on C-SPAN to see how people who speak on a regular basis use gestures as part of their overall delivery.

part 9

Portfolios

We gather together, or package, items all the time. Maybe you purchased this textbook in a package with a handbook. Maybe you or your parents have a range of investments referred to as a portfolio. In writing classes, we often pull together our assignments to create a writing portfolio. The following chapter offers advice on how to create a portfolio of the work you do over the course of a school term.

36 Compiling a Portfolio

Artists maintain portfolios of their work to show gallery owners, collectors, and other potential buyers. Money managers work with investment portfolios of stocks, bonds, and various mutual funds. And often as part of a writing class, student writers compile portfolios of their work. As with a portfolio of paintings or drawings, a portfolio of writing includes a writer's best work and, sometimes, preliminary and revised drafts of that work, along with a statement by the writer articulating why they consider it good. The *why* is as important as the work, for it provides you with an occasion for assessing your overall strengths and weaknesses as a writer. This chapter offers guidelines to help you compile both a *writing portfolio* and a *literacy portfolio*, a project that writing students are sometimes asked to complete as part of a literacy narrative.

Considering the Rhetorical Situation

As with the writing you put in a portfolio, the portfolio itself is generally intended for a particular audience but could serve a number of different purposes. It's a good idea, then, to consider these and the other elements of your rhetorical situation when you begin to compile a portfolio.

Purpose — Why are you creating this portfolio? To show your learning? To create a record of your writing? As the basis for a grade in a course? To organize your research? To explore your literacy? For something else?

Audience — Who will read your portfolio? What will your readers expect it to contain? How can you help them understand the context or occasion for each piece of writing you include?

Genre	What genres of writing should the portfolio contain? Do you want to demonstrate your ability to write one particular type of writing or in a variety of genres? Will your introduction to or assessment of the portfolio be in the form of a letter or an essay?
Stance	How do you want to portray yourself in this portfolio? What items should you include to create this impression? What stance do you want to take in your written assessment of its contents? Thoughtful? Enthusiastic? Something else?
Media/Design	Will your portfolio be in print? Or will it be electronic? Will it include multiple media? Whichever medium you use, how can you help readers navigate its contents? What design elements will be most appropriate to your purpose and medium?

A WRITING PORTFOLIO

What to Include

A portfolio developed for a writing course typically contains examples of your best work in that course, including any notes, outlines, preliminary drafts, and so on, along with your own assessment of your performance in the course. You might include any of the following items:

- freewriting, outlines, and other work you did to generate ideas
- drafts, rough and revised
- in-class writing assignments
- source material—copies of articles and online sources, observation notes, interview transcripts, and other evidence of your research
- tests and quizzes

- responses to your drafts
- conference notes, error logs, lecture notes, and other course materials
- electronic material, including visuals, blogs, and multimedia texts
- reflections on your work

What you include will vary depending on what your instructor asks for. You may be asked to include three or four of your best papers or everything you've written. You may also be asked to show work in several different genres. In any case, you will usually need to choose, and to do that you will need to have criteria for making your choices. Don't base your decision solely on grades (unless grades are one criterion); your portfolio should reflect *your* assessment of your work, not your instructor's. What do you think is your best work? your most interesting work? your most ambitious work? Whatever criteria you use, you are the judge.

Organizing a Portfolio

If you set up a way to organize your writing at the start of the course, you'll be able to keep track of it throughout the course, making your job at term's end much easier. Remember that your portfolio presents you as a writer, presumably at your best. It should be neat, well organized, and easy to navigate. Your instructor may provide explicit guidelines for organizing your portfolio. If not, here are some guidelines:

Paper portfolios. Choose something in which to gather your work. You might use a two-pocket folder, a three-ring binder, or a file folder, or you may need a box, basket, or some other container to accommodate bulky or odd-shaped items.

Label everything. Label each piece at the top of the first page, specifying the assignment, the draft, and the date: "Proposal, Draft 1, 9/12/18"; "Text Analysis, Final Draft, 10/10/18"; "Portfolio Self-Assessment, Final Draft, 11/11/18"; and so on. Write this information neatly on the page, or put it on a Post-it note. For each assignment, arrange your materials chronologically, with your earliest material (freewriting, for example) on the bottom, and each successive item (source materials, say, then your outline, then your first draft, and so on) on top of the last, ending with your final draft on top. That way readers can see how your writing changed from draft to draft.

Electronic portfolios. You might also create an electronic portfolio, or e-portfolio. E-portfolios typically consist of a network of **LINKED** documents that might include not only your writing and reflections on that writing, but also sources, writing, and art you did for other courses or for your own enjoyment, audio and video clips, and other resources. Tools that can help you create an e-portfolio include:

381–82

- ***Online tools.*** Several websites, including *Weebly* and *Wix*, offer free tools to help you create a preformatted e-portfolio. For example, *GoogleSites* provides templates you can use to build an e-portfolio, uploading documents, images, and videos from your computer.
- ***Blogging tools.*** You can create an e-portfolio using a blogging platform, like *Tumblr* or *WordPress*, which allows you to upload files and create a network of linked pages. Readers can then comment on your e-portfolio, just as they might on your blog entries.
- ***Wikis.*** Wiki-based e-portfolios differ from blog-based ones in the level of interactivity they allow. In addition to commenting, readers may—if you allow them—make changes and add information. *PBworks* is one free provider, as is *WikiSpaces*.
- ***Courseware.*** Your school may use a learning platform, such as *Blackboard*, *Brightspace*, or *Moodle*, that allows you to create an e-portfolio of your work.

It's also possible to create an electronic portfolio using word processing, spreadsheet, or presentation software. The programs available for your use and the requirements for publishing your portfolio vary from school to school and instructor to instructor; ask your instructor or your school's help desk for assistance.

Assessing Your Portfolio

An important part of your portfolio is your written self-assessment of your work. This is an opportunity to assess your work with a critical eye and to think about what you're most proud of, what you most enjoyed doing, what you want to improve. It's your chance to think about and say what you've learned during the class. Some instructors may ask you to write out your assessment in essay form, as an additional sample of your writing; others will want you to put it in letter form, which usually allows for a more relaxed and personal tone. Whatever form it takes, your statement should cover the following ground:

- *An evaluation of each piece of writing in the portfolio.* Consider both strengths and weaknesses, and give examples from your writing to support what you say. What would you change if you had more time? Which is your favorite piece, and why? your least favorite?
- *An assessment of your overall writing performance.* What do you do well? What still needs improvement? What do you *want* your work to say about you? What *does* your work say about you?
- *A discussion of how the writing you did in this course has affected your development as a writer.* How does the writing in your portfolio compare with writing you did in the past? What do you know now that you didn't know before? What can you do that you couldn't do before?
- *A description of your writing habits and process.* What do you usually do? How well does it work? What techniques seem to help you most, and why? Which seem less helpful? Cite passages from your drafts that support your conclusions.
- *An analysis of your performance in the course.* How did you spend your time? Did you collaborate with others? participate in peer review? have any conferences with your instructor? visit the writing center? Consider how these or any other activities contributed to your success.

A Sample Self-Assessment

Here is a self-assessment written by Nathaniel Cooney as part of his portfolio for his first-year writing class at Wright State University.

2 June 2018

Dear Reader,

It is my hope that in reading this letter you will gain an understanding of the projects contained in this portfolio. I enclose three works that I have submitted for an introductory writing class at Wright State University, English 102, Writing in Academic Discourse: an informative report, an argument paper, and a genre project based largely on the content of the argument paper. I selected the topics of these works for two reasons: First, they address issues that I believe to be relevant in terms of both the intended audience (peers and instructors of the course) and the times when they were published. Second, they speak to issues that are important to me personally. Below I present general descriptions of the works, along with my review of their strengths and weaknesses.

My purpose in writing the informative report "Higher Standards in Education Are Taking Their Toll on Students" was to present a subject in a factual manner and to support it with well-documented research. My intent was not to argue a point. However, because I chose a narrowly focused topic and chose information to support a thesis, the report tends to favor one side of the issue over the other. Because as a student I have a personal stake in the changing standards in the formal education system, I chose to research recent changes in higher education and their effects on students. Specifically, I examine students' struggles to reach a standard that seems to be moving further and further beyond their grasp.

I believe that this paper could be improved in two areas. The first is a bias that I think exists because I am a student presenting information from the point of view of a student. It is my hope, however, that my inclusion of unbiased sources lessens this problem somewhat and, furthermore, that it presents the reader with a fair and accurate collection of facts and examples that supports the thesis. My second area of concern is the overall balance in the paper between outside sources supporting my own thoughts and outside sources supporting opposing points of view. Rereading the paper, I notice many places where I may have worked too hard to include sources that support my ideas.

The second paper, "Protecting Animals That Serve," is an argument intended not only to take a clear position on an issue but also to argue for that position and convince the reader that it is a valid one. That issue is the need for legislation guaranteeing that certain rights of service animals be protected. I am blind and use a guide dog. Thus, this issue is especially important to me. During the few months that I have had him, my guide dog has already encountered a number of situations where intentional or negligent treatment by others has put him in danger. At the time I was writing the paper, a bill was being written in the Ohio House of Representatives that, if passed, would protect service animals and establish consequences for those who violated the law. The purpose of the paper, therefore, was to present the reader with information about service animals, establish the need for the legislation in Ohio and nationwide, and argue for passage of such legislation.

I think that the best parts of my argument are the introduction and the conclusion. In particular, I think that the conclusion does a good job of not only bringing together the various points but also conveying the significance of the issue for me and for others. In contrast, I think that the area most in need of further attention is the body of the paper. While I think the content is strong, I believe the overall organization could be improved. The connections between ideas are unclear in places, particularly in the section that acknowledges opposing viewpoints. This may be due in part to the fact that I had difficulty understanding the reasoning behind the opposing argument.

The argument paper served as a starting point for the genre project, for which the assignment was to revise one paper written for this class in a different genre. My genre project consists of a poster and a brochure. As it was for the argument paper, my primary goal was to convince my audience of the importance of a particular issue and viewpoint—specifically, to convince my audience to support House Bill 369, the bill being introduced in the Ohio legislature that would create laws to protect the rights of service animals in the state.

Perhaps both the greatest strength and the greatest weakness of the genre project is my use of graphics. Because of my blindness, I was limited in my use of some graphics. Nevertheless, the pictures were carefully selected to capture the attention of readers and, in part, to appeal to their emotions as they viewed and reflected on the material.

I put a great deal of time, effort, and personal reflection into each project. While I am hesitant to say that they are finished and while I am dissatisfied with some of the finer points, I am satisfied with the overall outcome of this collection of works. Viewing it as a collection, I am also reminded that writing is an evolving process and that even if these works never become exactly what I envisioned them to be, they stand as reflections of my thoughts at a particular time in my life. In that respect, they need not be anything but what they already are, because what they are is a product of who I was when I wrote them. I hope that you find the papers interesting and informative and that as you read them, you, too, may realize their significance.

Respectfully,

Nathaniel J. Cooney

Enclosures (3)

Cooney describes each of the works he includes and considers their strengths and weaknesses, citing examples from his texts to support his assessment.

A LITERACY PORTFOLIO

As a writing student, you may be asked to think back to the time when you first learned to read and write or to remember significant books or other texts you've read, and perhaps to put together a portfolio that chronicles your development as a reader and writer. You may also be asked to put together a literacy portfolio to accompany a literacy narrative.

What you include in such a portfolio will vary depending on what you've kept over the years and what your family has kept. You may have all of your favorite books, stories you dictated to a preschool teacher, notebooks in which you practiced writing the alphabet. Or you may have almost nothing. What you have or don't have is unimportant in the end: what's important is that you gather what you can and arrange it in a way that shows how you think about your development and growth as a literate person. What have been your experiences with reading and writing? What's your earliest memory of learning to write? If you love to read, what led you to love it? Who was most responsible for shaping your writing ability? Those are some of the questions you'll ask if you write a literacy narrative. You might also compile a literacy portfolio as a good way to generate ideas and text for that assignment.

What to Include in a Literacy Portfolio

- school papers
- drawings and doodles from preschool
- favorite books
- photographs you've taken
- drawings
- poems
- letters
- journals and diaries
- lists
- reading records or logs

- electronic texts you've created
- marriage vows
- speeches you've given
- awards you've received

Organizing a Literacy Portfolio

You may wish to organize your material chronologically, but there are other methods of organization to consider as well. For example, you might group items according to where they were written (at home, at school, at work), by genre (stories, poems, essays, letters, notes), or even by purpose (pleasure, school, work, church, and so on). Arrange your portfolio in the way that best conveys who you are as a literate person. Label each item you include, perhaps with a Post-it note, to identify what it is, when it was written or read, and why you've included it in your portfolio. Or you might create an e-portfolio, scanning print items to include in it with electronic items.

Reflecting on Your Literacy Portfolio

- Why did you choose each item?
- Is anything missing? Are there any other important materials that should be here?
- Why is the portfolio organized as it is?
- What does the portfolio show about your development as a reader and writer?
- What patterns do you see? Are there any common themes you've read or written about? Any techniques you rely on? Any notable changes over time?
- What are the most significant items, and why?

THEY SAY / I SAY CREDITS

TEXT

Editorial Staff of *The Eagle Eye*: Excerpt from "Our Manifesto to Fix America's Gun Laws," *The Guardian*, March 23, 2018. Copyright Guardian News & Media Ltd 2020. www.theguardian.com. Used with permission.

Kenneth Goldsmith: "Go Ahead: Waste Time on the Internet," *The Los Angeles Times*, August 12, 2016. Reprinted courtesy of Kenneth Goldsmith.

Chris Nowinski: Excerpt from "Youth Tackle Football Will Be Considered Unthinkable 50 Years from Now," Vox.com, April 3, 2019. https://www.vox.com/2019/3/27/18174368/football-concussion-brain-injury-cte-youth-football. Republished by permission of Vox Media, LLC.

Eric Schlosser: Excerpt from "A People's Democratic Platform." From *The Nation*. © 2004 The Nation Company. All rights reserved. Used under license.

Elizabeth Silkes: From "Cultural Heritage Reminds Us of Our Shared Humanity. That's Why Threats against Them Are So Dangerous," Time.com, January 10, 2020. Reused with permission of Elizabeth Silkes, Executive Director, International Coalition of Sites of Conscience.

David Zinczenko: "Don't Blame the Eater," *The New York Times*, November 23, 2002, p. A31. Reprinted by permission of the author.

PHOTOGRAPHS

About the Authors: Tricia Koning (Graff and Birkenstein).

Field Guide Credits

IMAGE ACKNOWLEDGMENTS

p. 312: Photo courtesy of www.donlaurencephotography.com; p. 286: Courtesy Dena Betz; p. 332: Courtesy Adam Karsten; p. 333: Courtesy Adalena Kavanagh; p. 334: Courtesy Julia Black; p. 335: Courtesy Darcy Vebber; p. 246 (all): Nicholas S. Holtzman, Simine Vazire, Matthias R. Mehl. "Sounds Like a Narcissist: Behavioral Manifestations of Narcissism in Everyday Life." *Journal of Research in Personality*; p. 248 (both): Houston Community College; p. 251: Permission to publish courtesy of EBSCO; pp. 254–55: Wright State University Libraries; p. 367: Used with the permission of Inter IKEA Systems B.V; p. 375 (left): National Gallery of Art; p. 375 (right): Library of Congress; p. 377 (all): RNGS/RTR/Newscom; p. 378 (top): NASA Image Collection/Alamy Stock Photo; p. 378 (center): This map was created by the National Renewable Energy; Laboratory for the U.S. Department of Energy; p. 381: Caricature of an artist painting vigorously, ca. 1885–1886. Francis Davis Millet and Millet family papers, 1858–1984, bulk 1858–1955. Archives of American Art, Smithsonian Institution; p. 384: Library of Congress; p. 385: Courtesy of Judy Davis

TEXT ACKNOWLEDGMENTS

Danielle Allen: From *Our Declaration: A Reading of the Declaration of Independence in Defense of Equality* by Danielle Allen. Copyright © 2014 by Danielle Allen. Used by permission of Liveright Publishing Corporation.

E. J. Bader: "Homeless on Campus" from *The Progressive*, July 2004. Copyright © The Progressive. Reprinted by permission.

Dennis Baron: "Don't Make English Official—Ban It Instead." Reprinted by permission of the author.

Tanya Barrientos: "Se Habla Español," from the August 2004 issue of *Latina*. Reprinted by permission of the author.

Dave Barry: "Introduction: Guys vs. Men" from *Dave Barry's Complete Guide to Guys: A Fairly Short Book* by Dave Barry, copyright © 1995 by Dave Barry. Used by permission of Random House, an imprint and division of Penguin Random House LLC. All rights reserved.

Lynda Barry: "Lost and Found" from "One Hundred Demons," Salon.com, November 17, 2000. This article first appeared in Salon.com, at http://www.Salon.com. An online version remains in the Salon archives. Reprinted with permission.

Bailey Basinger: "Tension, Contradiction, and Ambiguity: Gender Roles in 'A Rose for Emily.'" Copyright © 2018 by W. W. Norton & Company.

Cynthia Bass: Excerpt from "Gettysburg Address: Two Versions," *The San Francisco Examiner*, November 19, 1997. Reprinted by permission of the author.

Michael Benton, Mark Dolan & Rebecca Zisch: "Teen Film$: An Annotated Bibliography" from *Journal of Popular Film and Television*, Vol. 25, No. 2, Summer 1997, pp. 83–88. Reprinted by permission of the publisher Taylor & Francis Ltd, http://www.tandfonline.com

Hannah Berry: "The Fashion Industry: Free to Be an Individual." Copyright © 2012 by Hannah Berry.

Dylan Borchers: "Against the Odds: Harry S. Truman and the Election of 1948." Copyright © 2009 by Dylan Borchers.

danah boyd: "*Wikipedia* as a Site of Knowledge Production" from *It's Complicated: the social lives of networked teens* by danah boyd. Copyright © 2014 by danah boyd. Reprinted by permission of Yale University Press.

Rick Bragg: "All Over But the Shoutin'" from *All Over But the Shoutin'* by Rick Bragg, copyright © 1997 by Rick Bragg. Used by permission of Pantheon Books, an imprint of the Knopf Doubleday Publishing Group, a division of Penguin Random House LLC. All rights reserved.

Rachel Brinkley, Kenneth Ricker, and Kelly Tuomey: From "Esthetic Knowing with a Hospitalized Morbidly Obese Patient," *Journal of Undergraduate Nursing Scholarship*, Vol. 9, No. 1, Fall 2007. Reprinted by permission of The University of Arizona College of Nursing.

Nicholas Carr: "Is *Google* Making Us Stupid?" *The Atlantic*, July/August 2008. Copyright © 2008 The Atlantic Media Co., as first published in The Atlantic Magazine. All rights reserved. Distributed by Tribune Content Agency, LLC. Reprinted with permission.

Cameron Carroll: "Zombie Film Scholarship: A Review of the Literature" from UMW Blogs (http://www.umwblogs.org/). Reprinted by permission of the author.

Michael Chabon: "Kids' Stuff" from *Maps and Legends: Reading and Writing along the Borderlands*, published by HarperCollins. Copyright © Michael Chabon. Reprinted by permission of International Creative Management, Inc. All rights reserved.

Roy Peter Clark: "Why It Worked: A Rhetorical Analysis of Obama's Speech on Race" from Poynter.org, October 20, 2017. Reprinted by permission of the author.

Nathaniel Cooney: "Self-Assessment." Copyright © 2013 by Nathaniel Cooney.

Michaela Cullington: "Texting and Writing," *Young Scholars in Writing*, Vol. 8, 2011. Reprinted by permission of University of Missouri Press.

Judith Ortiz Cofer: "The Myth of the Latin Woman: I Just Met a Girl Named Maria" from *The Latin Deli: Prose and Poetry*. Copyright © 1993 by the University of Georgia Press. Reprinted by permission of the University of Georgia Press.

Matt de la Peña: "Becoming Whole" from "Sometimes the Tough Teen Is Quietly Writing Stories," originally published by NPR Code Switch, November 11, 2013. Reprinted by permission of Writers House LLC acting as agent for the author.

Eva Derzic: "In Defense of Writing Letters," UC Berkeley Comparative Literature Undergraduate Journal Blog, December 3, 2013. Reprinted by permission of the author.

Rita Dove: "The First Book," was originally published in *The Language of Life*, ed. Bill Moyers, Doubleday, New York 1995. Reprinted by permission of the author.

Jeremy Dowsett: "What My Bike Has Taught Me about White Privilege." A Little More Sauce Blog, August 20, 2014. Reprinted by permission of the author.

Andre Dubus III: "My Father Was a Writer" from *Townie: A Memoir* by Andre Dubus III. Copyright © 2011 by Andre Dubus III. Used by permission of W. W. Norton & Company, Inc.

Sarah Dzubay: "An Outbreak of the Irrational." Originally published on *Fresh Writing* at the University of Notre Dame, Vol. 17. Reprinted by permission of the author.

William Faulkner: "A Rose for Emily" from *Collected Stories of William Faulkner* by William Faulkner. Copyright © 1950 by Random House, Inc., and renewed 1977 by Jill Faulkner Summers. Reprinted by permission of W. W. Norton and Company. This selection may not be reproduced, stored in a retrieval system, or transmitted in any form or by any means without the prior written permission of the publisher.

Daniel Felsenfeld: "Rebel Music" from *The New York Times*, March 26, 2010 © 2010 The New York Times. All rights reserved. Used by permission and protected by the Copyright Laws of the United States. The printing, copying, redistribution, or retransmission of this Content without express written permission is prohibited.

Ashley Foster: "*Polyvore.com*: An Evaluation of How Fashion Is Consumed Online." Copyright © 2018 by W. W. Norton & Company.

Robert Frost: "The Road Not Taken" by Robert Frost from the book *The Poetry of Robert Frost* edited by Edward Connery Lathem. Copyright © 1916, 1969 by Henry Holt and Company. Copyright © 1944 by Robert Frost. Utilized by permission of Henry Holt and Company. All Rights Reserved.

Gallup: Figure: "Racial and Ethnic Composition of U.S. by Party ID," from "Democrats Racially Diverse; Republicans Mostly White," Gallup.com, February 8, 2013. Reprinted by permission of the publisher.

Diana George: "Changing the Face of Poverty: Nonprofits and the Problem of Representation" by Diana George from *Popular Literacy: Studies in Cultural Practices and Poetics*, edited by John Trimbur, © 2001. Reprinted by permission of the University of Pittsburgh Press.

Andreas Ghabrial, Alana Hardy, and Ogden Playground Committee: "Proposal for Ogden Playground Project," originally published on Ogden Junior Public School online, April 25, 2013. Reprinted by permission of Ogden Junior Public School.

Isabelle Gill: "Representation of Disney Princesses in the Media." Copyright © 2016 by Isabelle Gill. Originally published on *Young Scholars in Writing* at arc.lib.montana.edu. Reprinted by permission of the author.

Michael Granof: "Course Requirement: Extortion" from *The New York Times*, August 12, 2007 © 2007 The New York Times. All rights reserved. Used by permission and protected by the Copyright Laws of the United States. The printing, copying, redistribution, or retransmission of this Content without express written permission is prohibited.

Adrienne Green: "The Boldness of Roxanne Gay's 'Hunger,'" *The Atlantic*, June 13, 2017. Copyright © 2017 The Atlantic Media Co., as first published in The Atlantic Magazine. All rights reserved. Distributed by Tribune Content Agency, LLC. Reprinted with permission.

Kelly Green: "Researching Hunger and Poverty." Originally published on Arizona State University's e-Portfolios at asu.digication.com. Republished by permission of the author.

James Hamblin: "Living Simply in a Dumpster," *The Atlantic*, September 11, 2014. Copyright © 2014 The Atlantic Media Co., as first published in The Atlantic Magazine. All rights reserved. Distributed by Tribune Content Agency, LLC. Reprinted with permission.

Jason Hasler: "An Ancient Remedy Reexamined." Copyright © 2017 by Jason Hasler.

Langston Hughes: "Theme for English B" from *The Collected Poems of Langston Hughes* by Langston Hughes, edited by Arnold Rampersad with David Roessel, Associate Editor, copyright © 1994 by the Estate of Langston Hughes. Used by permission of Alfred A. Knopf, an imprint of the Knopf Doubleday Publishing Group, a division of Penguin Random House LLC. All rights reserved.

Analisa Johnson: "The Benefits of Prison Nursery Programs." Originally published in the *Boston University Arts & Sciences Writing Program Journal*, Issue 9. Reprinted by permission of the author.

Ana-Jamileh Kassfy: "Automotive Literacy." Originally published on ajkassfy.weebly.com. Reprinted by permission of the author.

Johnna S. Keller: "The Politics of Stairs," *Design Equilibrium*, Spring 2016. Reprinted by permission of AIA Atlanta.

Geeta Kothari: "If You Are What You Eat, Then What Am I?" from *The Best American Essays*. Reprinted by permission of the author.

Jonathan Kozol: "Chapter 7: Excluding Beauty" from *The Shame of the Nation: The Restoration of Apartheid Schooling in America* by Jonathan Kozol, copyright © 2005 by Jonathan Kozol. Used by permission of Crown Books, a division of Penguin Random House LLC. All rights reserved.

Nicholas Kristof: "Our Blind Spot about Guns" from *The New York Times*, July 30, 2014 © 2014 The New York Times. All rights reserved. Used by permission and protected by the Copyright Laws of the United States. The printing, copying, redistribution, or retransmission of this Content without express written permission is prohibited.

Steven D. Kurutz: "The Yeti, Uniting America" from *The New York Times*, September 28, 2017 © 2017 The New York Times. All rights reserved. Used by permission and protected by the Copyright Laws of the United States. The printing, copying, redistribution, or retransmission of this Content without express written permission is prohibited.

Edan Lepucki: "Our Mothers as We Never Saw Them" from *The New York Times*, May 10, 2017 © 2017 The New York Times. All rights reserved. Used by permission and protected by the Copyright Laws of the United States. The printing, copying, redistribution, or retransmission of this Content without express written permission is prohibited.

Joanna MacKay: "Organ Sales Will Save Lives." Originally published on DSpace@MIT.edu. Reprinted by permission of the author.

Jon Marcus: "The Reason College Costs More than You Think" from Time.com, September 23, 2014. Used by permission of The Hechinger Report.

Erin McHugh: From "Letting the Unspoken Speak: A Reexamination of the Pueblo Revolt of 1680," *Armstrong Undergraduate Journal of History* 5, no. 1 (April 2015). Reprinted by permission of the author.

Nicole Miles: "How I Learned to Draw Black People Like Me" from BuzzFeed News, February 24, 2017. Reprinted by permission of the author.

Matthew Miller: "Frost's Broken Roads." Copyright © 2017 by Matthew Miller.

Liz Moore: "Abuse of an Unnamed Wife: Is She Familiar?" Copyright © 2018 by Liz Moore.

Vann R. Newkirk II: "When Picture-Day Combs Don't Actually Comb," *The Atlantic*, February 22, 2017. Copyright © 2017 The Atlantic Media Co., as first published in The Atlantic Magazine. All rights reserved. Distributed by Tribune Content Agency, LLC. Reprinted with permission.

Beth Nguyen: "American Stories Are Refugee Stories" from Literary Hub, May 1, 2017. Reprinted by permission of the author.

Ana Pacheco: "Street Vendors: Harvest of Dreams." Copyright © 2017 by Ana Pacheco.

Anu Partanen: "What Americans Keep Ignoring about Finland's School Success." Originally published in *The Atlantic*, December 29, 2011. Reprinted by permission of the author.

Anna Quindlen: "Write for Your Life." Copyright © 2007 by Anna Quindlen. First appeared in *Newsweek*, January 22, 2007. Reprinted by permission of International Creative Management, Inc. All rights reserved.

Alberto Ríos: "Nani" from *Whispering to Fool the Wind*. Reprinted by permission of Sheep Meadow Press.

William Safire: "A Spirit Reborn" by William Safire. Copyright © 2002 by The Cobbett Corporation. Originally appeared in *The New York Times Magazine*. Reprinted by permission of the author's estate.

Sneha Saha: "The Wedding Carriage." Copyright © 2018 by Sneha Saha.

Michael J. Sandel: Excerpt from "What Wounds Deserve the Purple Heart?" from "Doing the Right Thing" from *Justice: What's the Right Thing to Do?* by Michael J. Sandel. Copyright © 2009 by Michael J. Sandel. Reprinted by permission of Farrar, Straus, and Giroux.

Frankie Schembri: "Edible Magic," *Angles* 2016. Reprinted by permission of the author.

Tatiana Schlossberg: "At This Academy, the Curriculum Is Garbage" from *The New York Times*, August 15, 2014 © 2014 The New York Times. All rights reserved. Used by permission and protected by the Copyright Laws of the United States. The printing, copying, redistribution, or retransmission of this Content without express written permission is prohibited.

David Sedaris: From *Dress Your Family in Corduroy and Denim*. Copyright © 2004 by David Sedaris. Reprinted with the permission of Little, Brown and Company. All rights reserved.

Ernie Smith: "A Brief History of the Modern-Day Straw, the World's Most Wasteful Commodity" from *Atlas Obscura*, July 7, 2017. Reprinted by permission of Atlas Obscura.

Natalie Standiford: "The Tenacity of Hope" from *The New York Times*, January 13, 2012 © 2012 The New York Times. All rights reserved. Used by permission and protected by the Copyright Laws of the United States. The printing, copying, redistribution, or retransmission of this Content without express written permission is prohibited.

Jude Stewart: "Boredom Is Good for You: The Surprising Benefits of Stultification," *The Atlantic*, June 2017. Copyright © 2017 The Atlantic Media Co., as first published in *The Atlantic Magazine*. All rights reserved. Distributed by Tribune Content Agency, LLC. Reprinted with permission.

Martha Stewart: "Oven Frites Recipe" from *Favorite Comfort Food: Classic Favorites and Great New Recipes* by Martha Stewart. Reprinted by permission of Martha Stewart Living Omnimedia.

Kelly Tams: Excerpt from "Kelly Tams' Teaching Portfolio: My Image of the Child" from tams.yolasite.com. Reprinted by permission of the author.

Amy Tan: "Mother Tongue." Copyright © 1990 by Amy Tan. First appeared in *The Threepenny Review*. Reprinted by permission of the author and the Sandra Dijkstra Literary Agency.

Catherine Thoms: "Social Media and Data Privacy." Copyright © 2018 by Catherine Thoms.

William Thorne: "Movie Review: *The Circle*" from *The Daily Bruin*, April 28, 2017. Reprinted by permission of The Daily Bruin.

Alina Tugend: "Multitasking Can Make You Lose . . . Um . . . Focus" from *The New York Times*, October 25, 2008 © 2008 The New York Times. All rights reserved. Used by permission and protected by the Copyright Laws of the United States. The printing, copying, redistribution, or retransmission of this Content without express written permission is prohibited.

Laurel Thatcher Ulrich: "Introduction: The Slogan" from *Well-Behaved Women Seldom Make History* by Laurel Thatcher Ulrich, copyright © 2007 by Laurel Thatcher Ulrich. Used by permission of Alfred A. Knopf, an imprint of the Knopf Doubleday Publishing Group, a division of Penguin Random House LLC. All rights reserved.

Emily Vallowe: "Write or Wrong Identity." Copyright © 2010 by Emily Vallowe.

Alex Weiss: "Should Video Gamers Be Prosecuted for Stealing Virtual Objects?" From *Slate*, February 7, 2012 © 2012 The Slate Group. All rights reserved. Used by permission and protected by the Copyright Laws of the United States. The printing, copying, redistribution, or retransmission of this Content without express written permission is prohibited.

Molly Worthen: "U Can't Talk to Ur Professor Like This" from *The New York Times*, May 14, 2017 © 2017 The New York Times. All rights reserved. Used by permission and protected by the Copyright Laws of the United States. The printing, copying, redistribution, or retransmission of this Content without express written permission is prohibited.

Malala Yousafzai: From *I Am Malala: The Girl Who Stood Up for Education and Was Shot by the Taliban* by Malala Yousafzai. Copyright © 2013. Reprinted by permission of Little, Brown and Company, an imprint of Hachette Book Group, Inc.

ACKNOWLEDGMENTS

THIS BOOK WOULD NEVER HAVE seen print if it weren't for Marilyn Moller, our superb editor at Norton, and the extraordinary job she has done of inspiring, commenting on, and rewriting (and then rewriting and rewriting again) our many drafts. Our friendship with Marilyn is one of the most cherished things to have developed from this project.

We are also particularly thankful to our current Norton editor Sarah Touborg, whose exemplary counsel, criticism, and hands-on intervention shaped the changes we have made to this edition. We are grateful for Sarah's unflagging patience with a couple of sometimes-recalcitrant authors. Assistant editor Emma Peters skillfully and cheerfully coordinated the many details involved in preparing our manuscript.

Our thanks go as well to Roby Harrington for his encouragement and astute suggestions (and great dinners) on his annual visits to Chicago. We extend our gratitude to Christine D'Antonio and Elizabeth Marotta for their superb work managing the editing and production of this edition; and to Joy Cranshaw and Katie Bolger for their energetic work creating the many digital resources that accompany the book. We appreciate Patricia Wong's excellent work as permissions editor and Ted Szczepanski's management of the photos for both versions of the book.

ACKNOWLEDGMENTS

Thanks to John Darger, our Norton representative, who offered early encouragement to write this book; to Debra Morton Hoyt and Mike Wood for their excellent work on the cover. Special thanks to Michele Dobbins, Elizabeth Pieslor, Kim Bowers, Emily Rowin, Lib Triplett, and the incomparable Norton travelers for the superb work they've done on behalf of our book.

We extend our deep thanks to Laura J. Panning Davies for her many contributions to this edition, including the new exercises, the new readings in "*They Say / I Say*" *with Readings*, and updating of the instructor's guide for the book, and for her ongoing work on **theysayiblog.com**. We owe a special debt of gratitude to Erin Ackerman for her expert contributions to the new chapter on research and for her chapter on writing in the social sciences. We also thank Chris Gillen for his chapter on writing in the sciences. Working with Erin and Chris proved to be an exhilarating experience; we learned a great deal by seeing how they applied our ideas to their disciplines.

A very special thanks goes to those who provided in-depth reviews of the new chapters on research and revising: Steven Bailey (Central Michigan University), Ana Cooke (Penn State University), Courtney Danforth (College of Southern Nevada), Africa Fine (Palm Beach State College), and Traci Klass (Palm Beach State College); and to those who provided detailed evaluations of the fourth edition: Joe Bizup (Boston University), Laura J. Panning Davies (SUNY Cortland), Karen Gocsik (University of California at San Diego), and Kelly Ritter (University of Illinois at Urbana–Champaign).

We are grateful to all of the instructors whose feedback was invaluable in shaping this fifth edition: Catherine Agar (Keuka College); Craig Albin (Missouri State University, West Plains Campus); Jason Barrett-Fox (Weber State); Jade Bittle

(Rowan-Cabarrus Community College); Roberta Brown (Western New Mexico University); William Burgos (LIU Brooklyn); Jackson Connor (University of Rio Grande); Charles Cook (Red Creek High School/Finger Lakes Community College); Amanda Corcoran (American River College); Linda Cowling (North Central Missouri College); Ginny Crisco (California State University, Fresno); Tamera Davis, (Northern Oklahoma College, Stillwater); Matt Dube (William Woods University); Mei Mei Evans (Alaska Pacific University); Anna Eyre (Merrimack College); Audrey Fessler (Appalachian State University); Jane Focht-Hansen (San Antonio College); Susan Gentry (Tunxis Community College); Sean Glassberg (Horry-Georgetown Technical College); Sarah Hallenbeck (University of North Carolina Wilmington); LewEllyn Hallett (University of Arkansas, Fayetteville); Natalie Hewitt (Hope International University); Lori Hughes (Lone Star College, Montgomery); Mark Hughes (Community College of Philadelphia); Elizabeth Inness-Brown (Saint Michael's College); Tim Jensen (Oregon State University); Alyssa Johnson (Horry-Georgetown Technical College); Gregory Johnson (Wake Technical Community College); Rhonda Jackson Joseph (Lone Star University Park); Alan Lindsay (New Hampshire Technical Institute); Jade Lynch-Greenberg (Purdue University Northwest); Gina MacKenzie (Holy Family University); Andrew Marvin (Three Rivers Community College); James Matthews (Fairmont State University); Gena McKinley (Rappahannock Community College, Warsaw Campus); Kelsey McNiff (Endicott College); Jeremy Meyer (Arizona State University, Tempe Campus); Jeannine Morgan (St. John's River State College); Janine Morris (Nova Southeastern University); Nichole Oechslin (Piedmont Valley Community College); Jessica Santini (Lake Region State College); Dagmar Scharold (University of Houston, Downtown);

Greta Skogseth (Montcalm Community College); Joshua Smith (University of North Carolina at Chapel Hill); Christian Smith (Coastal Carolina University); Kristen Snoddy (Indiana University Kokomo); Nicholas Vick (Pitt Community College); Tobin von der Nuell (University of Colorado Boulder); Sarah White (Purdue University Northwest); Lacey Wootton (American University); and Ali Zimmerman Zuckerman (University of Minnesota).

We owe a special thanks to our colleagues in the English department at the University of Illinois at Chicago: Mark Canuel, our former department head, for supporting our earlier efforts overseeing the university's Writing in the Disciplines requirement; Walter Benn Michaels, another former department head; and Ann Feldman, former director of university writing programs, for encouraging us to teach first-year composition courses at UIC in which we could try out ideas and drafts of our manuscript; Tom Moss, Diane Chin, Vainis Aleksa, and Matt Pavesich, who have also been very supportive of our efforts; and Matt Oakes, our former research assistant. We are also grateful to Ann Feldman, Diane Chin, and Mark Bennett for bringing us into their graduate course on the teaching of writing; and to Lisa Freeman, John Huntington, Walter Benn Michaels, and Ralph Cintron for inviting us to present our ideas in the keynote lecture at UIC's 2013 Composition Matters conference.

We are also especially grateful to Steve Benton and Nadya Pittendrigh, who taught a section of composition with us using an early draft of this book. Steve made many helpful suggestions, particularly regarding the exercises. We are grateful to Andy Young, a lecturer at UIC who has tested our book in his courses and who continues to give us extremely helpful feedback. And we thank Vershawn A. Young, whose work on code-meshing influenced our argument in Chapter 9, and Hillel Crandus, who inspired the chapter on "Entering Classroom Discussions."

We are grateful to the many colleagues and friends who've let us talk our ideas out with them and given extremely helpful responses. UIC's former dean, Stanley Fish, has been central in this respect, both in personal conversations and in his incisive articles calling for greater focus on form in the teaching of writing. Our conversations with Jane Tompkins have also been integral to this book, as was the composition course that Jane cotaught with Gerald, titled "Can We Talk?" Lenny Davis, too, offered both intellectual insight and emotional support, as did Heather Arnet, Jennifer Ashton, Janet Atwill, Kyra Auslander, Noel Barker, Mark Bauerlein, Jim Benton, Jack Brereton, Jim Burke, Tim Cantrick, Marsha Cassidy, David Chinitz, Lisa Chinitz, Pat Chu, Harry J. Cook, Duane Davis, Bridget O'Rourke Flisk, Steve Flisk, Judy Gardiner, Howard Gardner, Rich Gelb, Gwynne Gertz, Jeff Gore, Bill Haddad, Ben Hale, Scott Hammerl, Patricia Harkin, Andy Hoberek, John Huntington, Carol Jago, Joe Janangelo, Paul Jay, David Jolliffe, Nancy Kohn, Don Lazere, Sarah Levine, Jo Liebermann, Les Lynn, Steven Mailloux, Deirdre McCloskey, Maurice J. Meilleur, Alan Meyers, Greg Meyerson, Anna Minkov, Chris Newfield, Randy Olson, Jim Phelan, Paul Psilos, Bruce Robbins, Charles Ross, Eileen Seifert, Evan Seymour, David Shumway, Herb Simons, Jim Sosnoski, Kyle Stedman, David Steiner, Harold Aram Veeser, Chuck Venegoni, Marla Weeg, Jerry Wexler, Joyce Wexler, Virginia Wexman, Jeffrey Williams, Lynn Woodbury, Art Young, Vershawn Young, and the late Wayne Booth, whose friendship we dearly miss.

We are grateful for having had the opportunity to present our ideas to a number of colleges and high schools: University of

Arkansas at Little Rock, Augustana College, Brandeis University, Brigham Young University, Bryn Mawr College, California State University at Bakersfield, California State University at Northridge, University of California at Riverside, Case Western University, Central Michigan University, Clemson University, Columbia University, Community College of Philadelphia, Daemen College, Davidson College, University of Delaware, DePauw University, Drew University, Duke University, Duquesne University, Elmhurst College, Emory University, Fairfield University, Fontbonne University, Furman University, Gettysburg College, Harper College, Harvard University, Haverford College, Hawaii Office of Secondary School Curriculum Instruction, Hunter College, University of Illinois College of Medicine, Illinois State University, Illinois Wesleyan University, John Carroll University, Kansas State University, Lawrence University, the Lawrenceville School, University of Louisiana at Lafayette, MacEwan University, University of Maryland at College Park, Massachusetts Institute of Technology, University of Memphis, Miami University, Mills College, University of Missouri at Columbia, New Trier High School, North Carolina A&T University, University of North Florida, Northern Michigan University, Northwestern University Division of Continuing Studies, Norwalk Community College, University of Notre Dame, Ohio State University, Ohio Wesleyan University, Oregon State University, University of Portland, Purdue University at Calumet, University of Rochester, Rockford University, St. Ambrose University, St. Andrew's School, St. Charles High School, St. Francis University at Joliet, State University of New York at Geneseo, State University of New York at Stony Brook, Seattle University, South Elgin High School, University of South Florida, Southern Connecticut State University, University of Southern Mississippi, Stanford

University, Swarthmore College, Teachers College, University of Tennessee at Knoxville, University of Texas at Arlington, Tulane University, Union College, Ursinus College, Wabash College, Washington College, University of Washington, University of West Virginia at Morgantown, Western Michigan University, Westinghouse/Kenwood High Schools, Wheaton North High School, Wheaton Warrenville English Chairs, Winona State University, and the University of Wisconsin at Whitewater.

We particularly thank those who helped arrange these visits and discussed writing issues with us: Jeff Abernathy, Herman Asarnow, John Austin, Greg Barnheisel, John Bean, Crystal Benedicks, Joe Bizup, Sheridan Blau, Dagne Bloland, Chris Breu, Elizabeth Brockman, Mark Brouwer, Lizabeth Bryant, Joan Johnson Bube, John Caldwell, Gregory Clark, Irene Clark, Dean Philip Cohen, Cathy D'Agostino, Tom Deans, Gaurav Desai, Lisa Dresdner, Kathleen Dudden-Rowlands, Lisa Ede, Alexia Ellett, Emory Elliott, Anthony Ellis, Kim Flachmann, Ronald Fortune, Rosanna Fukuda, George Haggerty, Donald Hall, Joe Harris, Gary Hatch, Elizabeth Hatmaker, Donna Heiland, Harry Hellenbrand, Nicole Henderson, Doug Hesse, Van Hillard, Andrew Hoberek, Michael Hustedde, Sara Jameson, T. R. Johnson, David Jones, Ann Kaplan, Don Kartiganer, Linda Kinnahan, Dean Georg Kleine, Albert Labriola, Craig Lawrence, Lori Lopez, Tom Liam Lynch, Hiram Maxim, Michael Mays, Elizabeth McDermott, Thomas McFadden, Sean Meehan, Connie Mick, Robert Morace, Joseph Musser, Margaret Oakes, John O'Connor, Gary Olson, Tom Pace, Amy Pearson, Les Perelman, Jim Phelan, Emily Poe, Dominick Randolph, Clancy Ratliff, Monica Rico, Kelly Ritter, Jack Robinson, Warren Rosenberg, Laura Rosenthal, Dean Howard Ross, Deborah Rossen-Knill, Paul Schacht, Petra Schatz, Evan Seymour, Rose

Shapiro, Mike Shea, Cecilia M. Shore, Erec Smith, Kelly Smith, Nancy Sommers, Stephen Spector, Timothy Spurgin, Ron Strickland, Marcy Taylor, Michael Theune, Trig Thoreson, Josh Toth, Judy Trost, Aiman Tulamait, Charles Tung, John Webster, Robert Weisbuch, Sandi Weisenberg, Karin Westman, Martha Woodmansee, and Lynn Worsham.

We also wish to extend particular thanks to two Chicago-area educators who have worked closely with us: Eileen Murphy of CERCA and Les Lynn, formerly of the Chicago Debate League and now director of our joint organization, Argument-Centered Education. Lastly, we wish to thank two high school teachers for their excellent and inventive adaptations of our work: Mark Gozonsky in his *YouTube* video clip "Building Blocks," and Dave Stuart Jr. in his blogs, *Teaching the Core* and *Let's Make Teaching Better*.

We would also like to express our gratitude to several people who have published recent interviews with us about "*They Say / I Say*": Dave Stuart Jr., "A Conversation with Gerald Graff and Cathy Birkenstein" at **www.davestuartjr.com**; Erica Meltzer, "The Critical Reader Conversation with Gerald Graff and Cathy Birkenstein" at **www.thecriticalreader.com**; Park Howell, "How the Teaching of Argument Can Save American Education" at **www.businessofstory.com**; and Harold Aram Veeser, ed., in *The Rebirth of American Literary Theory and Criticism: Scholars Discuss Intellectual Origins and Turning Points* (2020).

For inviting us to present our ideas at their conferences, we are grateful to John Brereton and Richard Wendorf at the Boston Athenaeum; Wendy Katkin of the Reinvention Center of State University of New York at Stony Brook; Luchen Li of the Michigan English Association; Lisa Lee and Barbara Ransby of the Public Square in Chicago; Don Lazere of the University of Tennessee at Knoxville; Dennis Baron of the University of Illinois at Urbana–Champaign; Alfie Guy of Yale University; Irene Clark of the California State University of Northridge; George Crandell and Steve Hubbard, codirectors of the ACETA conference at Auburn University; Mary Beth Rose of the Humanities Institute at the University of Illinois at Chicago; Diana Smith of St. Anne's Belfield School and the University of Virginia; Jim Maddox and Victor Luftig of the Bread Loaf School of English; Jan Fitzsimmons and Jerry Berberet of the Associated Colleges of Illinois; Rosemary Feal, executive director of the Modern Language Association; Les Perelman of the Massachusetts Institute of Technology; and Bruce Herzberg of Bentley College and Chris Gallagher of Northeastern University.

We wish to thank several reviewers not already mentioned who provided feedback on the material for Chapter 9: Ana Cooke (Carnegie Mellon University); Elias Dominguez-Barajas (University of Arkansas); Douglas Kern (University of Maryland); Janine Morris (Nova Southeastern University); and Keith Walters (Portland State University).

Our thanks also go to those who helped develop the ideas for the chapter on online discussions: Karen Bruce (Ohio State University); Nick Carbone; Ana Cooke (Carnegie Mellon); Courtney Danforth (University of Southern Nevada); Lyra Hilliard (University of Maryland); Janine Morris (Nova Southeastern University); and Ilknur Sancak-Marusa (West Chester University).

A very special thanks goes to those who reviewed materials for the fourth edition: Teresa Alto (Itasca Community College); Darla Anderson (California State University, Northridge); Jan Andres (Riverside City College); Steven Bailey (Central Michigan University); Valerie Bell (Loras College); Tamara

Benson (Kent State University); Jade Bittle (Rowan-Cabarrus Community College); Jill Bonds (University of Phoenix); William Cantrell (Johnson Central High School); David Chase (Raritan Valley Community College); Barbara Cook (Mount Aloysius College); Jonathan Cook (Durham Technical Community College); Carol Lynne Lana Dalley (California State University, Fullerton); D'Arcangelis (Memorial University of Newfoundland); Nicholas DeArmas (Seminole State College of Florida); Elias Dominguez-Barajas (University of Arkansas); Ember Dooling (St. Joseph High School); Andrew Dunphy (Massasoit Community College); Justin Eells (Minnesota State University, Mankato); Africa Fine (Palm Beach State College); Valerie Fong (Foothill College); Reese Fuller (Episcopal School of Acadiana); Karen Gaffney (Raritan Valley Community College); Jacquelyn Geiger (Bucks County Community College); Joshua Geist (College of the Sequoias); Ashley Gendek (Kentucky Wesleyan College); Sean George (Dixie State University); Karen Gocsik (University of California, San Diego); Sarah Gray (Middle Tennessee State University); George Grinnell (University of British Columbia Okanagan); Lindsay Haney (Bellevue College); Catherine Hayter (Saddleback College); Stephen V. Hoyt (Obridge Academy/St. Joseph's College); Timothy Jackson (Rosemont College); Julie Jung-Kim (Trinity International University); Hannah Keller (Campbell University); Michael Keller (South Dakota State University); Nina Kutty (DePaul University); Lisa Lipani (University of Georgia); Judi Mack (Joliet Junior College); Anna Maheshwari (Schoolcraft College); Sarah F. McGinley (Wright State University); James McGovern (Germanna Community College); Liz McLemore (Minneapolis Community and Technical College) Jason Melton (Sacramento State University); Michael Mendoza (Seminole State College of Florida); Carey

Millsap-Spears (Moraine Valley Community College); Nicole Morris (Emory University); Shelley Palmer (Central Piedmont Community College); Jeff Pruchnic (Wayne State University); Tammy Ramsey (Bluegrass Community and Technical College); Cynthia Cox Richardson (Sinclair Community College); Rachel Rinehart (St. Edward's University); Kelly Ritter (University of Illinois Urbana–Champaign); Deborah Rossen-Knill (University of Rochester); Laura Rossi-Le (Endicott College); Julie Shattuck (Frederick Community College); Ellen Sorg (Owens Community College); Jennifer Stefaniak (Springfield Technical Community College); Heather Stringham (College of Southern Nevada); Stuart Swirsky (Seminole State College of Florida); Star Taylor (Riverside City College); Stephanie Tran (Foothill College); Alicia Trotman (Mercy College); Robert Williams (St. Edward's University); and Benjamin Woo (Carleton University).

A very special thanks goes to those who reviewed materials for the third edition: Carrie Bailey (Clark College); Heather Barrett (Boston University); Amy Bennett-Zendzian (Boston University); Seth Blumenthal (Boston University); Ron Brooks (Oklahoma State University); Jonathan Cook (Durham Technical Community College); Tessa Croker (Boston University); Perry Cumbie (Durham Technical Community College); Robert Danberg (Binghamton University); Elias Dominguez-Barajas (University of Arkansas); Nancy Enright (Seton Hall University); Jason Evans (Prairie State College); Ted Fitts (Boston University); Karen Gaffney (Raritan Valley Community College); Karen Gardiner (University of Alabama); Stephen Hodin (Boston University); Michael Horwitz (University of Hartford); John Hyman (American University); Claire Kervin (Boston University); Melinda Kreth (Central Michigan University); Heather Marcovitch (Red Deer College);

Christina Michaud (Boston University); Marisa Milanese (Boston University); Theresa Mooney (Austin Community College); Roxanne Munch (Joliet Junior College); Sarah Quirk (Waubonsee Community College); Lauri Ramey (California State University, Los Angeles); David Shawn (Boston University); Jennifer Sia (Boston University); Laura Sonderman (Marshall University); Katherine Stebbins McCaffrey (Boston University); K. Sullivan (Lane Community College); Anne-Marie Thomas (Austin Community College at Riverside); Eliot Treichel (Lane Community College); Rosanna Walker (Lane Community College); and Mary Erica Zimmer (Boston University). We also thank those who reviewed the literature chapter: Julie Bowman (Carnegie Mellon University); Jim Burke (Burlingame High School); Ana Cooke (Carnegie Mellon University); Thomas Cooley (Ohio State University); Lisa Ede (Oregon State University); Priscilla Glanville (State College of Florida); Melissa Goldthwaite (Saint Joseph's University); Rafey Habib (Rutgers University at Camden); Michael Hennessy (Texas State University); and Alexis Teagarden (Carnegie Mellon University).

Thanks to those who reviewed the materials for the second edition: Erin Ackerman (City University of New York–John Jay College); Mary Angeline (University of Northern Colorado); Ned Bachus (Community College of Philadelphia); Michelle Ballif (University of Georgia); Jonathan Barz (University of Dubuque); Mary Bauer Morley (University of North Dakota); Benjamin Bennett-Carpenter (Oakland University); Michelle Boswell (University of Maryland); Laura Bowles (University of Central Arkansas); E. Brand (Broome Community College); Beth Buyserie (Washington State University); Dana Cairns Watson (University of California, Los Angeles); Genevieve Carminati (Montgomery College); Brent Chesley (Aquinas

College); Joseph Colavito (Butler University); Tara DaPra (University of Minnesota); Emily Detmer-Goebel (Northern Kentucky University); J. Michael Duvall (College of Charleston); Adriana Estill (Carleton College); Ralph Faris (Community College of Philadelphia); Chris Gillen (Kenyon College); Patricia Gillikin (University of New Mexico Valencia Campus); Kenneth Grant (University of Wisconsin–Baraboo/Sauk County); Kevin Griffith (Capital University); Annemarie Hamlin (Central Oregon Community College); Rick Hansen (California State University, Fresno); John Hare (Montgomery College); Wendy Hayden (Hunter College of the City University of New York); Karen Head (Georgia Institute of Technology); Chene Heady (Longwood University); Nels Highberg (University of Hartford); Victoria Holladay (California State University, Los Angeles); D. Kern Holoman (University of California, Davis); Elizabeth Huergo (Montgomery College); Sara Jameson (Oregon State University); Joseph Jones (University of Memphis); Andrew Keitt (University of Alabama at Birmingham); Kurt Koenigsberger (Case Western Reserve University); Gary Leising (Utica College); Gary Lewandowski (Monmouth University); Michelle Maher (La Roche College); Lisa Martin (University of Wisconsin–Baraboo/Sauk County); Miles McCrimmon (J. Sargeant Reynolds Community College); Jacqueline Megow (Oklahoma State University); Bruce Michelson (University of Illinois at Urbana–Champaign); Megan Morton (Purdue University); Steven Muhlberger (Nipissing University); Lori Muntz (Iowa Wesleyan College); Ann Murphy (Assumption College); Sarah Perrault (University of Nevada, Reno); Christine Pipitone-Herron (Raritan Valley Community College); David Samper (University of Oklahoma); Rose Shapiro (Fontbonne University); Jennifer Stewart (Indiana University–Purdue University Fort Wayne);

Sandra Stollman (Broward College); Linda Sturtz (Beloit College); Mark Sutton (Kean University); Tobin von der Nuell (University of Colorado at Boulder); Brody Waybrant (Bay Mills Community College); Gina Weaver (Southern Nazarene University); Amy Whitson (Missouri State University); and Susan Wright (Montclair State University).

Thanks also to those who reviewed the manuscript for the original version of *They Say*; their suggestions contributed enormously to this book: Alan Ainsworth (Houston Community College); Rise Axelrod (University of California, Riverside); Bob Baron (Mesa Community College); David Bartholomae (University of Pittsburgh); Diane Belcher (Georgia State University); Michel De Benedictis (Miami Dade College); Joseph Bizup (Boston University); Patricia Bizzell (College of the Holy Cross); John Brereton (Harvard University); Richard Bullock (Wright State University); Charles Cooper (University of California, San Diego); Christine Cozzens (Agnes Scott College); Sarah Duerden (Arizona State University); Russel Durst (University of Cincinnati); Joseph Harris (Duke University); Paul Heilker (Virginia Polytechnic Institute); Michael Hennessy (Texas State University); Karen Lunsford (University of California, Santa Barbara); Libby Miles (University of Rhode Island); Mike Rose (University of California, Los Angeles); William H. Smith (Weatherford College); Scott Stevens (Western Washington University); Patricia Sullivan (University of Colorado); Pamela Wright (University of California, San Diego); and Daniel Zimmerman (Middlesex Community College).

Finally, a special thank you to David Bartholomae for suggesting the phrase that became the subtitle of this book.

INDEX OF TEMPLATES

LISTEN BEFORE YOU LEAP

(PP. 10–11)

- While I understand the impulse to ____________, my own view is ____________.
- While I agree with X that ____________, I cannot accept her overall conclusion that ____________.
- While X argues ____________, and I argue ____________, in a way we're both right.

THE TEMPLATE OF TEMPLATES

(P. 11)

- In recent discussions of ____________, a controversial issue has been whether ________________. On the one hand, some argue that __________. From this perspective, __________. On the other hand, however, others argue that ____________. In the words of ____________, one of this view's main proponents, "____________." According to this view, ____________. In sum, then, the issue is whether __________ or __________.

  My own view is that ______________. Though I concede that

___________, I still maintain that ___________. For example, _________. Although some might object that _________, I would reply that _________. The issue is important because _________.

INTRODUCING WHAT "THEY SAY"

(P. 23)

- A number of ___________ have recently suggested that ___________.
- It has become common today to dismiss ___________.
- In their recent work, Y and Z have offered harsh critiques of ___________ for ___________.

INTRODUCING "STANDARD VIEWS"

(PP. 23–24)

- Americans have always believed that ___________.
- Conventional wisdom has it that ___________.
- Common sense seems to dictate that ___________.
- The standard way of thinking about topic X has it that ___________.
- It is often said that ___________.
- My whole life I have heard it said that ___________.
- You would think that ___________.
- Many people assume that ___________.

Index of Templates

MAKING WHAT "THEY SAY" SOMETHING *YOU* SAY
(PP. 24–25)

- I've always believed that ____________.
- When I was a child, I used to think that ____________.
- Although I should know better by now, I cannot help thinking that ____________.
- At the same time that I believe ____________, I also believe ____________.

INTRODUCING SOMETHING IMPLIED OR ASSUMED
(P. 25)

- Although none of them have ever said so directly, my teachers have often given me the impression that ____________.
- One implication of X's treatment of ____________ is that ____________.
- Although X does not say so directly, she apparently assumes that ____________.
- While they rarely admit as much, ____________ often take for granted that ____________.

INTRODUCING AN ONGOING DEBATE
(PP. 25–28)

- In discussions of X, one controversial issue has been ____________. On the one hand, ____________ argues ____________. On the other hand, ___________ contends ___________. Others even maintain ___________. My own view is ___________.

- When it comes to the topic of ___________, most of us will readily agree that ___________. Where this agreement usually ends, however, is on the question of ___________. Whereas some are convinced that ___________, others maintain that ___________.
- In conclusion, then, as I suggested earlier, defenders of ___________ can't have it both ways. Their assertion that ___________ is contradicted by their claim that ___________.

CAPTURING AUTHORIAL ACTION

(PP. 41–44)

- X acknowledges that ___________.
- X agrees that ___________.
- X argues that ___________.
- X believes that ___________.
- X celebrates the fact that ___________.
- X claims that ___________.
- X complains that ___________.
- X concedes that ___________.
- X demonstrates that ___________.
- X denies/does not deny that ___________.
- X deplores the tendency to ___________.
- X emphasizes that ___________.

- X insists that ___________.
- X observes that ___________.
- X questions whether ___________.
- X refutes the claim that ___________.
- X reminds us that ___________.
- X reports that ___________.
- X suggests that ___________.
- X urges us to ___________.

INTRODUCING QUOTATIONS

(P. 51)

- X states, "___________."
- As the prominent philosopher X puts it, "___________."
- According to X, "___________."
- X himself writes, "___________."
- In her book, ___________, X maintains that "___________."
- Writing in the journal ___________, X complains that "___________."
- In X's view, "___________."
- X agrees when she writes, "___________."
- X disagrees when he writes, "___________."
- X complicates matters further when he writes, "___________."

EXPLAINING QUOTATIONS

(P. 52)

- Basically, X is warning ___________.
- In other words, X believes ___________.
- In making this comment, X urges us to ___________.
- X is corroborating the age-old adage that ___________.
- X's point is that ___________.
- The essence of X's argument is that ___________.

DISAGREEING, WITH REASONS

(P. 62)

- I think X is mistaken because she overlooks ___________.
- X's claim that ___________ rests upon the questionable assumption that ___________.
- I disagree with X's view that ___________ because, as recent research has shown, ___________.
- X contradicts herself / can't have it both ways. On the one hand, she argues ___________. On the other hand, she also says ___________.
- By focusing on ___________, X overlooks the deeper problem of ___________.

AGREEING

(PP. 64–66)

- I agree that ________ because my experience ________ confirms it.
- X surely is right about ________ because, as she may not be aware, recent studies have shown that ________.
- X's theory of ________ is extremely useful because it sheds insight on the difficult problem of ________.
- Those unfamiliar with this school of thought may be interested to know that it basically boils down to ________.
- I agree that ________, a point that needs emphasizing since so many people believe ________.
- If group X is right that ________, as I think they are, then we need to reassess the popular assumption that ________.

AGREEING AND DISAGREEING SIMULTANEOUSLY

(PP. 68–69)

- Although I agree with X up to a point, I cannot accept his overall conclusion that ________.
- Although I disagree with much that X says, I fully endorse his final conclusion that ________.
- Though I concede that ________, I still insist that ________.
- X is right that ________, but she seems on more dubious ground when she claims that ________.

- While X is probably wrong when she claims that ___________, she is right that ___________.
- Whereas X provides ample evidence that ___________, Y and Z's research on ___________ and ___________ convinces me that ___________ instead.
- I'm of two minds about X's claim that ___________. On the one hand, I agree that ___________. On the other hand, I'm not sure if ___________.
- My feelings on the issue are mixed. I do support X's position that ___________, but I find Y's argument about ___________ and Z's research on ___________ to be equally persuasive.

SIGNALING WHO IS SAYING WHAT

(PP. 75–76)

- X argues ___________.
- According to both X and Y, ___________.
- Politicians, X argues, should ___________.
- Most athletes will tell you that ___________.
- My own view, however, is that ___________.
- I agree, as X may not realize, that ___________.
- But ___________ are real and, arguably, the most significant factor in ___________.
- But X is wrong that ___________.
- However, it is simply not true that ___________.
- Indeed, it is highly likely that ___________.
- X's assertion that ___________ does not fit the facts.

- X is right that ___________.
- X is wrong that ___________.
- X is both right and wrong that ___________.
- Yet a sober analysis of the matter reveals ___________.
- Nevertheless, new research shows ___________.
- Anyone familiar with ___________ should agree that ___________.

EMBEDDING VOICE MARKERS

(P. 79)

- X overlooks what I consider an important point about ___________.
- My own view is that what X insists is a ___________ is in fact a ___________.
- I wholeheartedly endorse what X calls ___________.
- These conclusions, which X discusses in ___________, add weight to the argument that ___________.

ENTERTAINING OBJECTIONS

(P. 86)

- At this point I would like to raise some objections that have been inspired by the skeptic in me. She feels that I have been ignoring ___________.
- Yet some readers may challenge the view that ___________.
- Of course, many will probably disagree with this assertion that ___________.

NAMING YOUR NAYSAYERS

(PP. 87–88)

- Here many ___________ would probably object that ___________.
- But ___________ would certainly take issue with the argument that ___________.
- ___________, of course, may want to question whether ___________.
- Nevertheless, both followers and critics of ___________ will probably argue that ___________.
- Although not all ___________ think alike, some of them will probably dispute my claim that ___________.
- ___________ are so diverse in their views that it's hard to generalize about them, but some are likely to object on the grounds that ___________.

INTRODUCING OBJECTIONS INFORMALLY

(PP. 88–89)

- But is my proposal realistic? What are the chances of its actually being adopted?
- Yet is it always true that ___________? Is it always the case, as I have been suggesting, that ___________?
- However, does the evidence I've cited prove conclusively that ___________?
- "Impossible," some will say. "You must be reading the research selectively."

MAKING CONCESSIONS WHILE STILL STANDING YOUR GROUND (P. 93)

- Although I grant that ________, I still maintain that ________.
- Proponents of X are right to argue that ________. But they exaggerate when they claim that ________.
- While it is true that ________, it does not necessarily follow that ________.
- On the one hand, I agree with X that ________. But on the other hand, I still insist that ________.

INDICATING WHO CARES (PP. 99–100)

- ________ used to think ________. But recently [or within the past few decades] ________ suggests that ________.
- These findings challenge the work of earlier researchers, who tended to assume that ________.
- Recent studies like these shed new light on ________, which previous studies had not addressed.
- Researchers have long assumed that ________. For instance, one eminent scholar of cell biology, ________, assumed in ________, her seminal work on cell structures and functions, that fat cells ________. As ________ herself put it, "________" (2012). Another leading scientist, ________, argued that fat cells "________" (2011). Ultimately, when it came to the nature of fat, the basic assumption was that ________.

But a new body of research shows that fat cells are far more complex and that ____________.

- If sports enthusiasts stopped to think about it, many of them might simply assume that the most successful athletes ____________. However, new research shows ____________.

- These findings challenge neoliberals' common assumptions that ____________.

- At first glance, teenagers appear to ____________. But on closer inspection ____________.

ESTABLISHING WHY YOUR CLAIMS MATTER

(PP. 102–3)

- X matters / is important because ____________.

- Although X may seem trivial, it is in fact crucial in terms of today's concern over ____________.

- Ultimately, what is at stake here is ____________.

- These findings have important consequences for the broader domain of ____________.

- My discussion of X is in fact addressing the larger matter of ____________.

- These conclusions / This discovery will have significant applications in ____________ as well as in ____________.

- Although X may seem of concern to only a small group of ____________, it should in fact concern anyone who cares about ____________.

Index of Templates

COMMONLY USED TRANSITIONS

(PP. 111–12)

ADDITION

also
and
besides
furthermore
in addition
in fact
indeed
moreover
so too

ELABORATION

actually
by extension
in other words
in short
that is
to put it another way
to put it bluntly
to put it succinctly
ultimately

EXAMPLE

after all
as an illustration
consider
for example
for instance
specifically
to take a case in point

CAUSE AND EFFECT

accordingly
as a result
consequently
hence
since
so
then
therefore
thus

INDEX OF TEMPLATES

COMPARISON

along the same lines
in the same way
likewise
similarly

CONTRAST

although
but
by contrast
conversely
despite
even though
however
in contrast
nevertheless
nonetheless
on the contrary
on the other hand
regardless
whereas
while
yet

CONCESSION

admittedly
although it is true that
granted
of course
naturally
to be sure

CONCLUSION

as a result
consequently
hence
in conclusion
in short
in sum
therefore
thus
to sum up
to summarize

Index of Templates

TRANSLATION RECIPES

(PP. 126–27)

- Scholar X argues, "__________." In other words, __________.
- Essentially, X argues __________.
- X's point, succinctly put, is that __________.
- Plainly put, __________.

ADDING METACOMMENTARY

(PP. 140–46)

- In other words, __________.
- What __________ really means by this is __________.
- My point is not __________, but __________.
- Ultimately, my goal is to demonstrate that __________.
- To put it another way, __________.
- Chapter 2 explores __________, while Chapter 3 examines __________.
- Even more important, __________.
- Incidentally, __________.
- In sum, then, __________.
- My conclusion, then, is that, __________.
- In short, __________.
- Having just argued that __________, let us now turn our attention to __________.
- Although some readers may object that __________, I would answer that __________.

LINKING TO WHAT "THEY SAY"

(P. 182)

- As X mentions in this article, " _________."
- In making this comment, X warns that _________.
- Economists often assume _________; however, new research by X suggests _________.

GERALD GRAFF, Emeritus Professor of English and Education at the University of Illinois at Chicago and the 2008 President of the Modern Language Association of America, has had a major impact on teachers through such books as *Professing Literature: An Institutional History*, *Beyond the Culture Wars: How Teaching the Conflicts Can Revitalize American Education*, and *Clueless in Academe: How Schooling Obscures the Life of the Mind*. The Common Core State Standards for K–12 cite his work on the importance of argument literacy for college and career readiness. **CATHY BIRKENSTEIN**, a lecturer at the University of Illinois at Chicago, has published essays on writing, most recently in *College English*, and, with Gerald, in *The Chronicle of Higher Education*, *Academe*, and *College Composition and Communication*. She and Gerald have given over a hundred lectures and workshops at colleges, conferences, and high schools—and are at present working on a book contending that our currently confusing school and college curriculum needs to be clarified by making the practice of argument the common thread across all disciplines.